AF291909

EXTRAORDINARY ART EXPERIENCES IN AMERICA:

An Insider's Guide

EXTRAORDINARY ART EXPERIENCES IN AMERICA:
An Insider's Guide

Linda Fischbach

with Tracey Pruzan

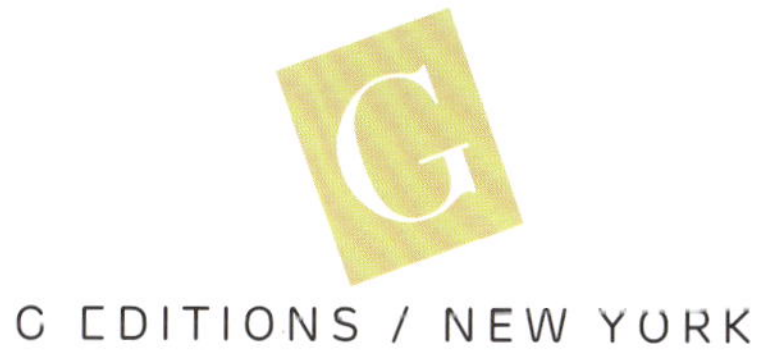

G EDITIONS / NEW YORK

First published in 2023 by

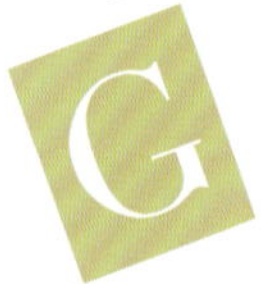

G Editions
New York, New York
www.geditions.com/media@geditions.com

First edition, 2023

Library of Congress Cataloging-in-Publication data is available from the publisher.

Hardcover editions ISBN: 978-1-943876-25-9
Printed and bound in China
10 9 8 7 6 5 4 3 2 1

Contents

Introduction

NEW ART VENUES evolving from private collections are emerging all over the globe. Some have become full-fledged, well-known museums. Others remain private and may seem available only to those who "know someone." I have visited many of these sites and can share that most are open to the public and often free of charge. Truly, they are the perfect destinations for art lovers to take advantage of awesome art experiences.

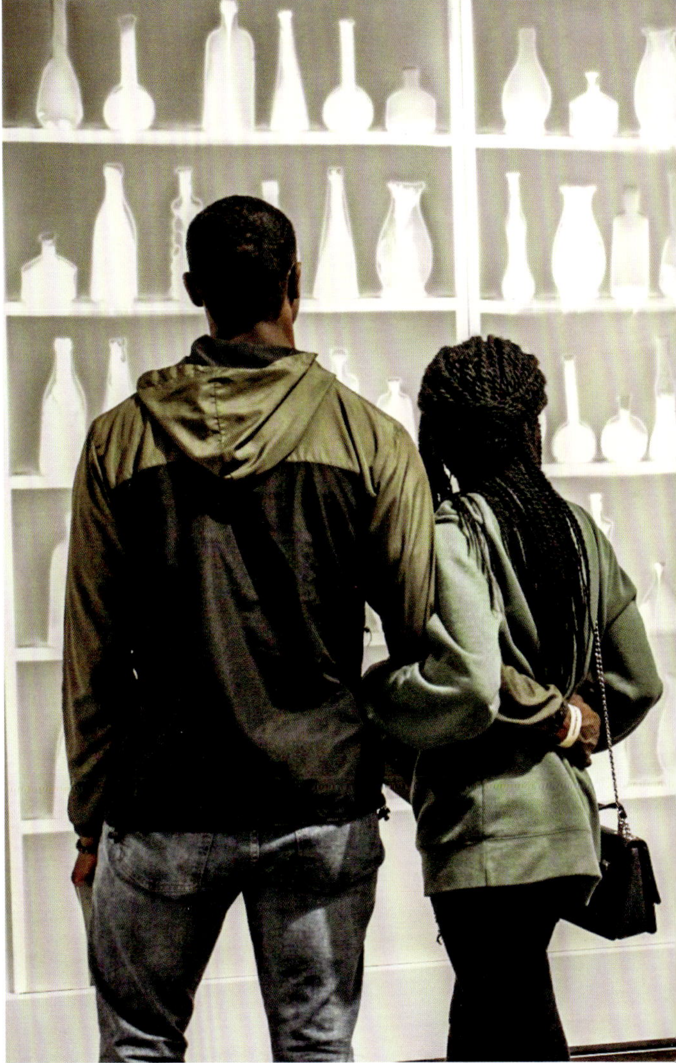

In this book, I will introduce you to a variety of art institutions, many of which began as private collections. Art lovers can find them inside of converted industrial warehouses or in structures designed by star architects, or even in homes left intact for visitors to see how the collectors lived with their art. World-class curators fill their exhibition calendars with innovative shows in every medium from painting and sculpture to performance and photography. The art is borrowed and loaned just like larger public museums.

In all these locations, the programming is cohesive and purposeful. Education often drives a desire to reach out to the community at large. It is hard to overstate the positive impact these institutions can have on a locality both financially and esthetically. Many are in small cities that don't have a world-class, nationally funded museum.

From California to Arkansas, from Miami to New York, collectors and curators are changing what it means to spend time with art. This transformation of the art landscape is taking place before our eyes.

I am passionate about art, and I love to travel. I also love to share information, and I have written this book as a guide to share what I know about these art experiences in America with you—the reader, the traveler, the art world enthusiast—because if you don't know, you'll never go!

Linda Fischbach

American Visionary Art Museum

A unique and educational destination for the whole family in Baltimore. **AVAM.ORG/ART-MUSEUM**

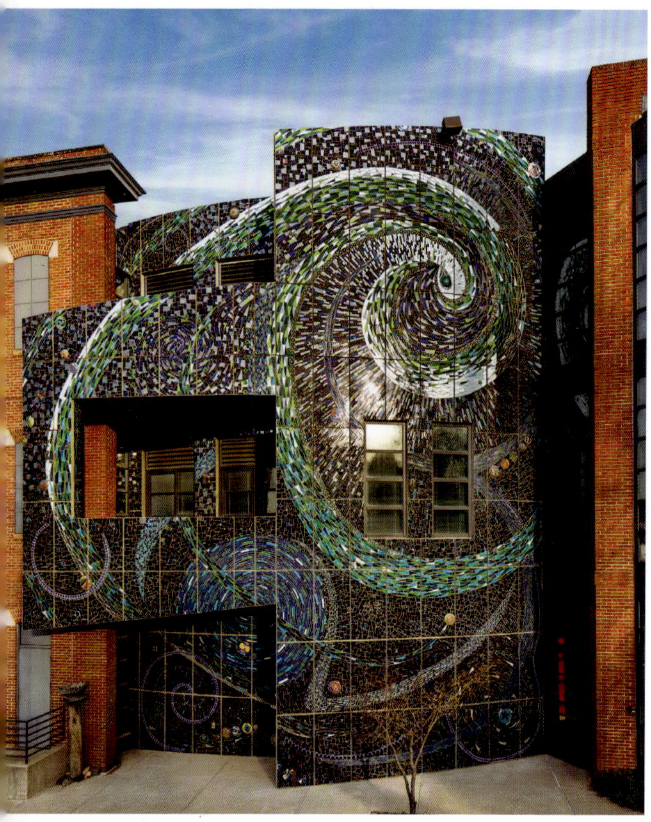

This striking *Aurora Borealis Mosaic Wall* was created by at-risk youth from the community.
On the facing page, the central staircase invites you to linger, as it leads to the exhibitions highlighting education, climate change, and outsider art.

THE AMERICAN VISIONARY ART Museum (AVAM) in Baltimore specializes in the preservation and display of outsider art, mostly by artists who are self-taught. Their thematic shows combine art, science, philosophy, humor, and social justice.

The AVAM is in three main structures consisting of a main building, an event space, and a large warehouse that stores ten-foot-high fluffy poodle sculptures, among other things. The exterior façade of the main building is a mirrored mosaic created by youth-at-risk apprentices, which I found fascinating and very beautiful. Across from the AVAM is a public park where outdoor movies shown against the warehouse building are enjoyed by people in the community.

On the day we visited, we ran into Rebecca Alban Hoffberger, founder, curator, and director of the AVAM. Hoffberger was guiding two friends through the museum and allowed us to join her for a tour. What a treat!

The installation we saw was titled *The Secret Life of Earth*, and the galleries were so unique and lively that walking through them felt more like an outing to a science fair than to a museum. The exhibition displayed an abundance of information about nature and the natural world, as the artists were making an artistic statement about ecology and the planet.

In the entry was an installation by ecological artists Judith and Richard Lang, whose work cautions us that plastics last forever, polluting our once pristine water,

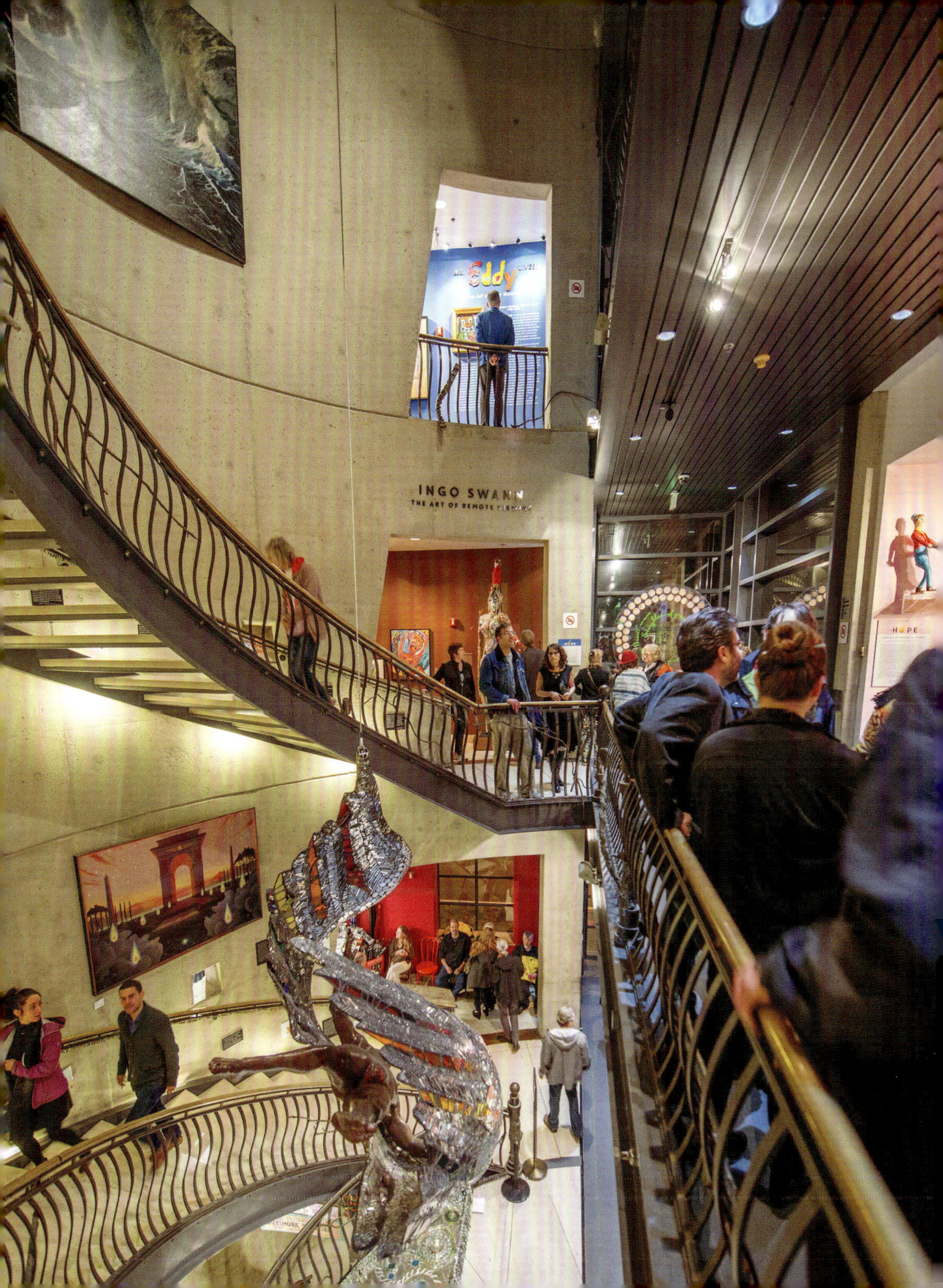
INGO SWANN
THE ART OF REMOTE VIEWING

The vivid blue
of the entrance
ceiling is hung
with surprisingly
beautiful debris
collected by the
artists Judith and
Richard Lang,
adding to the sense
of anticipation
created by the
architectural
design.

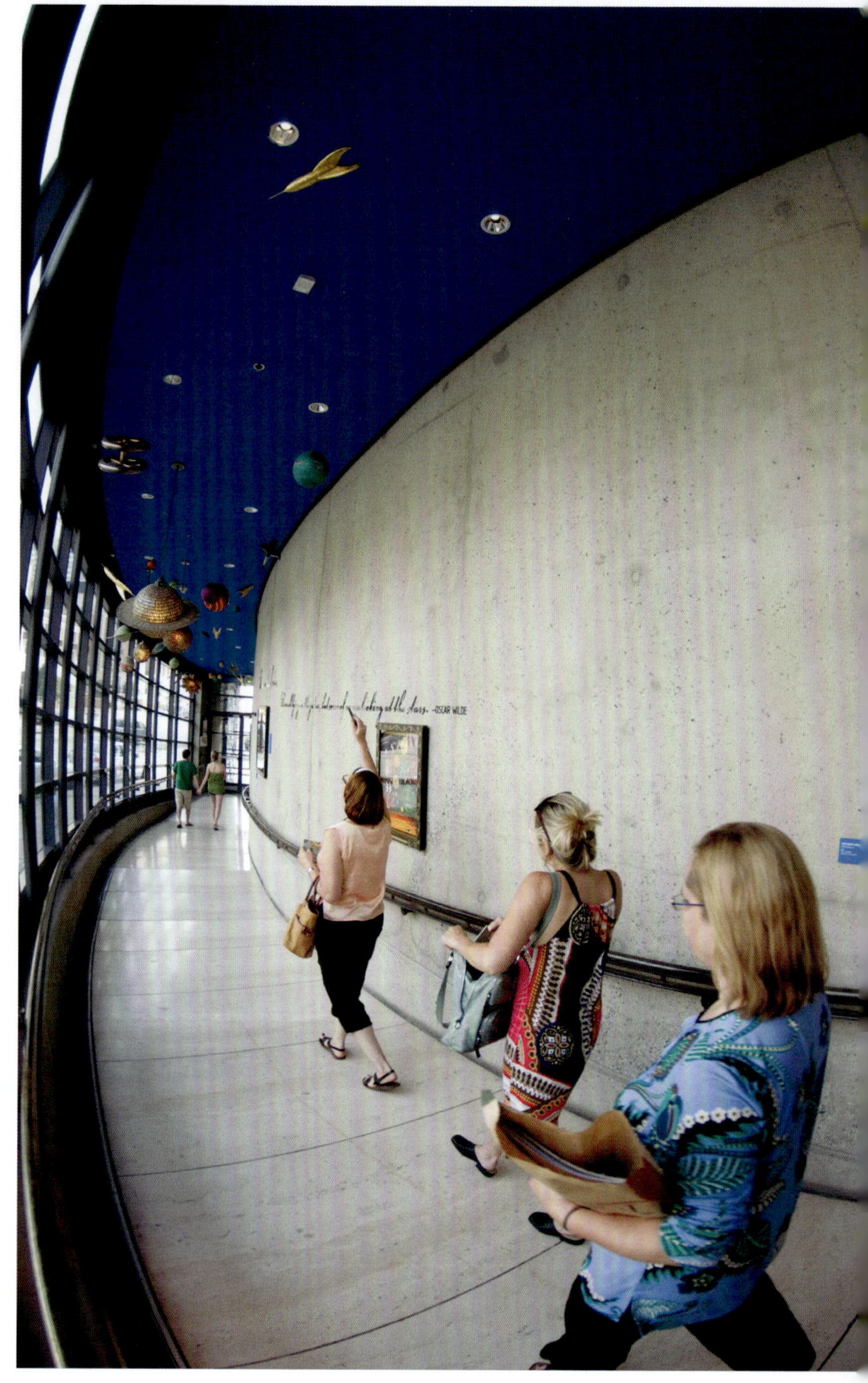

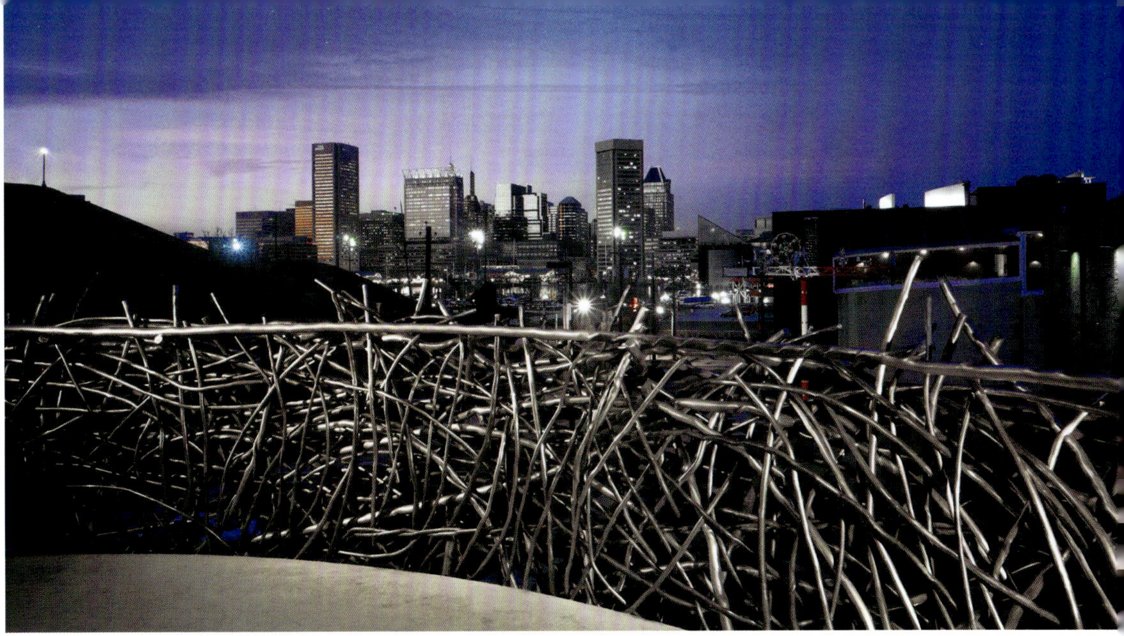

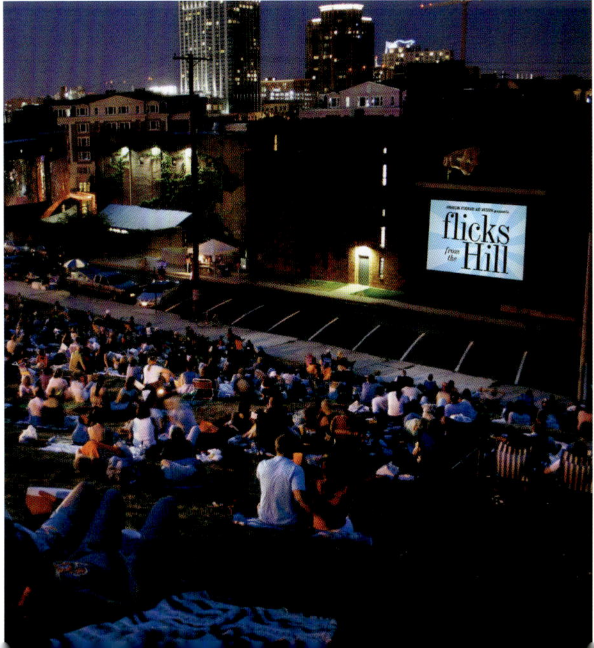

beaches, and shorelines. They painted the ceiling a beautiful blue and covered it with plastic objects that dangle down from overhead. Each piece of plastic was lovingly removed from the debris left on the Kehoe Beach in the Point Reyes National Seashore.

In one gallery, we learned about the marvelous Paulownia tree. It grows five to twenty feet in its first year and can be harvested in ten years. The Paulownia consumes eleven times more carbon dioxide than other trees and is three times stronger than pine. An installation by Johanna Burke called *Chimps, Bonobos, and Us* states that humans share 98 percent of our DNA with chimpanzees and bonobos. Larger-than-life green-beaded chimps cast a verdant glow over the space. Burke, an artist/fabricator who also creates the famed holiday windows for Bergdorf Goodman, states, "Green is an incredible color to work with—uplifting and wonderful on the eyes."

As one walks through the museum, they will notice many inspiring, informative, and funny signs. One quote by Jonathan Swift was deeply touching: "Vision is the art of seeing things invisible." Rebecca Alban Hoffberger is a visionary whose desires to spread art and information come together in this splendid museum.

Perched on the façade of the museum, the *Birds Nest Balcony*, by Hess Industries, entices the viewer to step out and enjoy the view. Below, movies play against the outside wall on summer nights, an inviting instance of the museum's community-friendly approach.

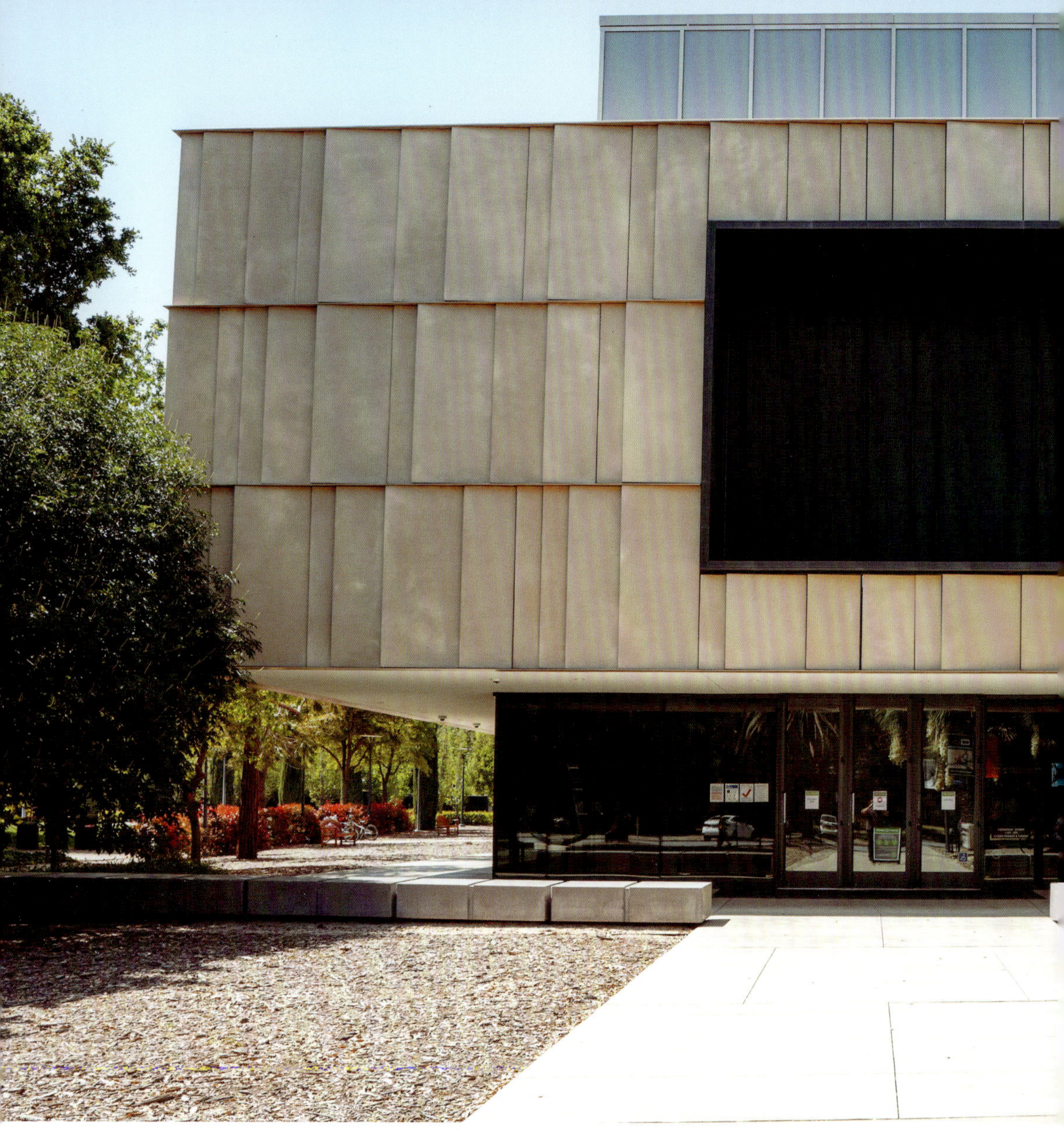

Anderson Collection At Stanford University

One family's passion for collecting postwar and abstract expressionist art turned into a world-class museum in Northern California. **ANDERSON.STANFORD.EDU**

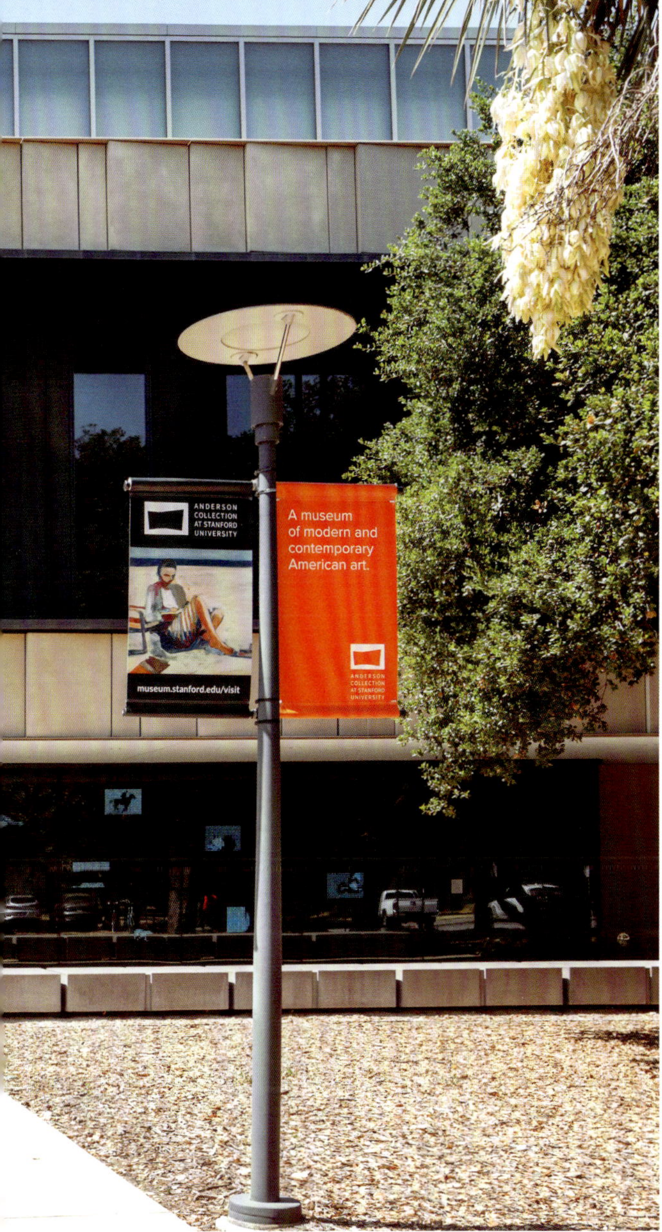

Set within the Stanford campus, a view of the entrance to the Ennead Architects-designed building.

MANY YEARS AGO, I had the good fortune to visit the home of Harry (Hunk) and Mary Margaret (Moo) Anderson in Northern California. I vividly recall my surprise at seeing masterpieces by well-known artists hung in a relatively modest ranch-style house. Everywhere I looked, I spotted a famous painting, including over their daughter's bed—a Jackson Pollock!

Harry Anderson cofounded the food service company Saga Foods. In the 1960s, Anderson and Moo visited Paris and started collecting French impressionist art. They soon changed their focus to collecting postwar and abstract expressionist art by artists such as Clyfford Still, Richard Diebenkorn, Mark Rothko, and Jackson Pollock. Their philosophy was always that they tried to buy the best work from the best artist.

The Anderson Collection at Stanford University in Stanford was a gift from the Andersons who built the collection over their lifetimes. Ennead Architects designed this jewel of a contemporary building that fits very well into the beautiful campus landscape. San Francisco Bay Area artists who might not be known to visitors outside of the Bay Area are highlighted here, including Manuel Neri and Nathan Oliveira. Besides the extraordinary permanent collection, there are also temporary shows such as a recent one titled, *Formed & Fired: Contemporary American Ceramics*, which highlighted four contemporary ceramic artists including the famed multi-faceted artist Simone Leigh.

When visiting the Anderson, the first thing one should do is go to the library on the first floor to see the video about the Andersons' lifelong passion for collecting art. Although they are now deceased, the video features images of their house, the one I visited, and explains how they started collecting and how their deep passion for art developed over time. It also shows the intricate and interesting process of how these masterpieces were packed up to be sent to their museum.

The Cantor Arts Center, located next to the Anderson Collection, is an encyclopedic museum and worth a visit. The Arts Center has an impressive twenty-six pieces by Richard Diebenkorn and over 250 works by Auguste Rodin. On a beautiful day, you can have lunch outside and enjoy the Rodin sculpture garden.

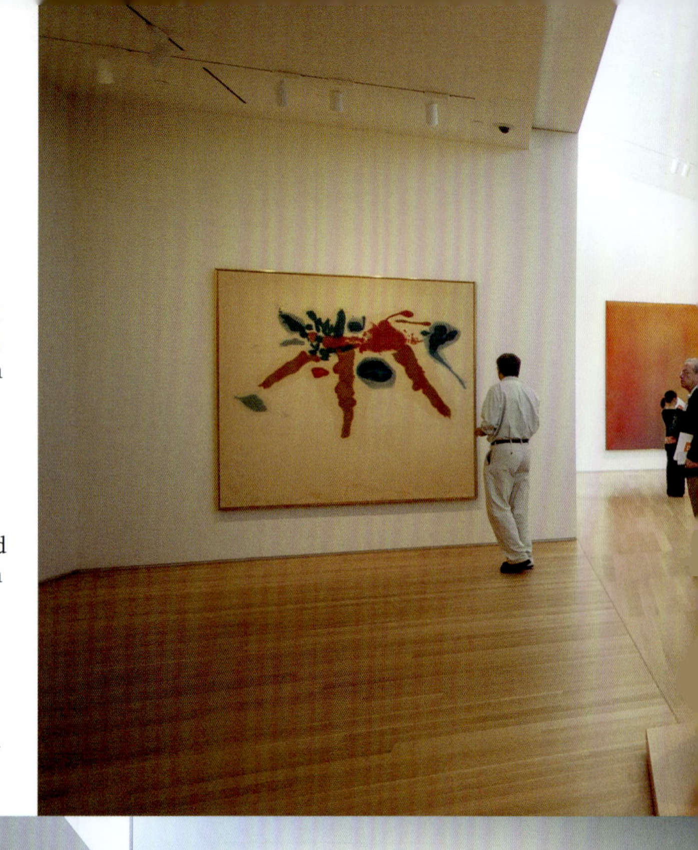

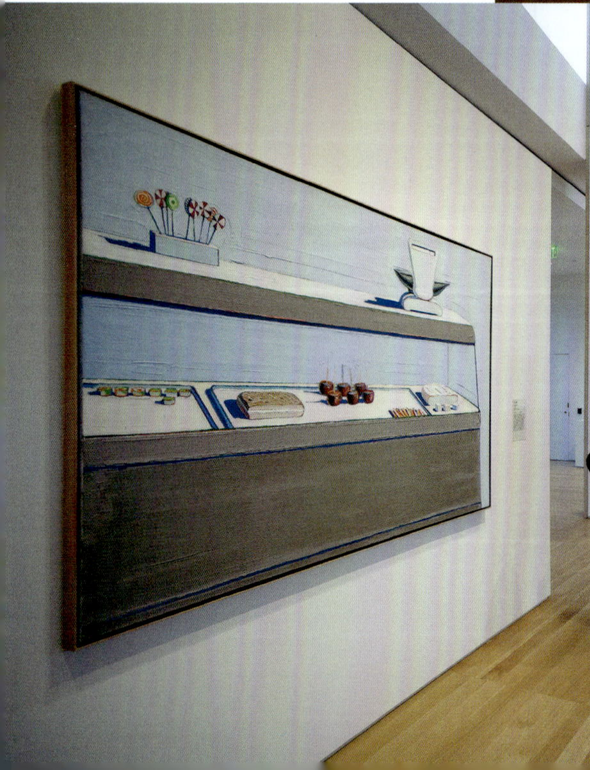

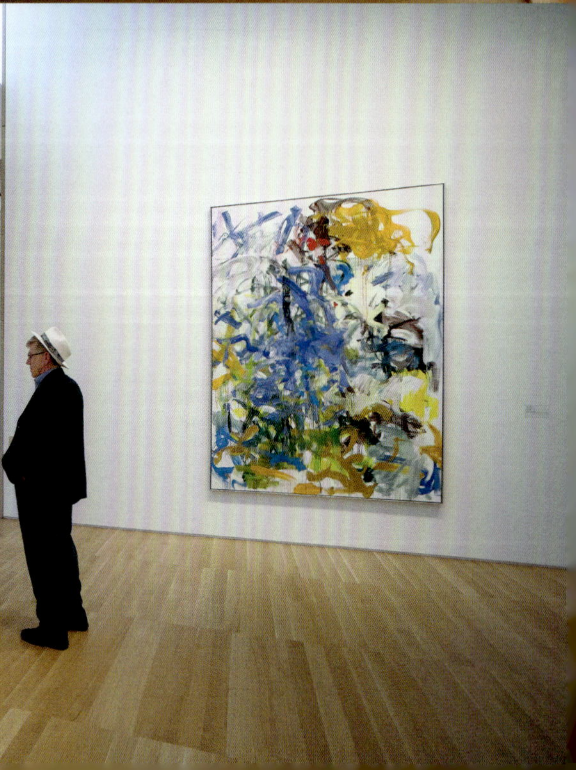

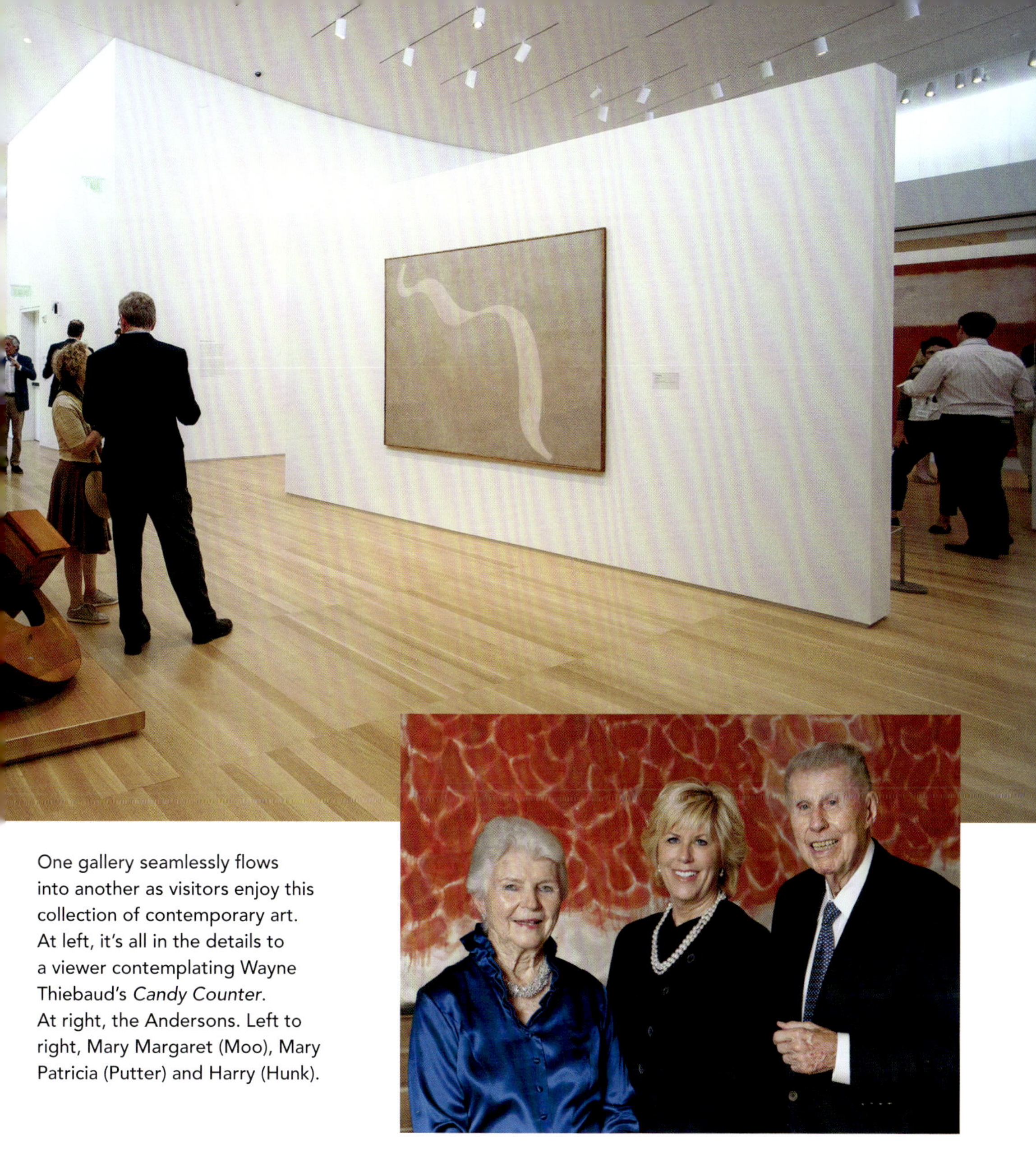

One gallery seamlessly flows into another as visitors enjoy this collection of contemporary art. At left, it's all in the details to a viewer contemplating Wayne Thiebaud's *Candy Counter*. At right, the Andersons. Left to right, Mary Margaret (Moo), Mary Patricia (Putter) and Harry (Hunk).

Art Barge and Victor D'amico Institute of Art

Inspiring vistas for art classes on the
East End of Long Island.
DAMICO-ART.ORG

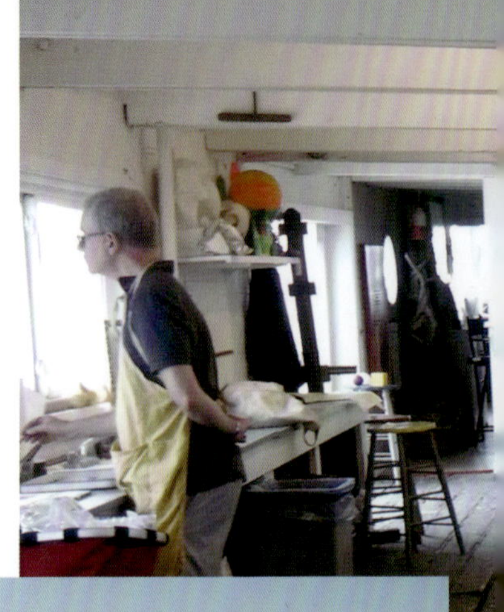

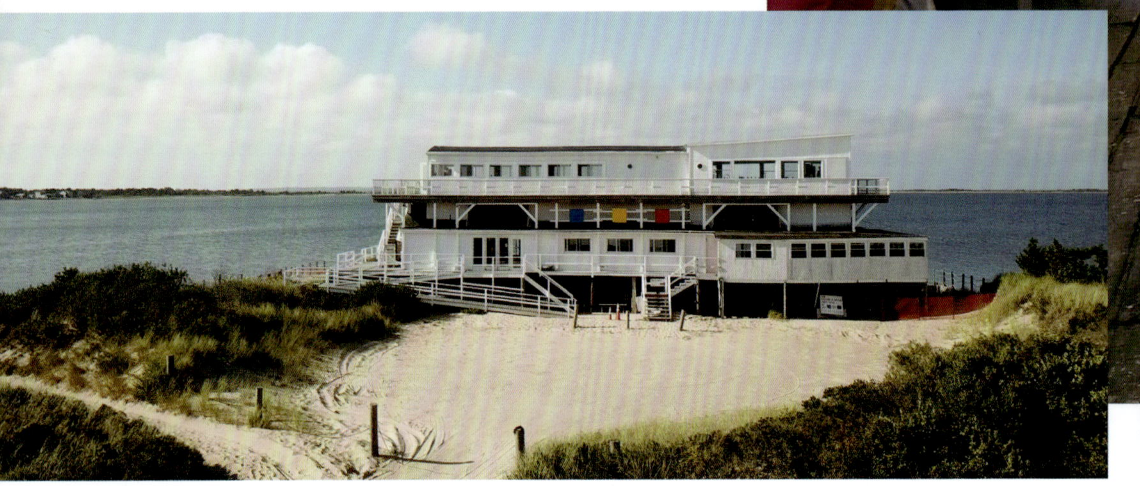

IF YOU WOULD LIKE TO TAKE ART CLASSES, I know the most amazing venue in the Hamptons. It is called the Art Barge, and it is located on Napeague Beach in Amagansett, New York.

The Art Barge was the idea of Victor D'Amico, who taught art through the auspices of the Department of Education at the Museum of Modern Art and was the first director of their Art Education Department.

The Barge was originally used by the navy in World War II but retired. In 1960, the Barge was towed from New Jersey to its new location in Amagansett by D'Amico. He choreographed the move to one of the most beautiful settings in the world, as he thought it would be an inspirational place to teach his art philosophies to students.

Every summer for more than sixty years, art students of all ages have participated in classes including Painting,

The famously beautiful light on the East End of Long Island washes over the Art Barge. Above right, art students, inspired by the 360 degree views of the sea and shore, can take a variety of classes in this free yet structured environment. Far right, Mabel's studio at the D'Amico house highlights her collections and her inspiring life in art.

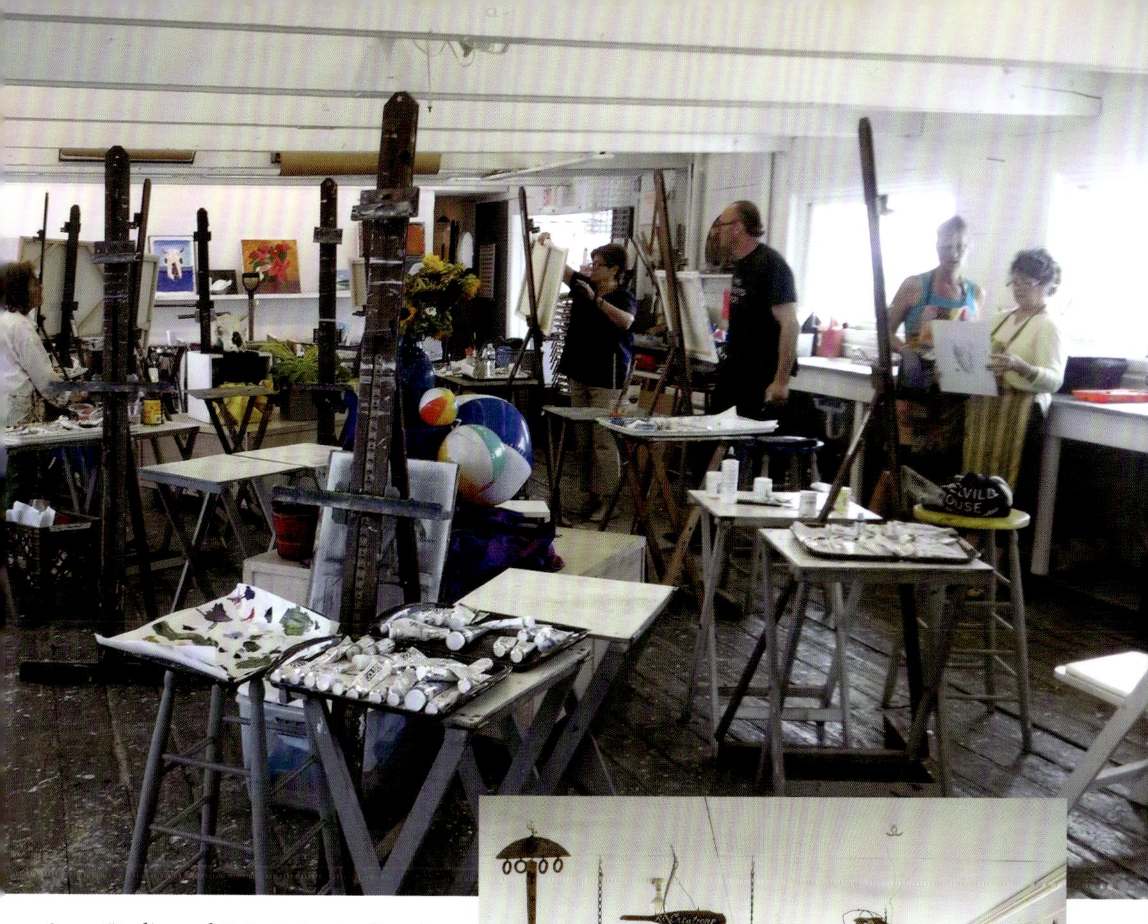

Open Studio, and Orientation to Creativity. There are also special workshops on collage, watercolor, and pastel.

Not far from the Barge is the home that Victor and Mabel D'Amico built together. The house, with its majestic views, is a very simply constructed yet innovative house for its time—one of the first modern beach homes. It is a wonderful show case for Mabel's glass artworks, her found and made constructions, her collections, and her ceramics.

The house recently became a designated local historical landmark in the town of East Hampton and part of the Historic Artists' Homes and Studios Program (HAHS).

For tour reservations, it is best to call 631-267-3172.

Barnes Foundation

Re-imagining a collector's vision of what art is—from a blanket chest and humble hardware to paintings by van Gogh and Cezanne.
BARNESFOUNDATION.ORG

ALBERT BARNES ESTABLISHED the Barnes Foundation in 1922 with the desire to promote the appreciation of art. Originally located in Merion, over time the museum created unwanted local traffic, while also experiencing a downturn in its financial status. In 2012, the Barnes collection moved out of the suburbs and into the city of Philadelphia. Though the move was controversial, as Barnes's original intention was to bring art to an area that would not have otherwise had it, the fact is that the new location near the Philadelphia Museum of Art and the outdoor Rodin Sculpture Museum is more accessible and creates a vibrant and vital artistic destination for the city. In addition, their financial base has been renewed because many more

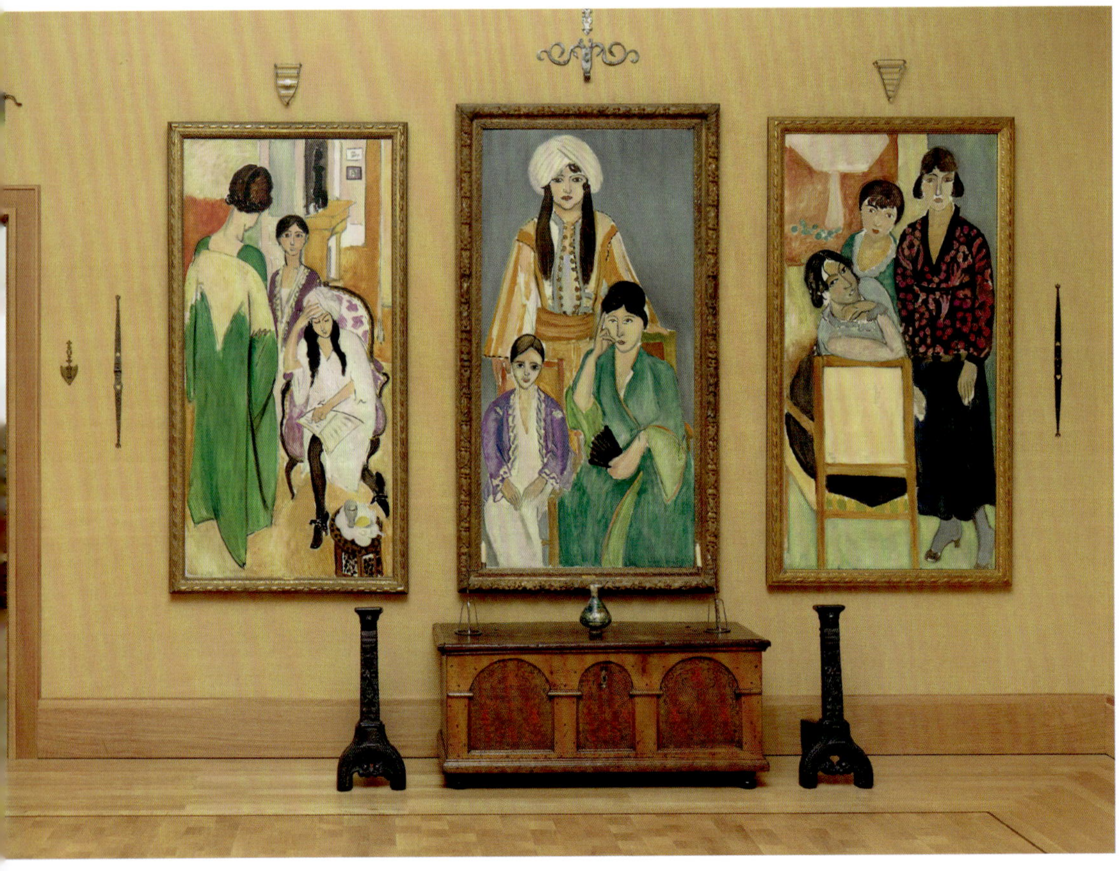

visitors, from local residents to school children to tourists, are enjoying the collection.

The new building by Tod Williams and Billie Tsien was created with the understanding that the quirky and very specific arrangement of the artworks and other furniture within the galleries would maintain the experience—the scale, proportion, and configuration of the original galleries in Merion—as Albert Barnes intended. Whenever I visit, I am always delighted to reacquaint myself with his esoteric collection of impressionist and post-impressionist art, including work by Matisse and Picasso. Two of my favorites are *The Postman* by van Gogh and *The Card Players* by Cezanne. I can't recommend highly enough that visitors to Philadelphia should be sure to enjoy an hour or two spent in quiet contemplation at the Barnes.

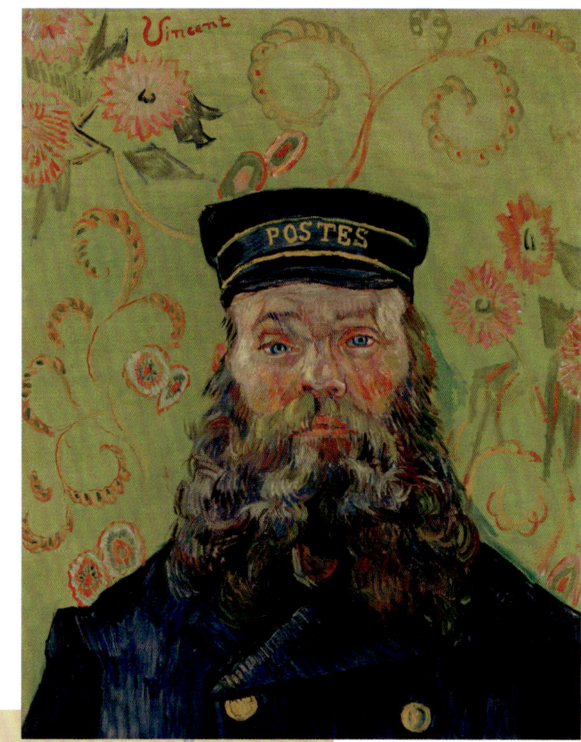

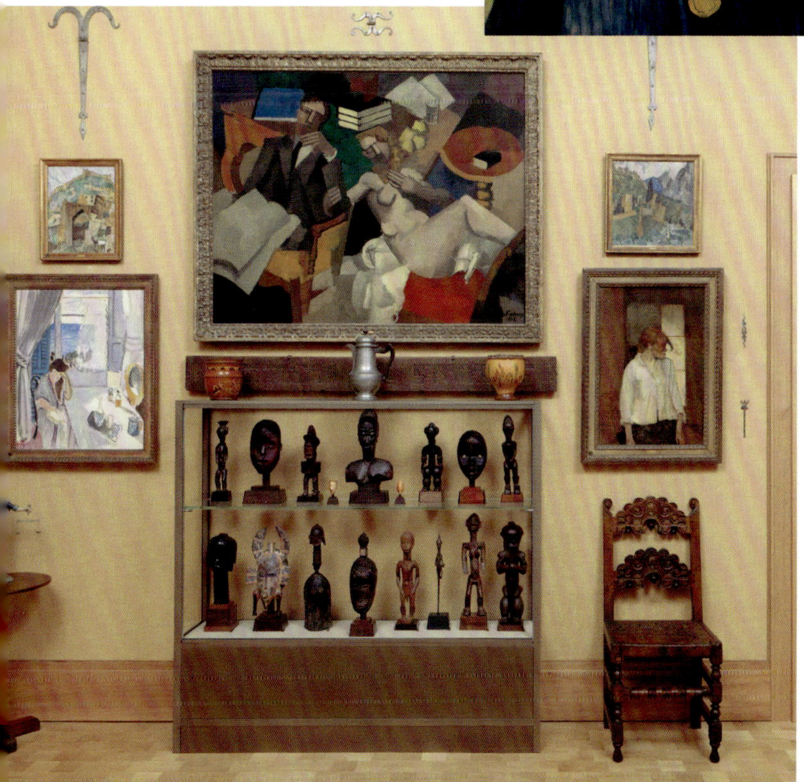

The Postman by Vincent van Gogh is one of the most popular paintings for visitors at the Barnes. At left, this eclectic collection emphasizes Albert Barnes's discerning eye and passion for a variety of art forms. Facing page, an ensemble of paintings and objets d'art in the Matisse room.

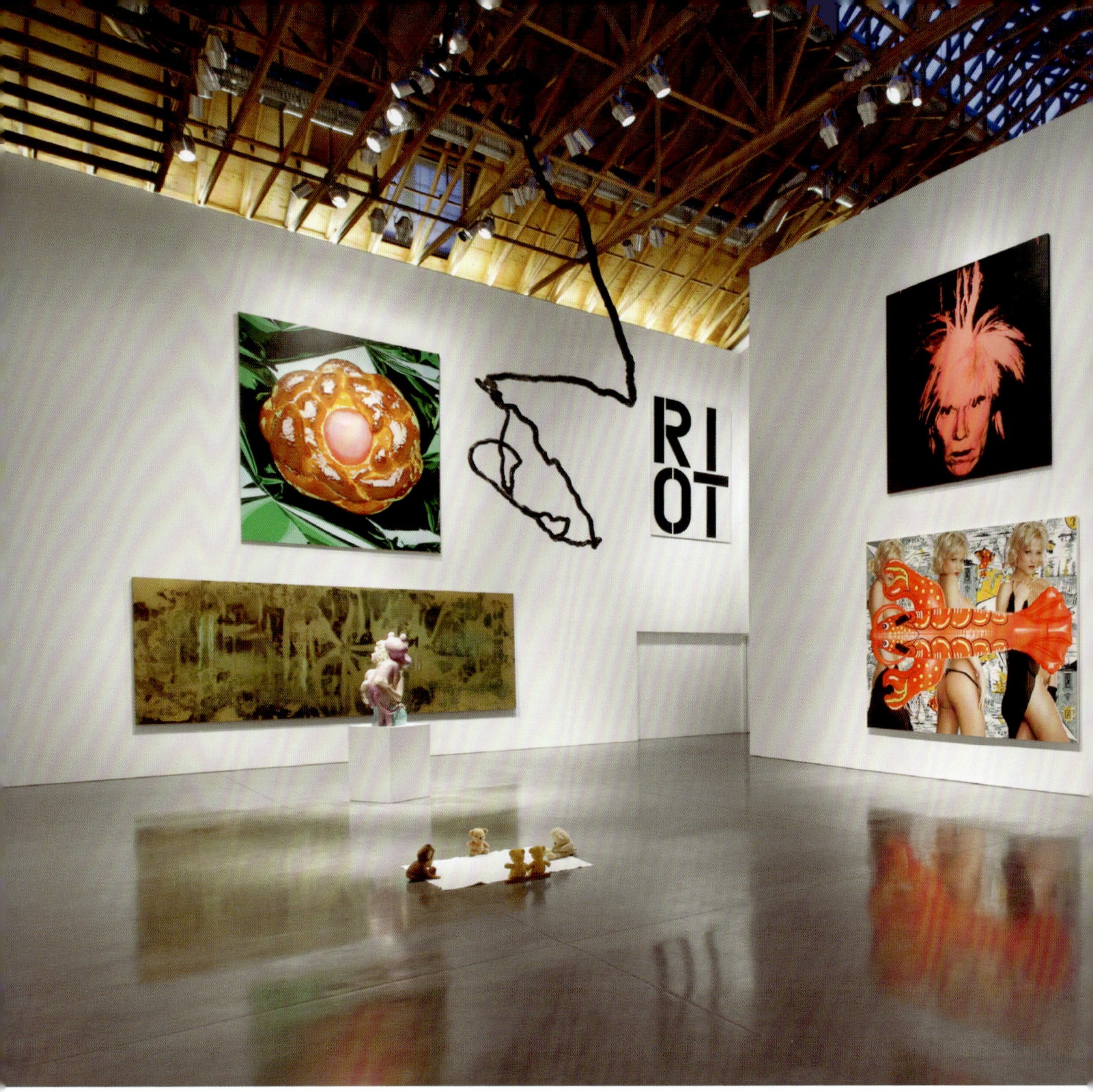

GREENWICH, CT/NEW YORK, NY

The Brant Foundation

Peter Brant has generously opened his private collection to the public in Greenwich, Connecticut and on the Lower East Side. At both locations, there are curated shows of contemporary art.

BRANTFOUNDATION.ORG

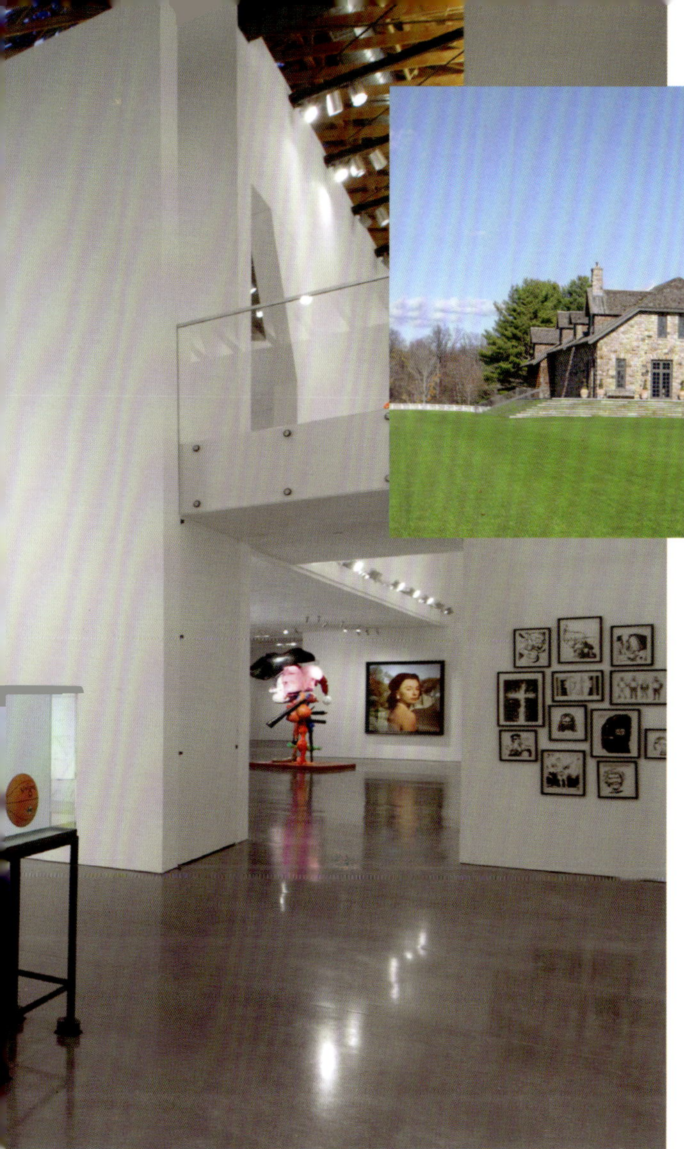

The open space of the main gallery features an exposed wooden ceiling. A 2009 group show of contemporary artists including Cindy Sherman and Jeff Koons, dazzled the eye and provoked the mind. Above right, the beautiful grounds of the Foundation's Greenwich, Connecticut, location, with an Urs Fischer's sculpture, *To Be Titled (Big Clay No. 3)*.

THE BRANT FOUNDATION was founded in 1996 by Peter M. Brant, a passionate art collector since his teens. Brant followed the guidance of his renowned mentors, the gallerists Bruno Bischofberger and Leo Castelli, and amassed a significant collection of art, which was the basis of the Foundation, and which has grown over time. The Brant Foundation has a mission to promote the appreciation of contemporary art and design by making these works available to the public for scholarly study and examination. There are two locations: one in Greenwich, Connecticut, and one on the Lower East Side of Manhattan.

When the Brant Foundation first opened in Greenwich, I visited often to enjoy the museum-quality art in the idyllic setting. The Foundation's exhibitions are always thoughtful, stimulating, and informative. Whenever one chooses to visit, in the fall with the leaves changing or in winter with a light snow, the location and the museum never disappoint.

The Brant Foundation's Greenwich space, designed by Richard Gluckman of Gluckman Tang Architects, was originally constructed from local stones and historically used as a cold storage warehouse.

When we visited, a Dan Colen show featured a

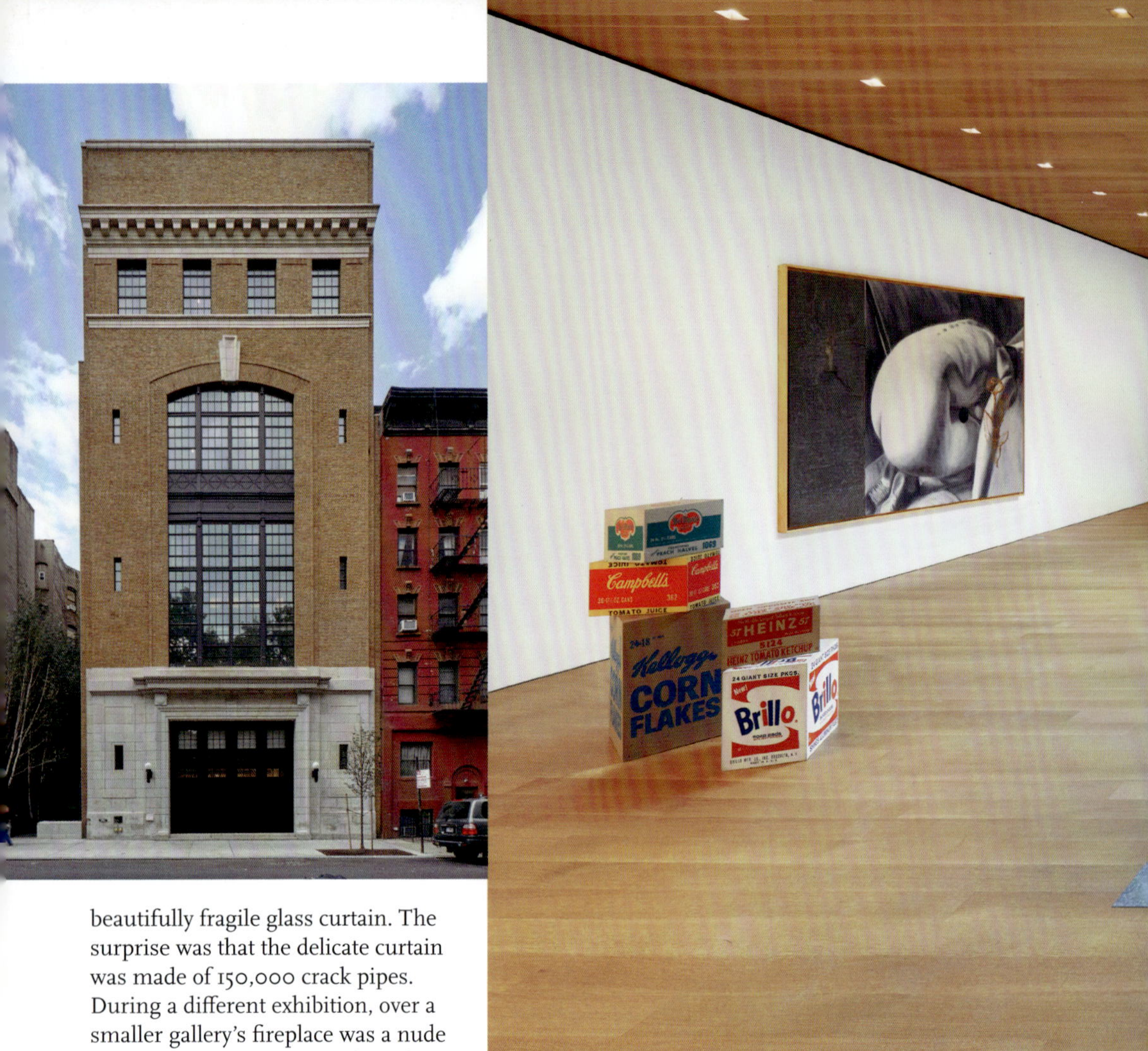

beautifully fragile glass curtain. The surprise was that the delicate curtain was made of 150,000 crack pipes. During a different exhibition, over a smaller gallery's fireplace was a nude bust of eighties supermodel Stephanie Seymour by Maurizio Cattelan. Seymour is Brant's wife, and here she appears like the figurehead on the bow of a ship.

The Brant Foundation's New York space is located on a graffitied street in the East Village. Be prepared to be knocked out visually by your visit. Whether you arrive by foot or by car, take note of a beautiful private garden to the left of the entrance, which is part of the Foundation.

For a personal touch, staff welcome guests into the space, which was originally a substation for Con Ed and later the studio and home of artist Walter De Maria. In 2016, Brant hired Gluckman Tang architects to renovate the building for the Brant Foundation's New York space.

On a recent visit, on view was a Julian Schnabel show of his plate paintings titled *Self-Portraits of Others*, in which he examines the theme of portraiture in art history. Throughout the building were his portraits of artists such as Vincent van Gogh, Diego Velázquez, and Frida Kahlo made from plates, oil, and Bondo (a permanent resin-like material.)

The enormous gallery on the fourth floor, distinguished with a beautiful wood ceiling pierced by a skylight, has great views of the Lower East

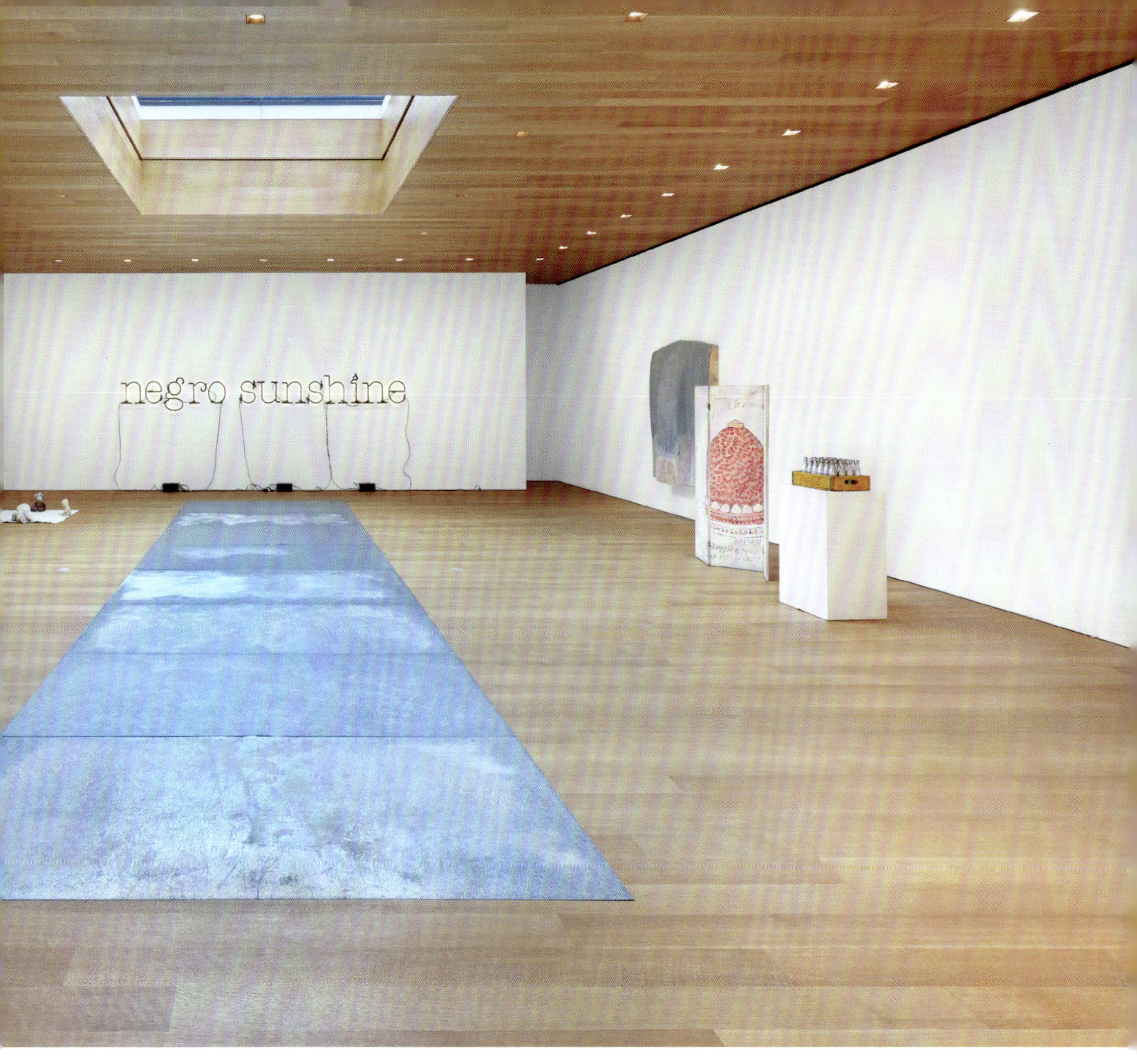

Side. The third-floor gallery, also with great views, has a concrete ceiling. The second-floor gallery has an exposed brick façade. The first floor houses the gift shop where one can find exclusive products by artists such as Keith Haring and Andy Warhol.

On my first visit, I saw a truly amazing show of work by Jean-Michel Basquiat. The Brant Foundation has extensive programs for public outreach such as an Internship Program, Lecture Series, and a Library and Loan Program. Whether one visits the Brant Foundation in Greenwich or in Manhattan, each space has incredible art and architecture to offer the viewing public.

Wonderful daylight illuminates the contemporary art in this generously proportioned gallery. Far left, the unassuming façade of the Lower East Side Brant Foundation belies it's fabulous collections.

The Broad

Architecturally exciting, The Broad is a landmark in the burgeoning downtown Los Angeles art scene.

THEBROAD.ORG

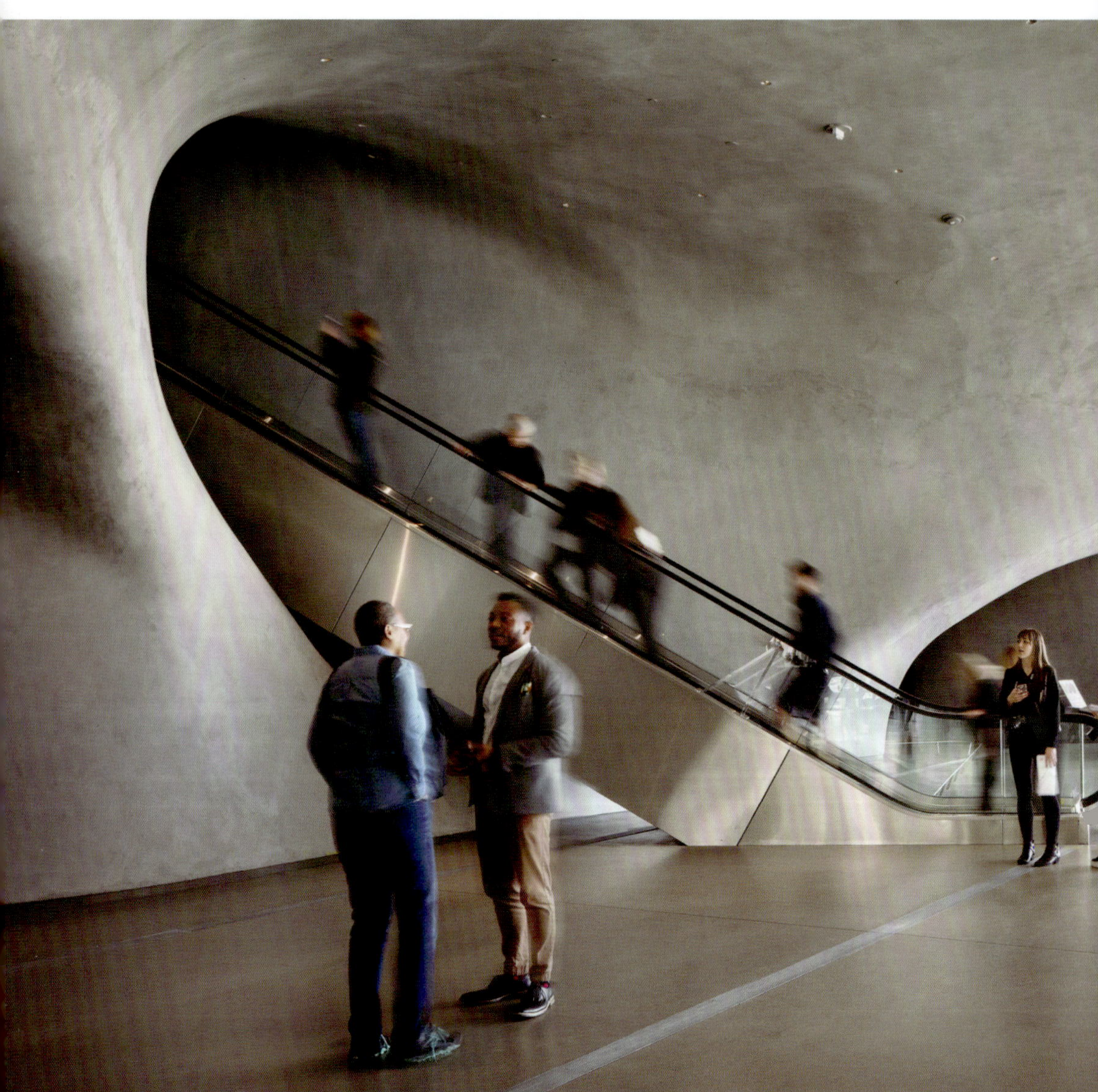

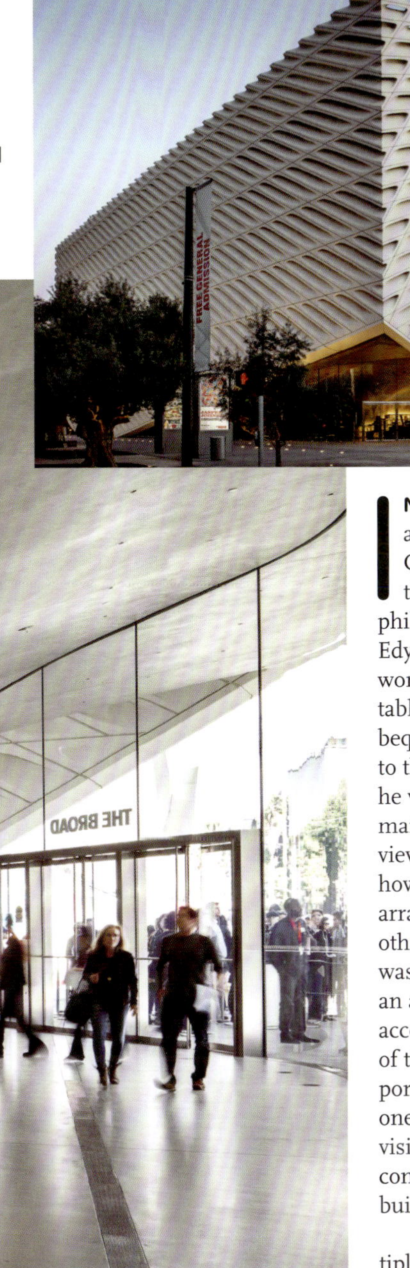

The spectacular lobby entrance to The Broad was designed by the world renowned architectural firm Diller Scofidio + Renfro in collaboration with Gensler. Its striking exterior at right.

IN DOWNTOWN LOS ANGELES, across from the Museum of Contemporary Art and close to the Walt Disney Concert Hall, philanthropists and collectors Edythe and Eli Broad created a world-class art institution. By establishing The Broad rather than bequeathing their entire collection to the LA County Museum, where he was a board member, they maintained their own point of view with the goal of controlling how the work would be viewed, arranged, and experienced. Another hallmark of their approach was to collect in great depth across an artist's career, which provides access to the historical panorama of the work of individual contemporary artists and is undoubtedly one of the great visual treats when visiting The Broad. The Broad continues to make acquisitions to build the collection.

In addition to seeing multiple works by individual artists, what struck me the most on my initial visit was the storage floor. Rather than create a basement storage room or find an off-site location, the museum was designed to incorporate the storage facilities in between the gallery floors. As a visitor, you feel like you are in Mr. Broad's head, surrounded by his gorgeous art. This makes the museum feel very current and energized, as it poses an interesting idea about how to deal with art and storage of collections. The "unseen" artworks become part of the galleries.

The other highlight for me is the *Infinity Mirrored Room-The Souls of Millions of Light Years Away*, from 2013, by Yayoi Kusama. Kusama's mirrored rooms never disappoint, and this one is especially fascinating and quite large. Be sure to secure reserved time tickets ahead of your visit for both the museum and the Kusama Room, which requires its own ticket, to avoid waiting in a long line, as they are both top-of-the-list for most visitors to LA.

The location is not an accident. In recent years, this area of downtown LA has been revitalized and is truly worth a visit to see the shops and restaurants, galleries, and food trucks. The overall experience is the perfect bridge for entering the museum.

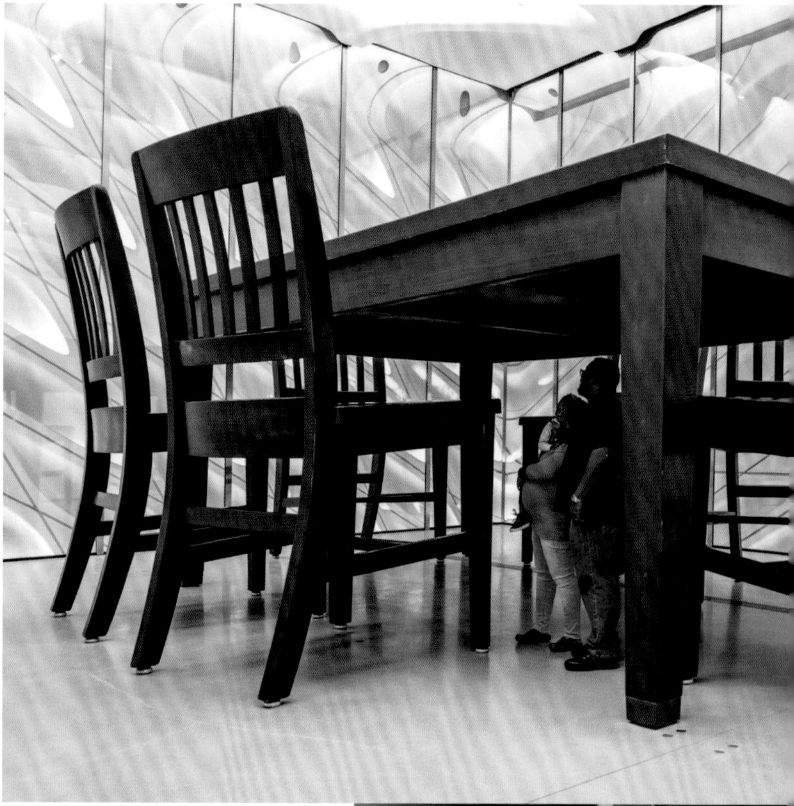

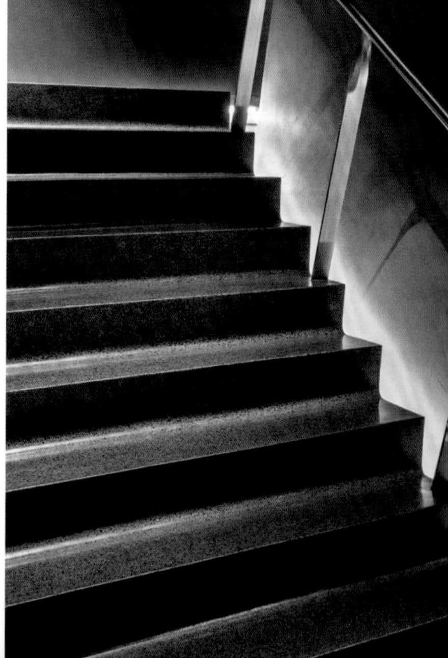

Clockwise from above, visitors enjoy the disruptive scale of Robert Therrien's *Under the Table*, 1994. Iconic works by Jeff Koons toy with our expectations of materiality. More dramatic spaces are found throughout the museum, as in this spectacular staircase with an unexpected window to a storage space.

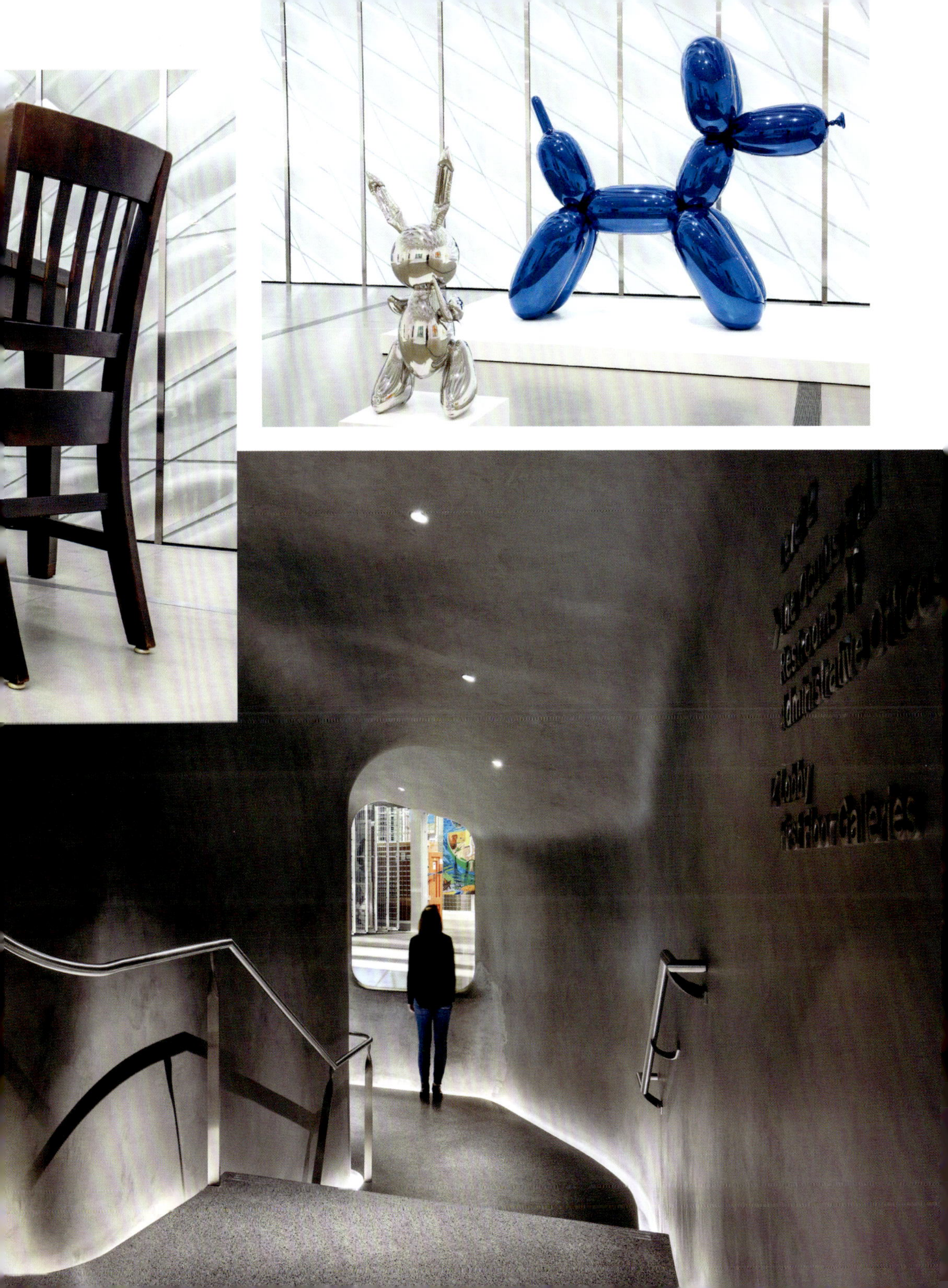

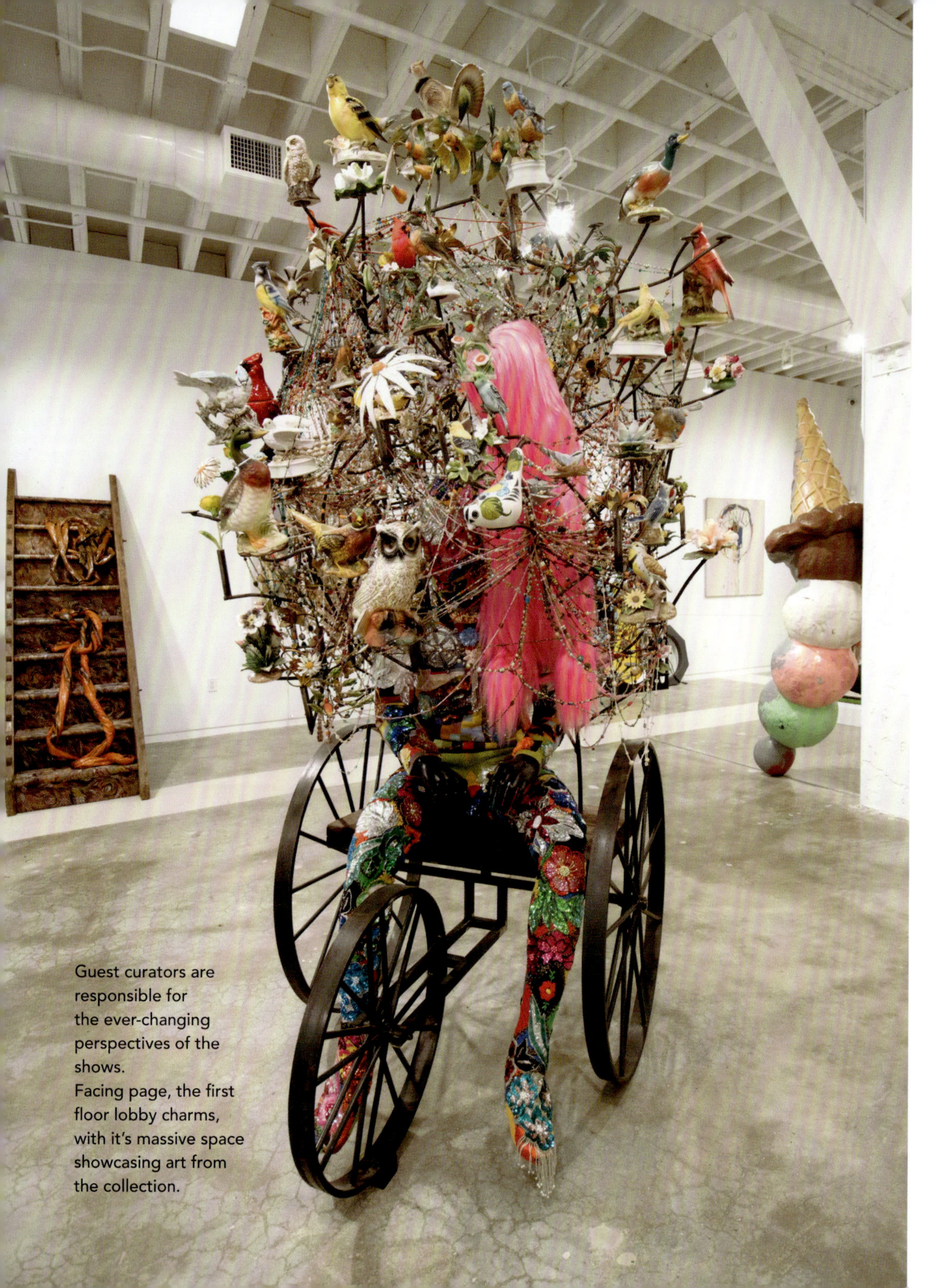

Guest curators are
responsible for
the ever-changing
perspectives of the
shows.
Facing page, the first
floor lobby charms,
with it's massive space
showcasing art from
the collection.

The Bunker Artspace

A little-known gem in West Palm Beach jam packed with art both high and low. Shows by world-class curators provide a one-of-a-kind art experience. **THEBUNKERARTSPACE.COM**

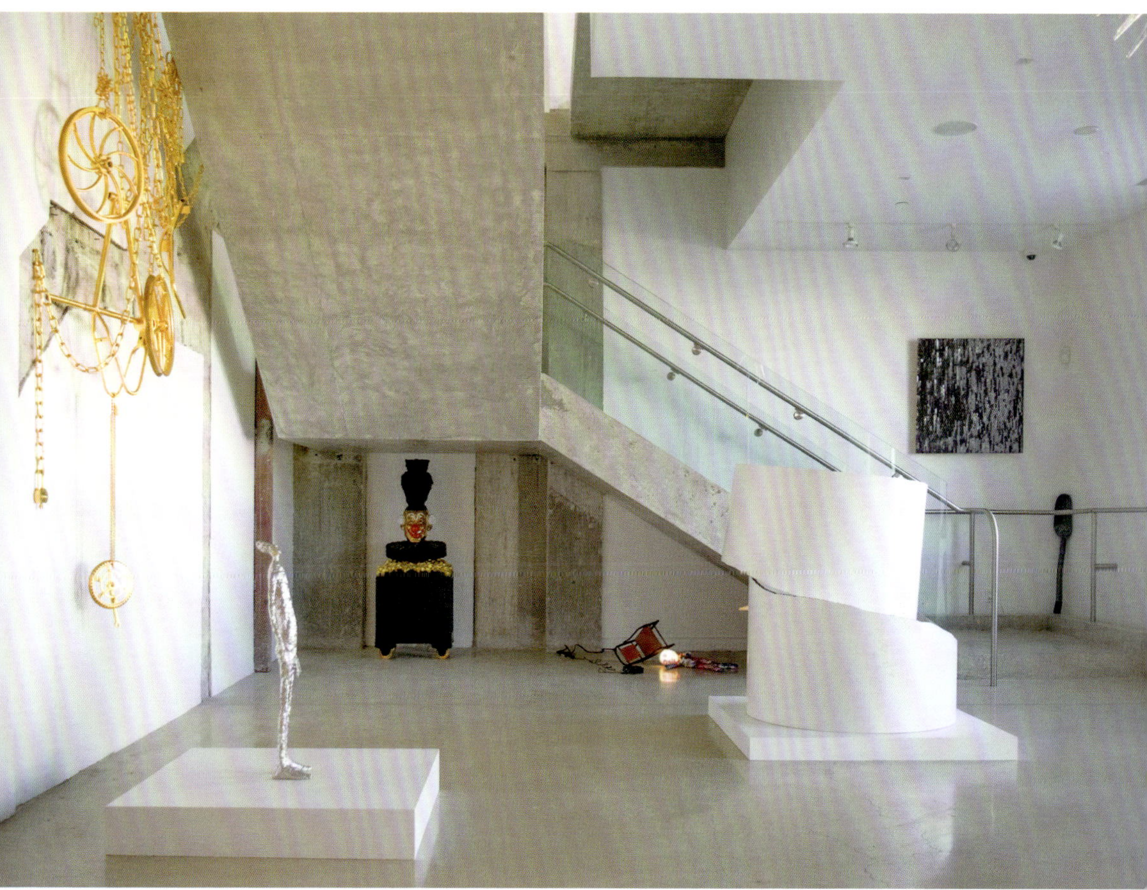

BETH RUDIN DEWOODY is a well-known philanthropist and art collector who buys and supports emerging artists, under-appreciated artists, and established art stars. I have been to her extraordinary art-filled home in New York and to her home in Palm Beach, and not only is she an all-around nice person, but she has a black belt in contemporary art collecting.

DeWoody has been collecting since she was a teenager and has more than ten thousand objects in her collection. A simple conversation is a reminder of her genius, as she remembers every name and every story behind each of her acquisitions. In 2017, she found a large venue to store and show her art works in West Palm Beach when a twenty-thousand-square-foot structure became available on Bunker Road, hence the name, The Bunker Artspace. The location, down the street from the Norton Museum, is near the chic section of West Palm Beach filled with furniture, antiques, and design boutiques. DeWoody renovated the building, and it is frequently opened in December to coincide with the opening of Art Basel Miami, but it is also possible to make reservations to visit.

A visit to The Bunker is dazzling, and visitors should follow the installation maps that are provided for guidance. The Bunker has two full-time curators as well as guest curators who are invited to create shows using the collection as a base for their inspiration. DeWoody's innate genius and sense of order guide her purchases and curatorial choices in the most exceptional and interesting ways.

The Bunker consists of two floors jam-packed with objects both high and low—from sculpture, prints, paintings, and drawings to furniture, Lucite pieces, and objects from the sea. Many of the artists are unknown but interwoven with artists' names we all know, while each piece is valued for itself, be it a vase, a piece of coral, or a masterpiece. I especially love that the library is tucked behind galleries on the second floor. Instead of the institutional-type library that we might see elsewhere, this library is both fun and serious—and especially inviting. Interspersed within the many books and catalogues are small art pieces as well as ephemera, such as comic books and a basketball. If you look closely, you will see works by Ugo Rondinone, Sylvie Fleury, and Ed Ruscha.

Of exceptional note is that De-Woody has always supported and encouraged unknown and under-appreciated female artists. Throughout her collection, you can see the work of women now in their eighties and nineties whom she has been quietly collecting for years.

Beth Rudin DeWoody's support of young artists is also legendary; she is a patron in the truest sense of the word. I remember an interview with Kehinde Wiley in which he said that if it hadn't been for DeWoody's support early in his

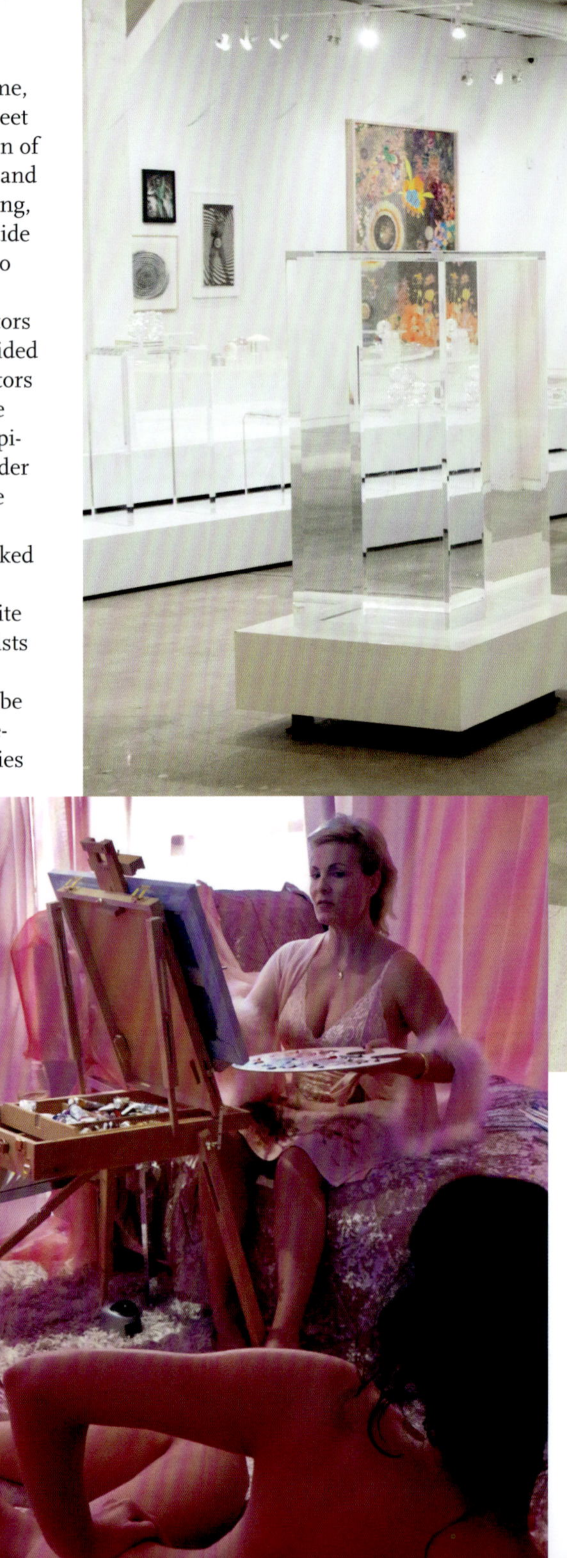

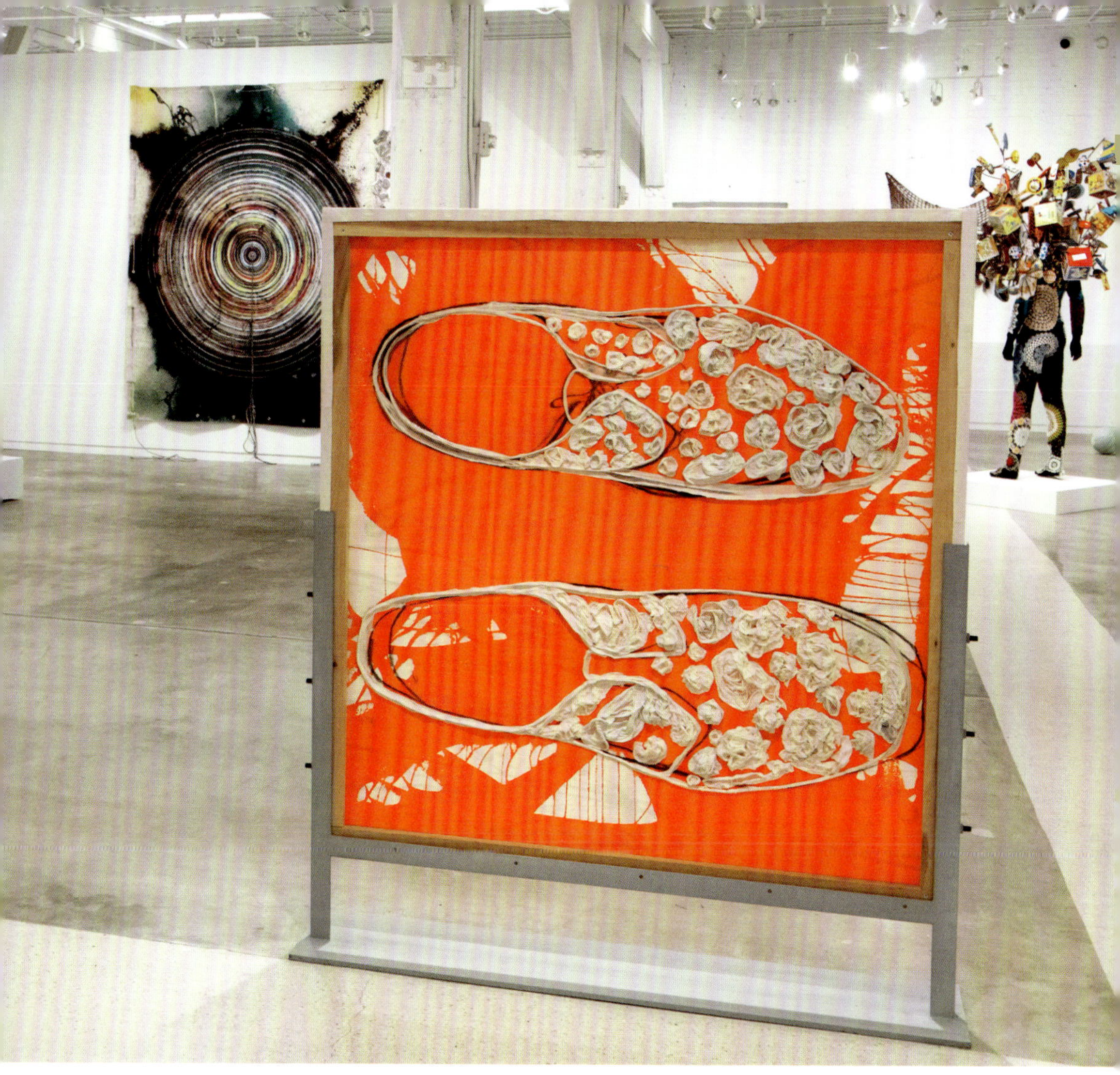

career, he would have had to stop painting. On my most recent visit to The Bunker, I saw a large painting by famed and impossible-to-get artist Amoako Boafo. DeWoody explained that she was able to buy two large paintings from Vienna where Boafo had a studio, and that she was instrumental in helping him get an Artist in Residency with the Rubell Art Museum in Miami. The Bunker is a monument to DeWoody's discerning eye and especially to her generosity and brilliance.

Visiting The Bunker is an extraordinary art experience one will always remember.

The scale of the galleries creates the space to marvel at the major works Beth DeWoody has collected, mingled with works from artists less well known.

At left, the support and encouragement of women artists is a hallmark of the DeWoody vision.

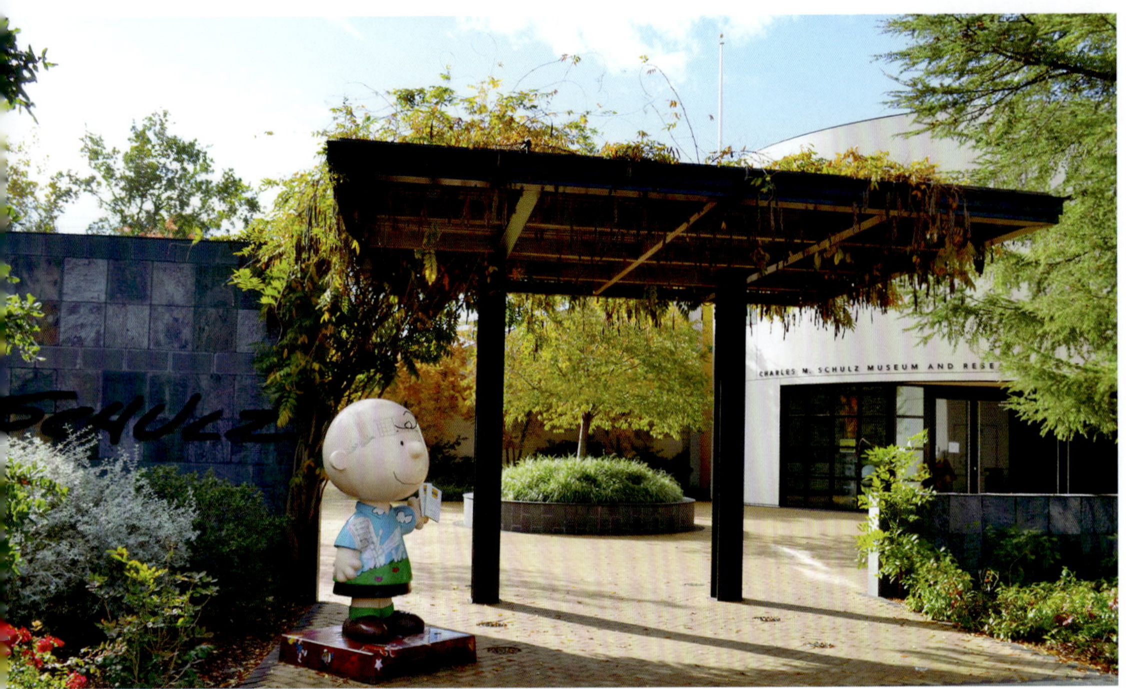

Charles M. Schulz Museum And Research Center

A mecca for the *Peanuts* obsessed who start their day with the much-beloved comic strip.

SCHULZMUSEUM.ORG

The entrance to this family-friendly Museum is warm and charming with Charlie Brown himself welcoming visitors. Facing page, on the first floor, a large, striking pastiche of published comic strips commands the space.

THE CHARLES M. SCHULZ Museum and Research Center is a forty-minute drive on Route 12 from Sonoma to the museum that winds through the hills past charming villages, small forests, and rolling acres of grape vines. In the warmer months, a visit to the museum—and Snoopy's Home Ice (an indoor ice arena) across the street—is a wonderful way to cool off.

Just outside the museum, a small Charlie Brown sculpture welcomes visitors. When you enter, tucked in an alcove on the first floor is a must-see video of Schulz's life that presents him as the artist and cartoonist we think of, as well as a dedicated family man and an integral part of the Santa Rosa community. Within walking distance from the museum is an ice hockey rink and a baseball field, both of which he donated to the town. An avid sports enthusiast, Schulz

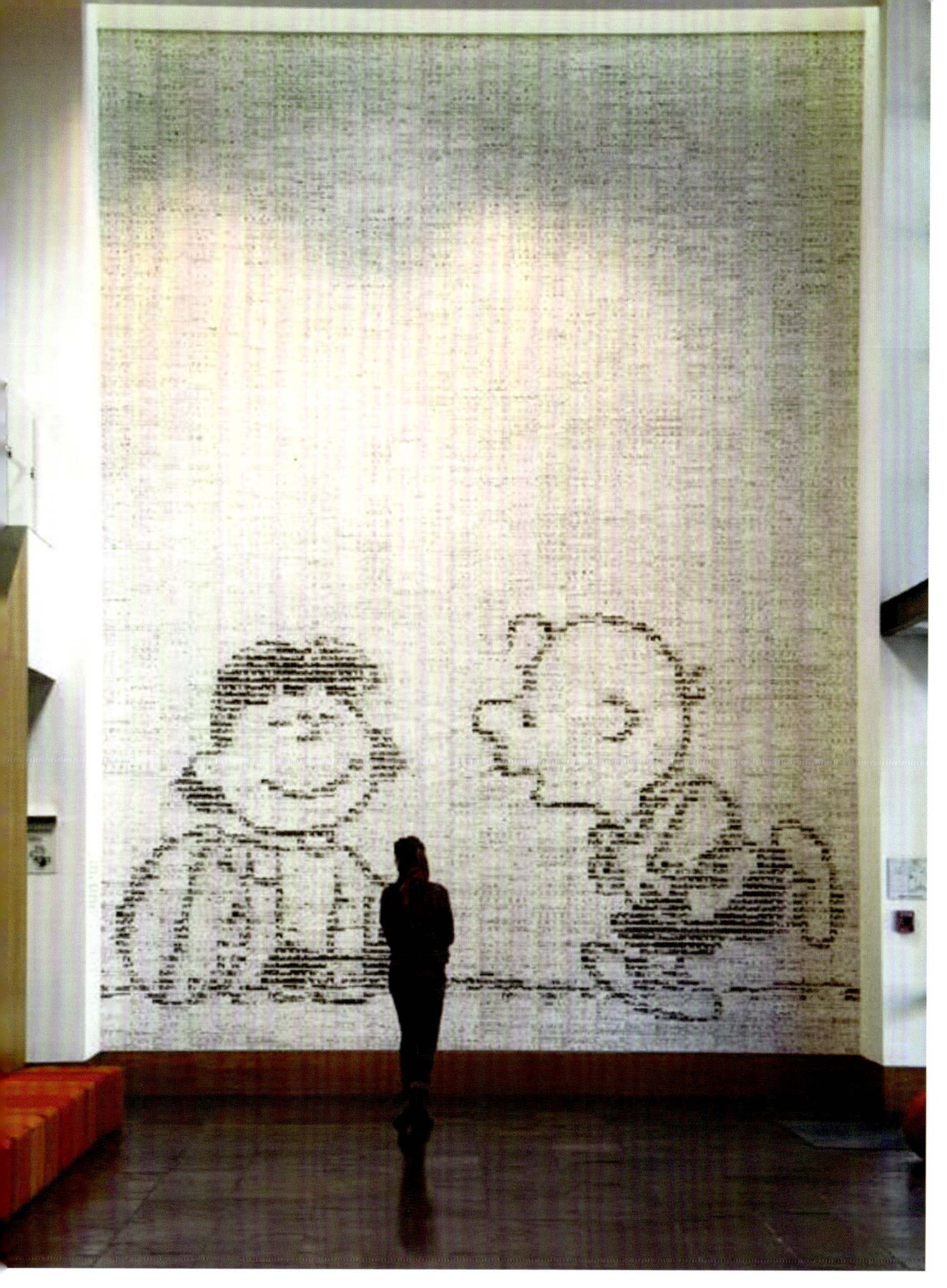

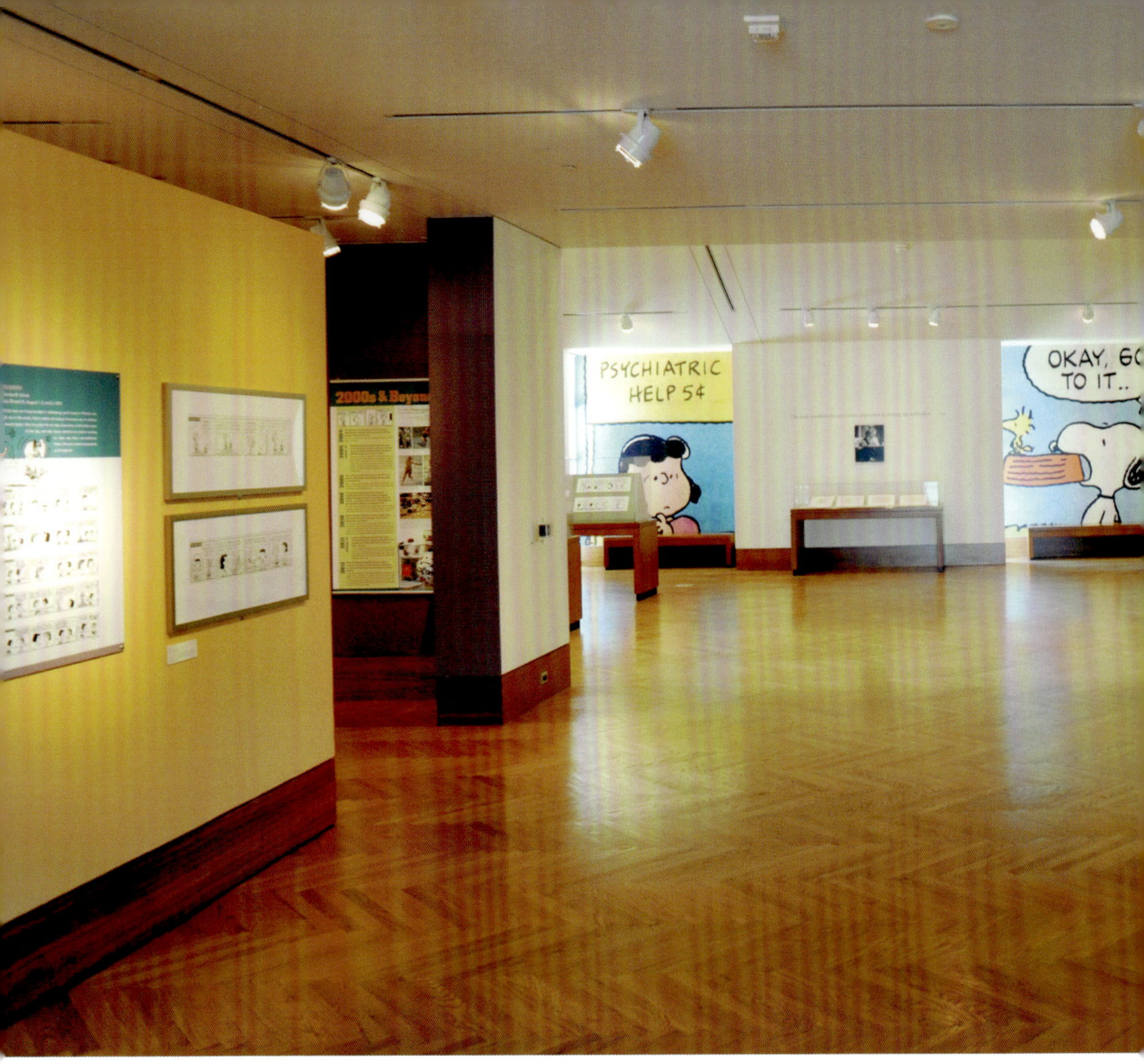

often drew Charlie Brown and friends playing football, baseball, and ice hockey in many of the daily comic strips. To Schulz, sports were a metaphor for life's ups and downs.

When we visited, there was a marvelous and very relevant installation of *LUCY! Fussbudget to Feminist*. On the second floor, there is a permanent re-creation of Schulz's art studio with tools, gifts from family, and personal memorabilia. With just a few black lines, Schulz created an intimate world defined by his philosophy of life by highlighting universal themes such as frustration, insecurity, night-mares, sibling rivalry, arrogance, friendship, and love. In one cartoon strip, Charlie Brown asks Lucy for a hug because he is going to the dentist. She declines. What could be more human than needing support from a friend?

I love this quote from Schulz: "A cartoonist is someone who draws the same thing day after day without repeating himself." Charles M. Schulz was an artist and a philosopher, and this little gem of a museum is worth a visit if you are in Northern California.

The spacious galleries are designed with the room to study Charles Schulz's original art and presentations with areas to slow down and take it all in. Below, the drawing board where inspiration struck on a daily schedule. Schulz's original studio is re-created with personal memorabilia and his tools of the trade.

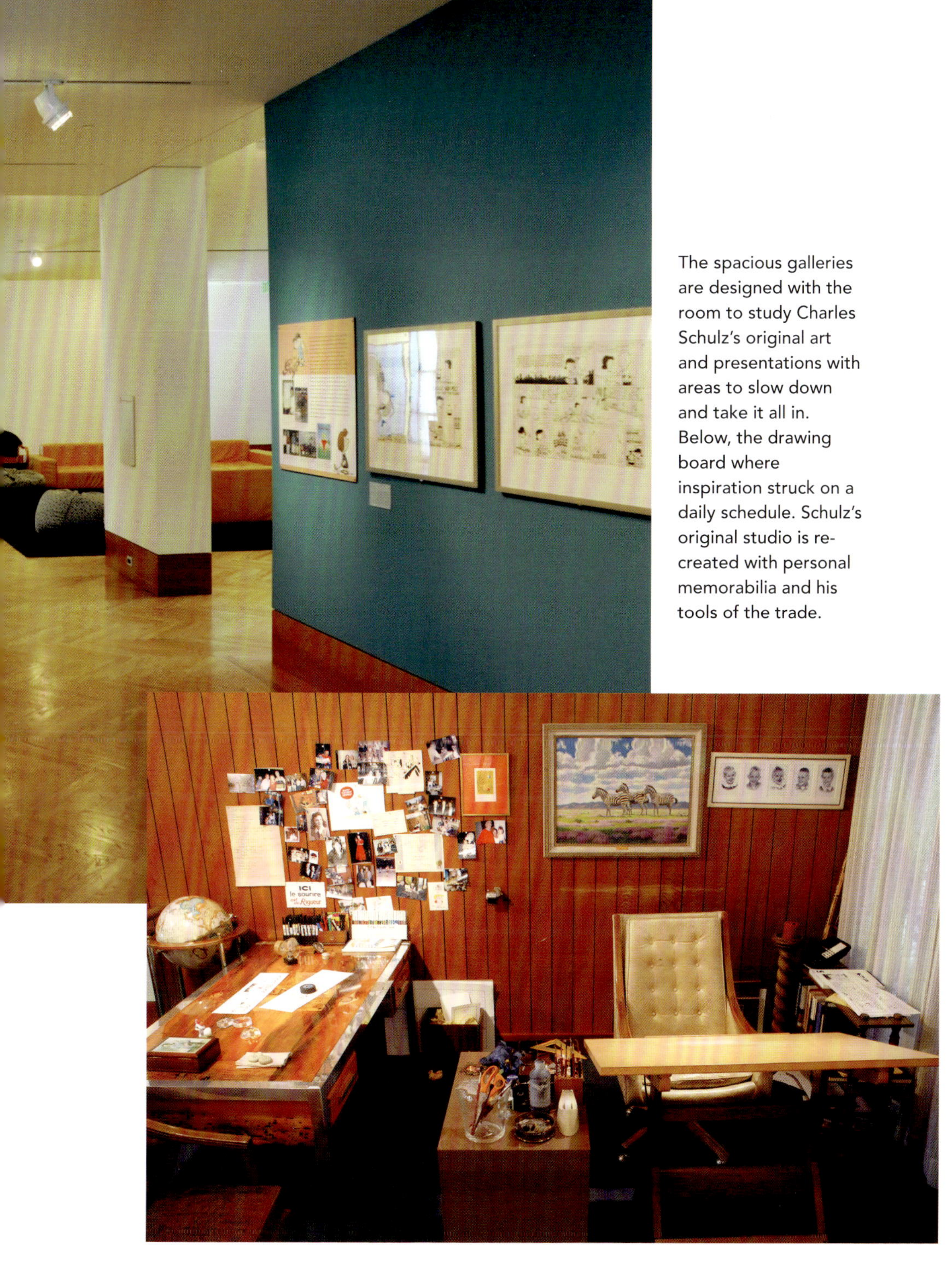

Chihuly Collection

The fragility, the danger, and the sheer beauty of these monumental glass installations is dramatically revealed as you walk through the galleries. **MOREANARTSCENTER.ORG**

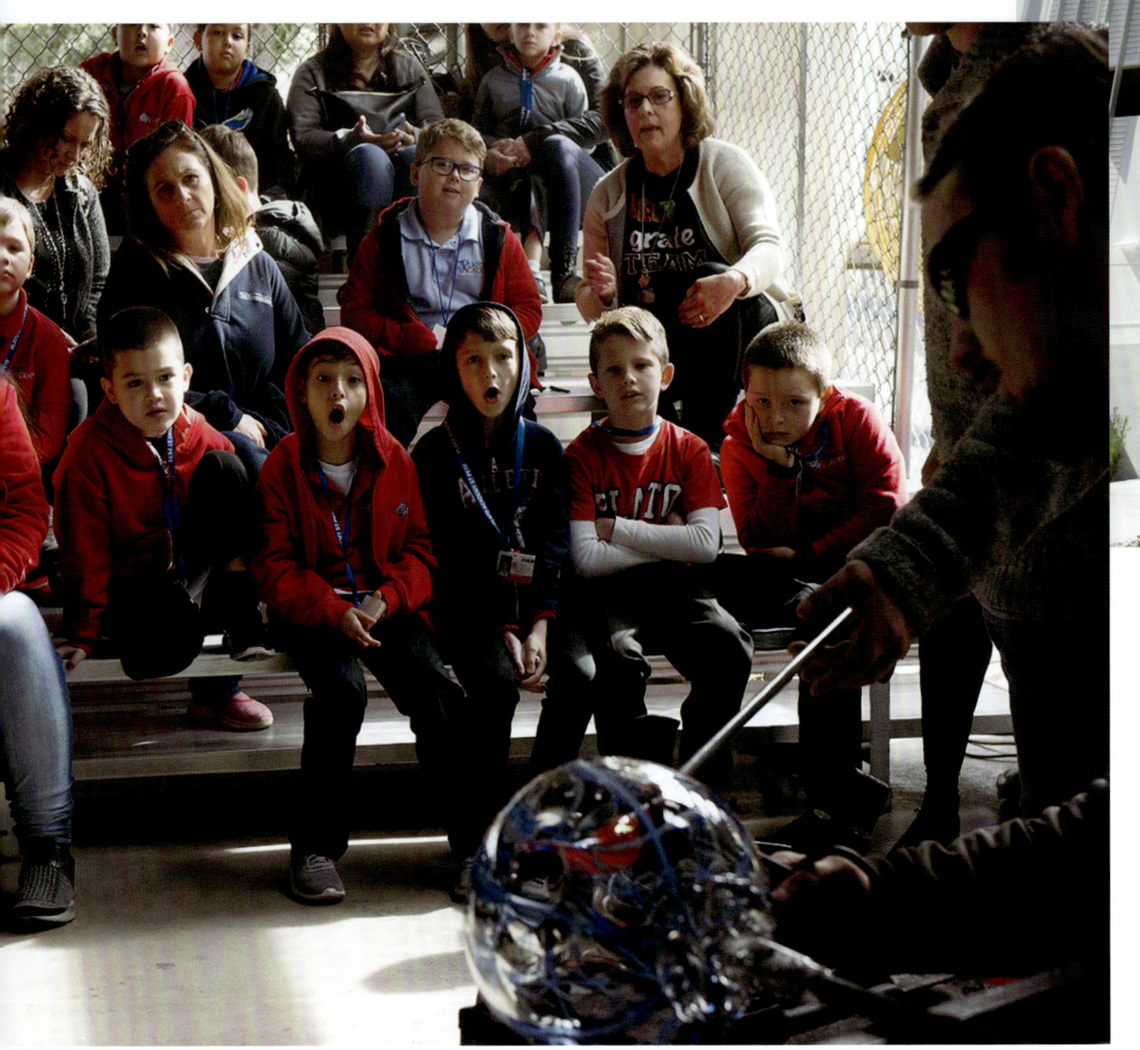

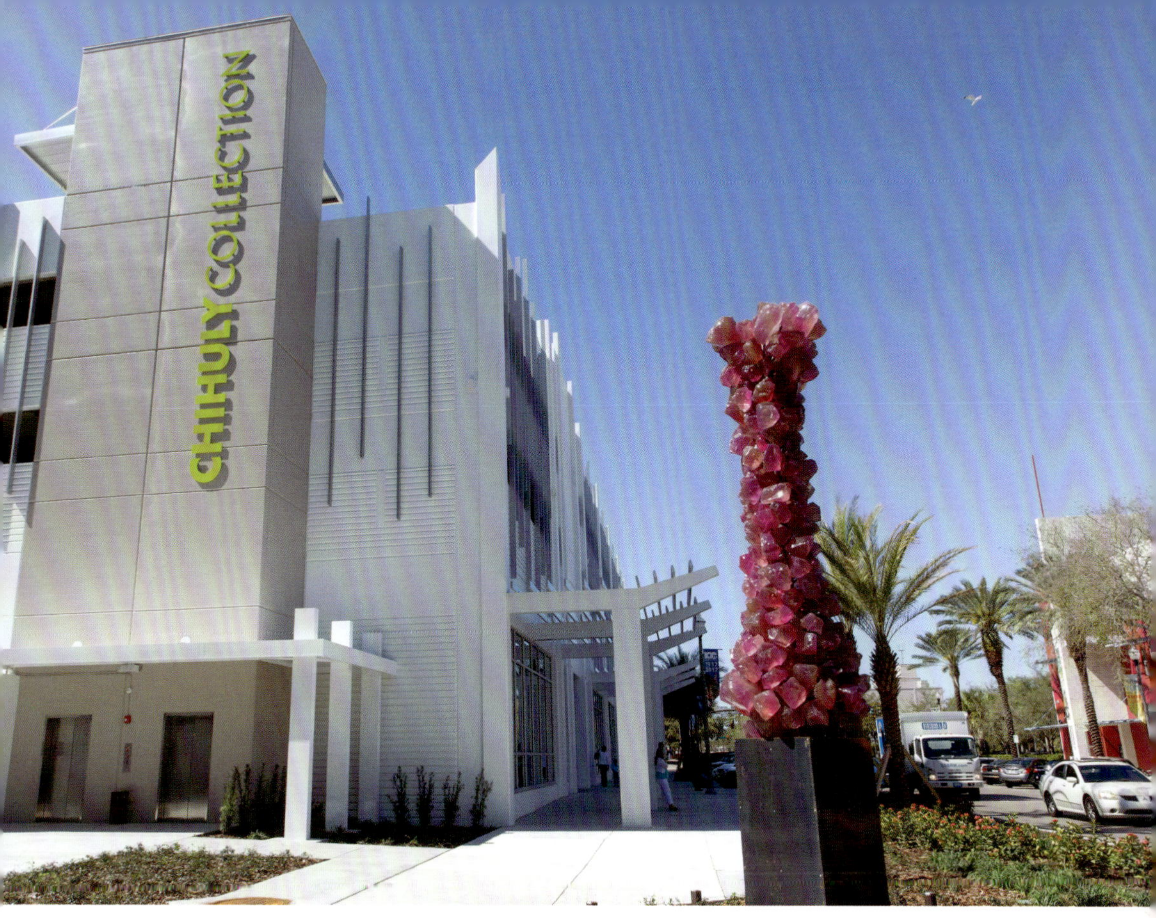

WHEN IN ST. PETERSBURG, Florida, it is definitely worth a visit to the Chihuly Collection, a permanent installation of Dale Chihuly's sensational works. Chihuly is a pioneer in glassblowing techniques and is known around the world for his dramatic art installations.

Under the auspices of the Morean Arts Center, which is located just across the street, the architecture of the building was specifically designed to highlight Chihuly's art. Each breathtaking gallery is intended to enhance the artwork with dramatic lighting that highlights the fragility of these twisted and dangerous works of art. Additionally, many of the pieces were created especially for the site, and seeing these along with his "best of the best" creations is an impressive visual experience.

Demonstrations in glassblowing can be seen at the Morean Glass Studio across the street from the Chihuly Collection. Visitors can book private lessons and even sign up for a "date night." The feeling of involvement and of demystifying the ancient art of glassblowing is a true gift to the community and will draw art tourism for many years to come.

In 2000, more than one million visitors toured the Tower of Da-

The Chihuly Collection, located across the street from the Morean Arts Center, features large glass works announcing Chihuly's artistry. Facing page, the magical transformation of molten glass into blown and decorated fantastic shapes is reflected in the faces of children enjoying a demonstration at the Morean Glass Studio.

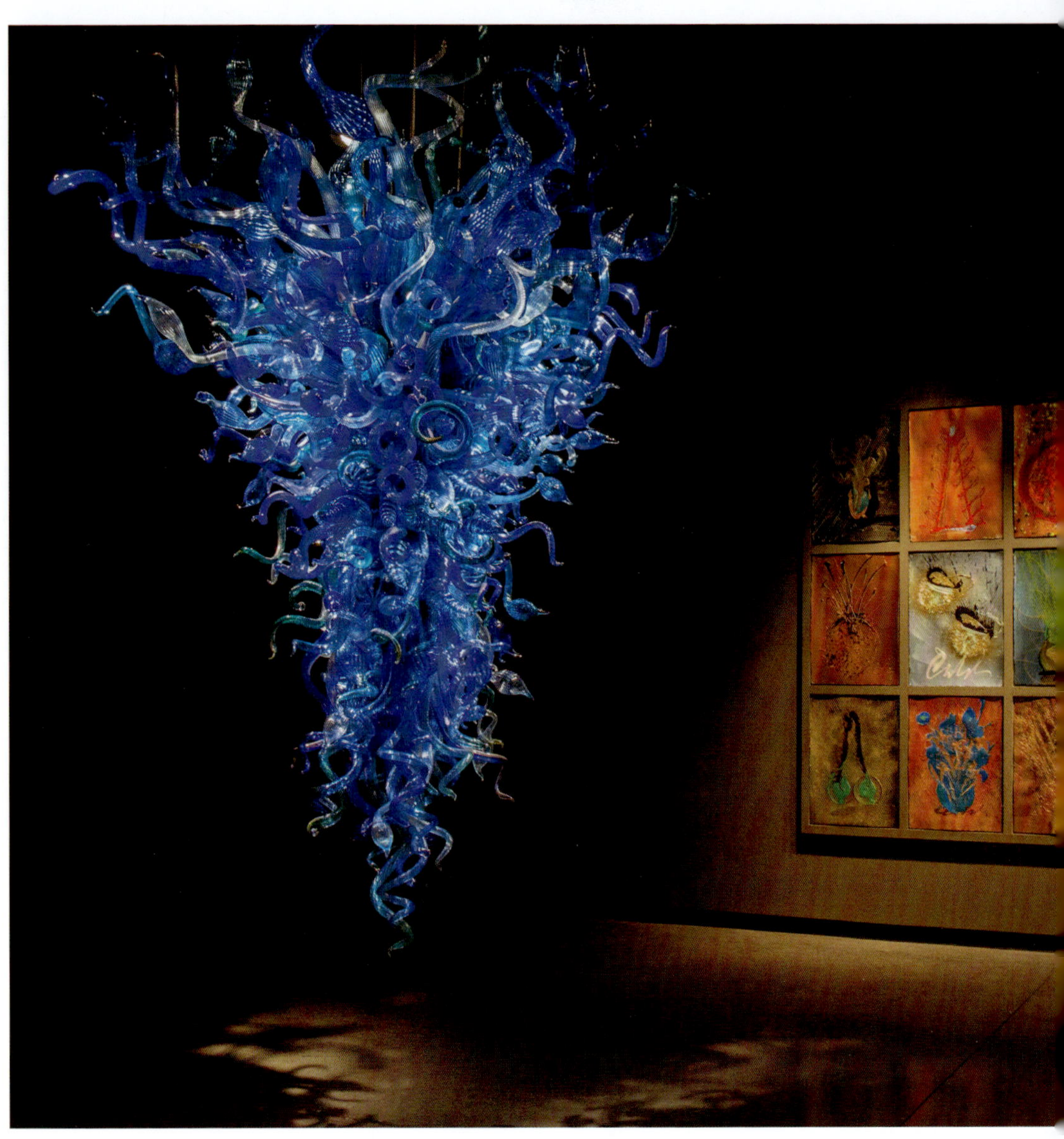

vid Museum in Jerusalem to see Chihuly's show *Light of Jerusalem*, breaking world attendance records for a temporary exhibit. I was privileged to see this remarkable installation, as well as his exhibitions in Venice and in the Botanical gardens in Denver and in New York. To learn more about this incredible artist, the Chihuly Garden and Glass Museum in Seattle, Washington, is also a must-see art venue. Established by Chihuly with the Wright family of Seattle, the Garden and Glass Museum maintains a large and comprehensive collection of his work and strongly supports arts education and involvement with the cultural community of the northwest.

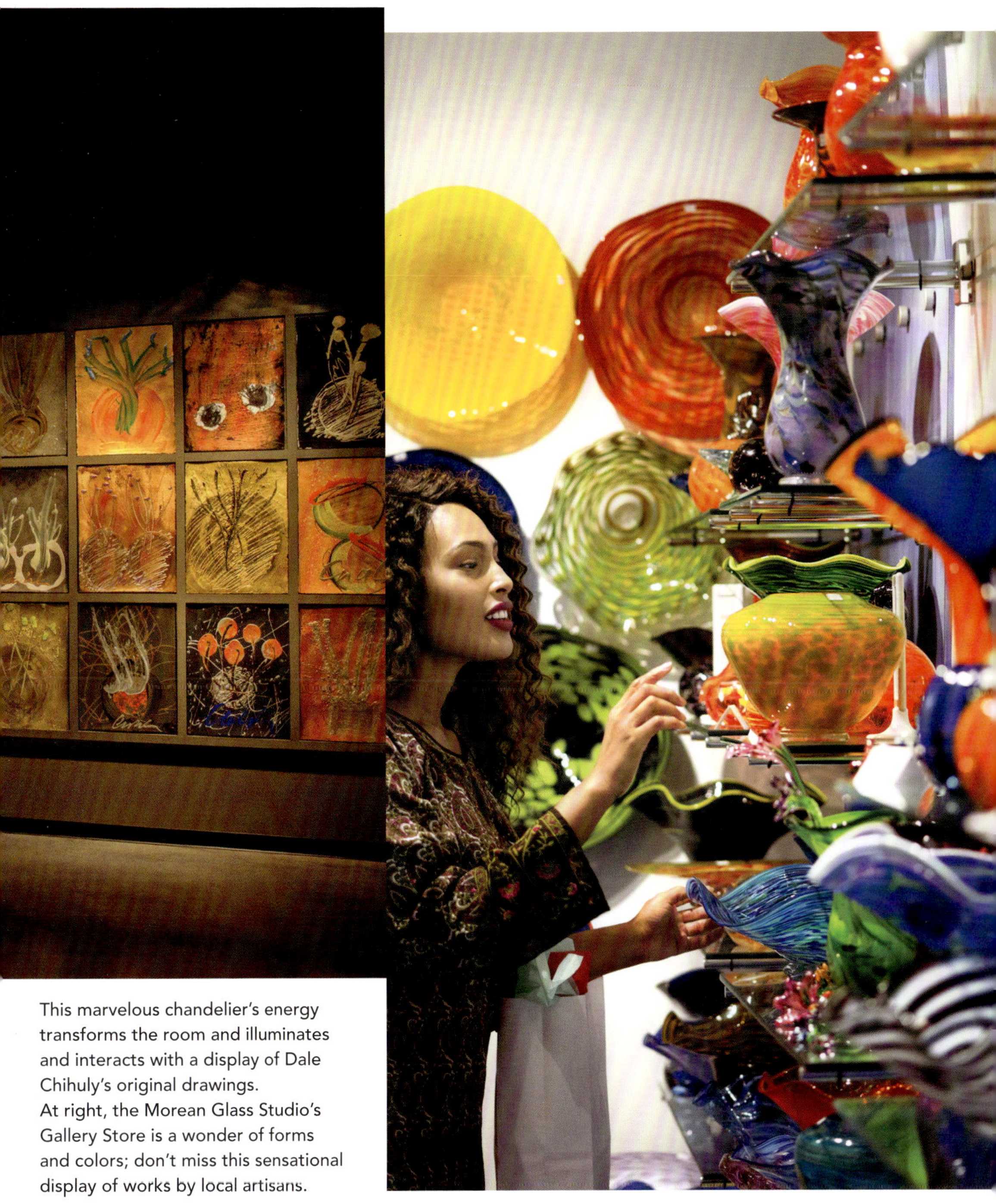

This marvelous chandelier's energy transforms the room and illuminates and interacts with a display of Dale Chihuly's original drawings.
At right, the Morean Glass Studio's Gallery Store is a wonder of forms and colors; don't miss this sensational display of works by local artisans.

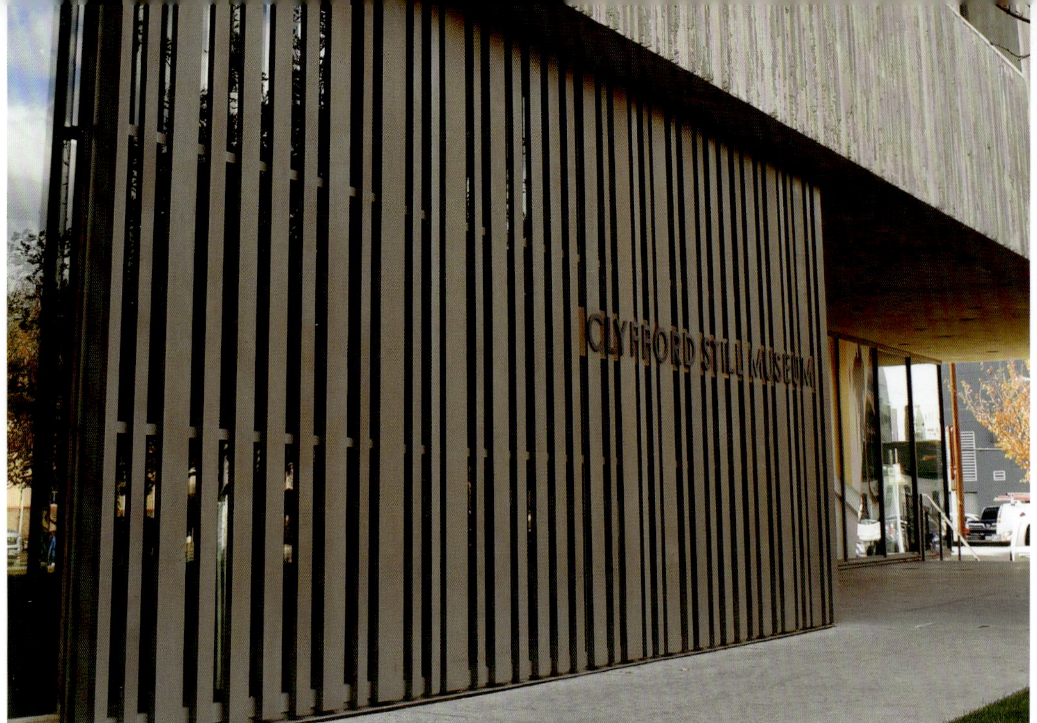

Clyfford Still Museum

Bravo to Denver, Colorado, that had the foresight to win the
Clyfford Still estate and create a museum that pays homage
to his astonishing legacy. A go-to art destination in America.
CLYFFORDSTILLMUSEUM.ORG

When you come upon
the façade, the brutalist
architecture hints at the
austere interior galleries.
Facing page, the
voluminous interiors with
soaring ceilings easily
accommodate these
monumental and thought-
provoking works.

ONE OF THE MAIN ATTRACTIONS for any visitor to Denver, Colorado, is the Clyfford Still Museum, which is home to one of the world's most intact public collections of a major artist. The story of the creation of the museum is unique and certainly worth considering before a visit.

Clyfford Still was one of the founders of the Abstract Expressionist movement in America. Still's philosophy of viewing art was that an individual artist's works should be seen together; the viewer should not be distracted by another artist's art. True to his vision, Still never sold most of his enormous body of work, and upon his death, it was part of his estate, in contrast to many other artists who sold their works while still alive. To that end, his single-page will bequeathed this entire collection of work, 95 percent of his lifetime output, to an American city that would

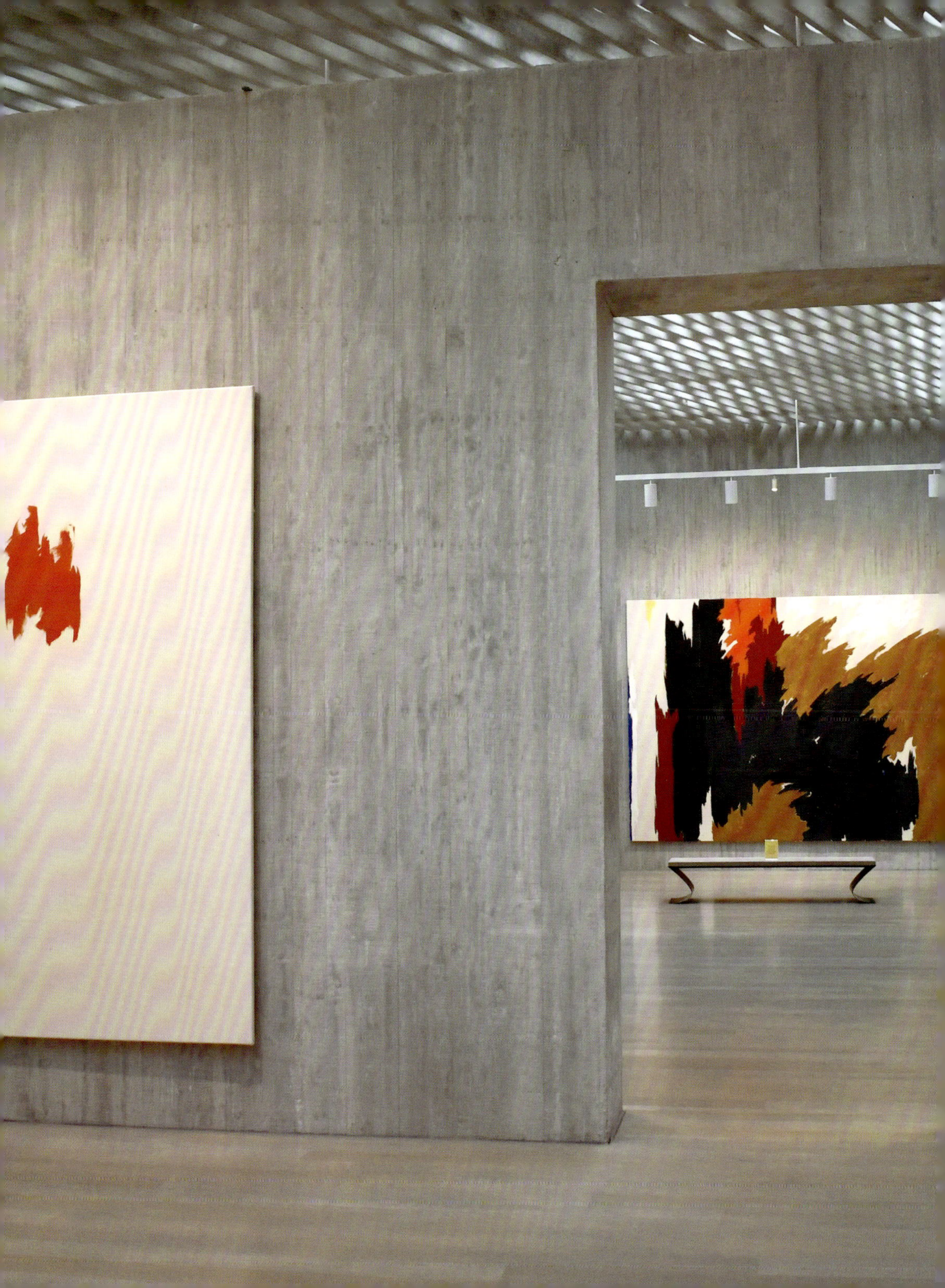

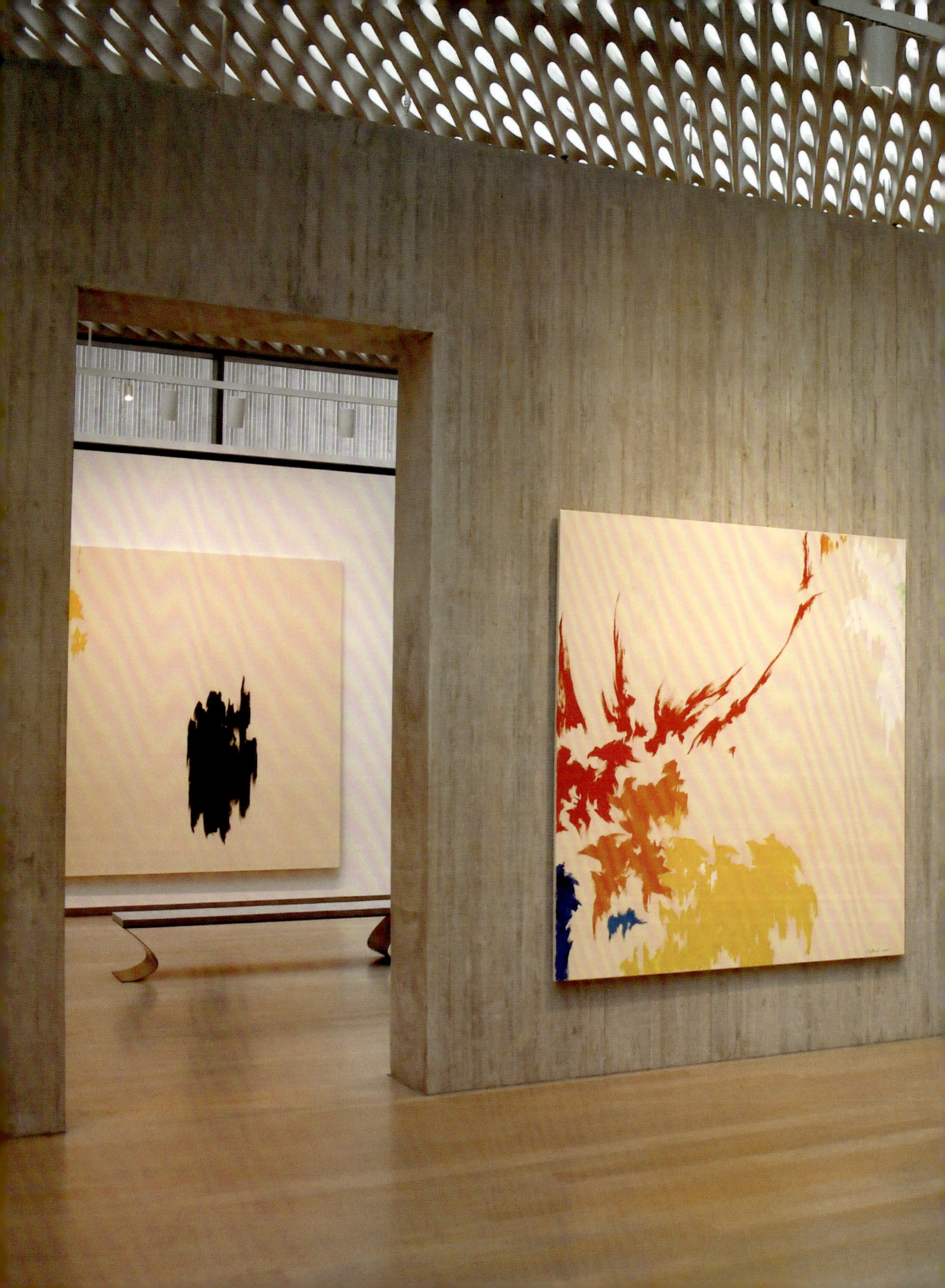

agree to design, build, and maintain permanent quarters exclusively for these works of art with the stipulation that nothing could be sold or exchanged.

Many cities vied for the prestigious collection. One of the difficulties was that many substantial museums could not maintain the collection intact in the necessary manner according to the details of the will, but Denver won the opportunity to exhibit and house this extraordinary body of work. To support the endowment, the city of Denver sold four Still paintings for $114 million at Sotheby's. Designed by Brad Cleopfil and Allied Works Architecture, the freestanding museum in a brutalist design opened to the public on November 15, 2011.

As the visitor enters the museum, one should first see the well-produced video about Clyfford Still and the philosophy of the museum. The second floor is a firework of colors, with room after room of monumental paintings. It is visually exciting and vibrant to the point of being almost overwhelming.

The Clyfford Still Museum is an art jewel and should be a stop for any art lover in Denver. The museum stores and displays Still's paintings and works on paper as well as historic photos, objects, and letters from his archives. There are 500 paintings yet to be unrolled and stretched. There are interactive features, outdoor spaces, and views into the storage and conservation areas. The museum engages with the community by including a hands-on creation studio as well as other programs and events. As former governor John Hickenlooper expressed, "Its presence will make the city an international destination for twentieth-century art."

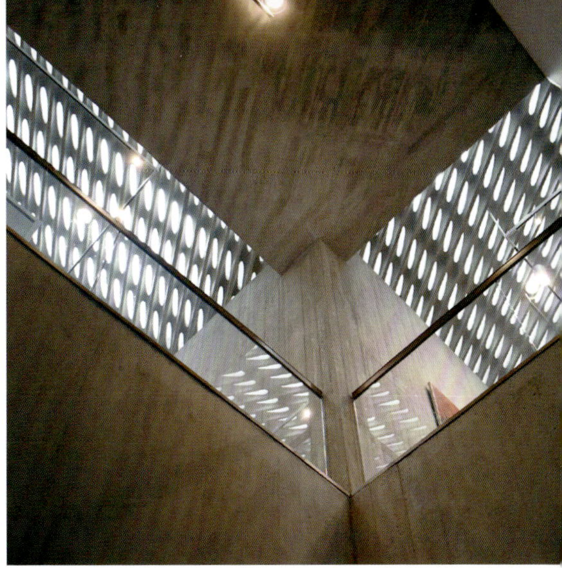

The light filled galleries showcase Still's work in a setting true to the artist's contention that the work should not be seen with competing visuals, but in the context of the artist's other work.

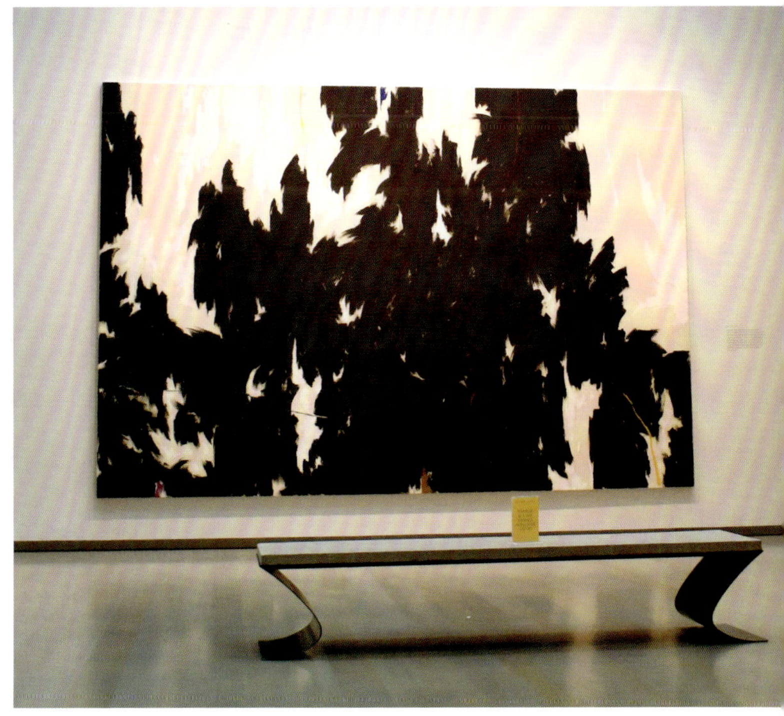

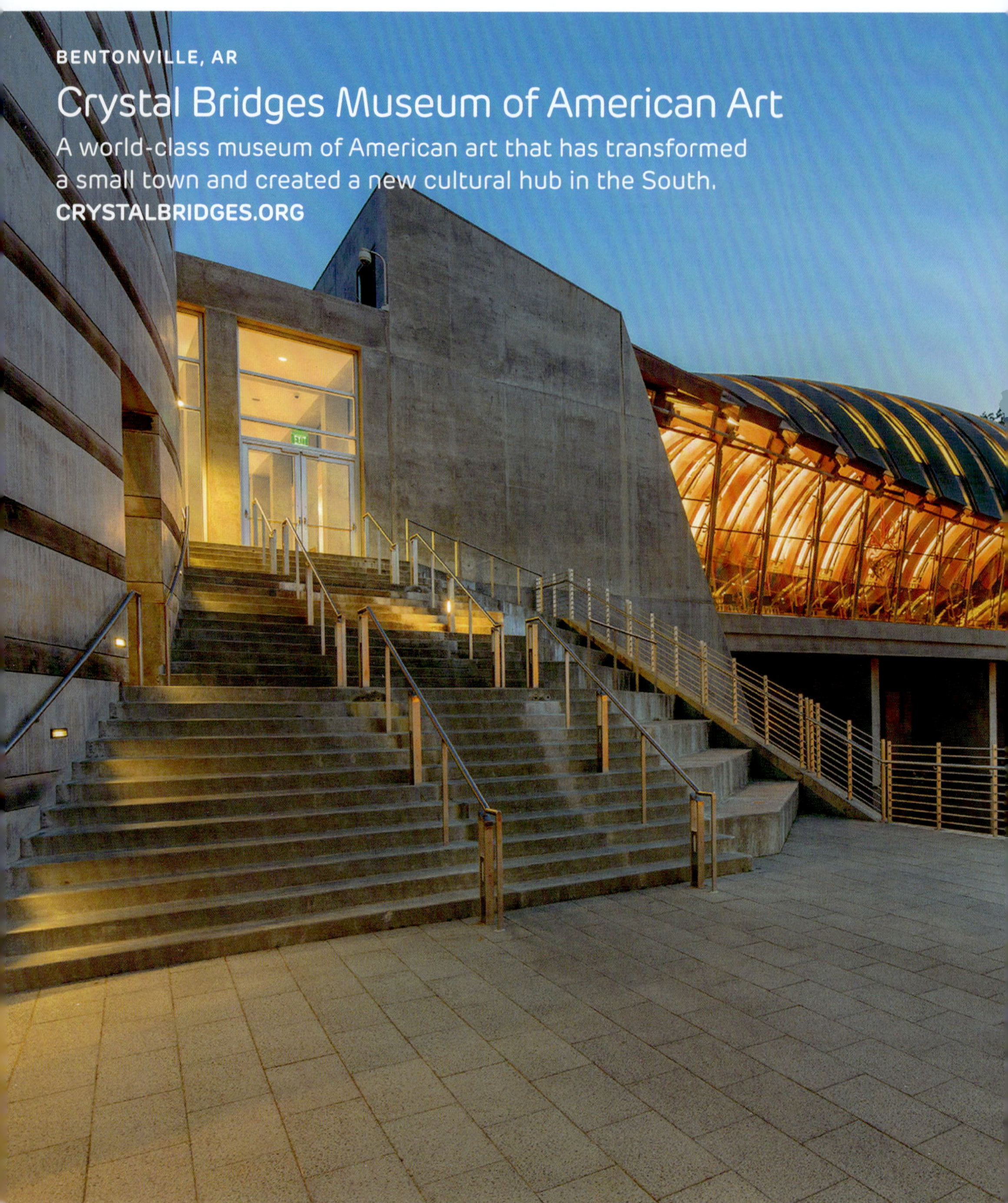

Crystal Bridges Museum of American Art

A world-class museum of American art that has transformed a small town and created a new cultural hub in the South.
CRYSTALBRIDGES.ORG

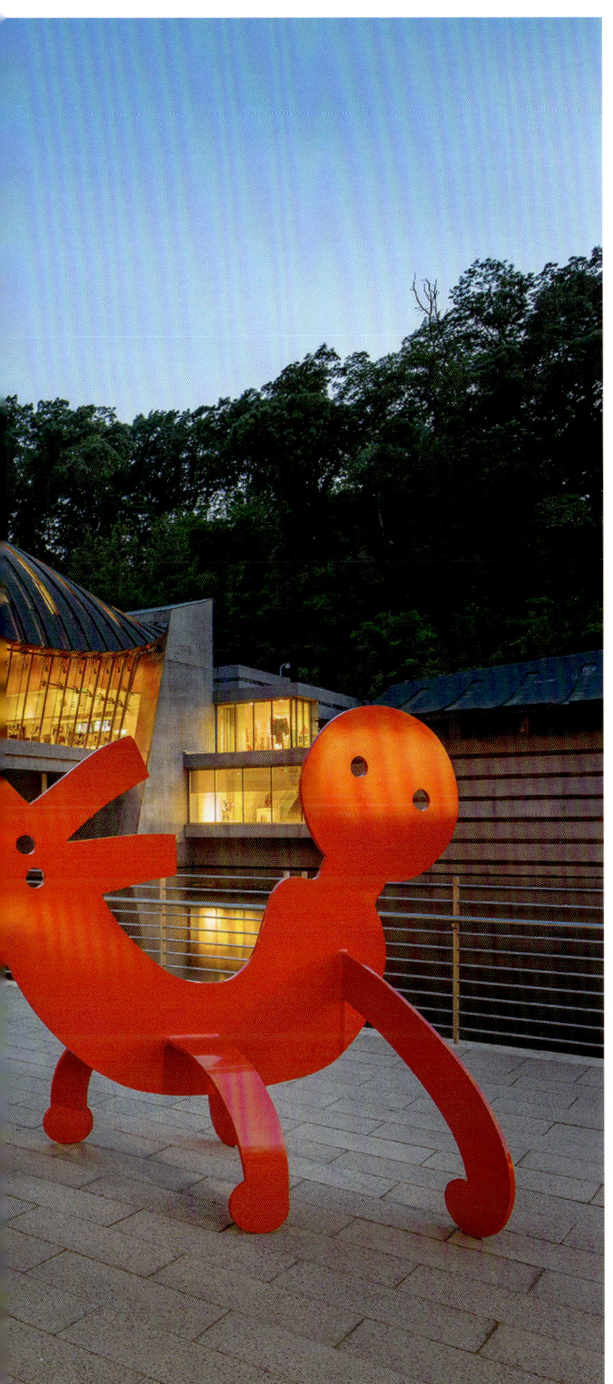

Lighting and a playful Keith Haring sculpture beckon visitors to the restaurant on Walker Landing.

IN 1997, I HAD THE OPPORTUNITY to go to the opening of Bilbao, a Guggenheim Museum built in the Catalonian region of Spain. At that time, Bilbao was a decaying industrial center, an unattractive venue without charming hotels, good restaurants or interesting boutiques.

Famed architect Frank Gehry designed the building, the Guggenheim ran the programming, and the government of Spain lent its support by providing substantial funding for the curators to buy art. Hopes were high that this new museum would change the city's landscape. Sure enough, when I returned ten years later, I found a different reality with attractive hotels, boutiques, and restaurants. There were beautifully landscaped parks, bike paths, and people enjoying the Bilbao experience.

When I visited Crystal Bridges the first time in 2011, just after the museum opened, I expected the museum would have a Bilbao effect on Bentonville, a sleepy town in Arkansas. After first visiting the museum, which was extraordinary, we visited the small city of Bentonville and the 5 & 10 Store, which was the original Walmart. Half family history museum and half souvenir shop, it boasts memorabilia from the Walton family, including their first truck. But, since there was nothing else to see or do at that time, we left for the airport. Five years later, we returned to Crystal Bridges and were happily surprised at how much the museum had expanded and how it had impacted the nearby town of Bentonville. Now, you will find cool restaurants, cute retail shops, and a 21C Museum Hotel, which is also filled with exciting art.

The cornerstone of the Crystal Bridges' collection is Alice Walton's own collection of masterpieces by American artists, including Asher Brown Duran, Winslow Homer, Edward Hopper, Norman Rockwell, and Andy Warhol. Most compelling is the range of programs and active community enhancement that have served as an example for private collectors and art enthusiasts to benefit the local community and beyond.

About a mile and half away from the museum, a former Kraft cheese plant has reopened as a multidisciplinary art space called the Momentary. Acting as a satellite to Crystal Bridges, this new center adds 24,000 square feet for performance, film, and art exhibitions.

By bringing a new cultural and educational experience to the area, this wonderful institution has changed the perception of what a "museum" is. Alice Walton has exposed and educated her community and given joy through art and the visual experience.

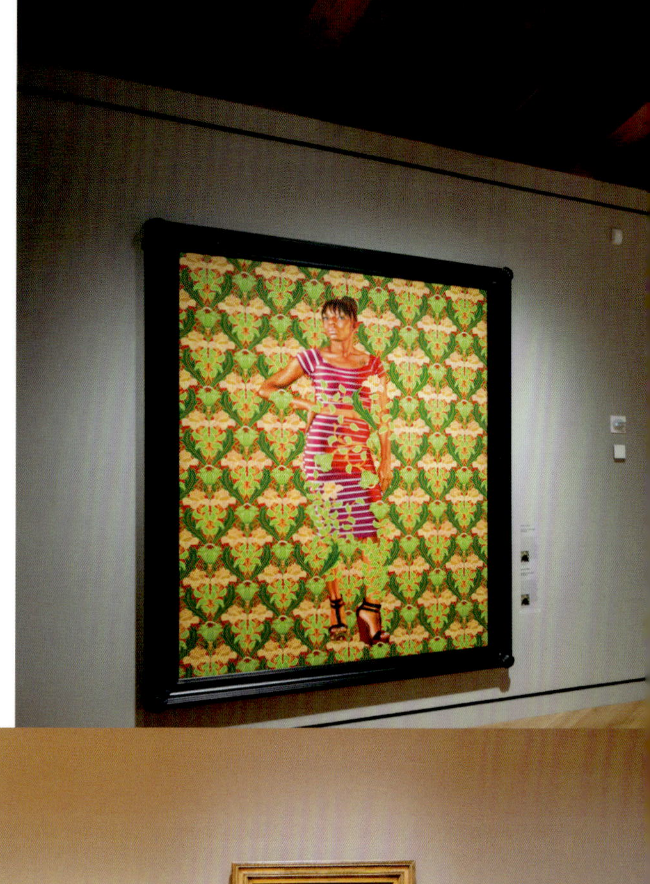

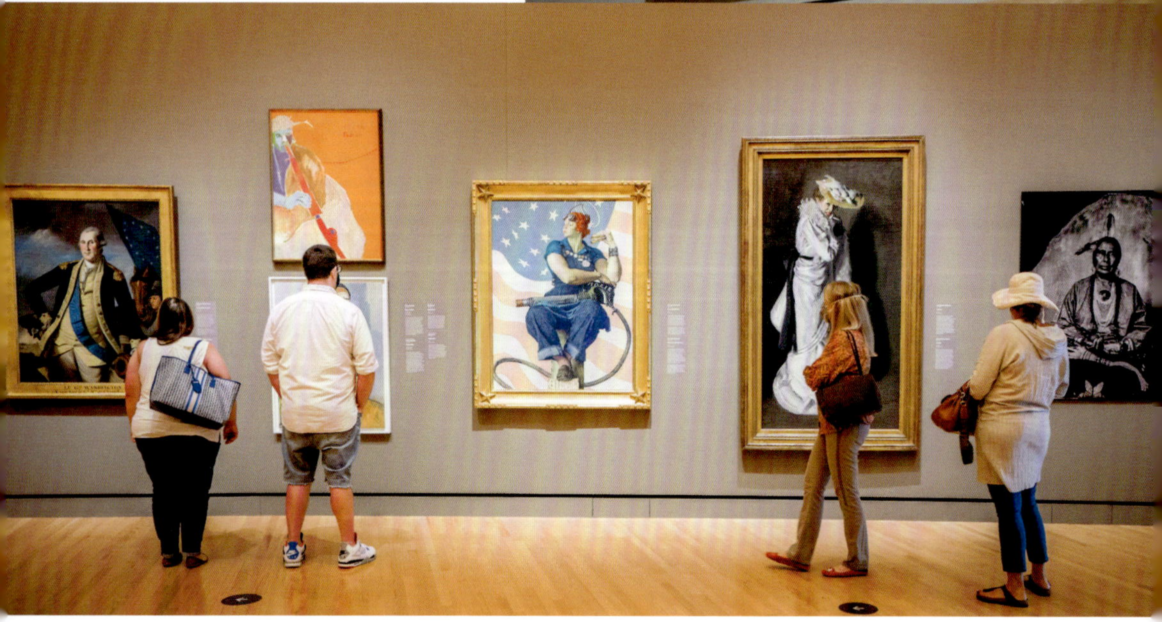

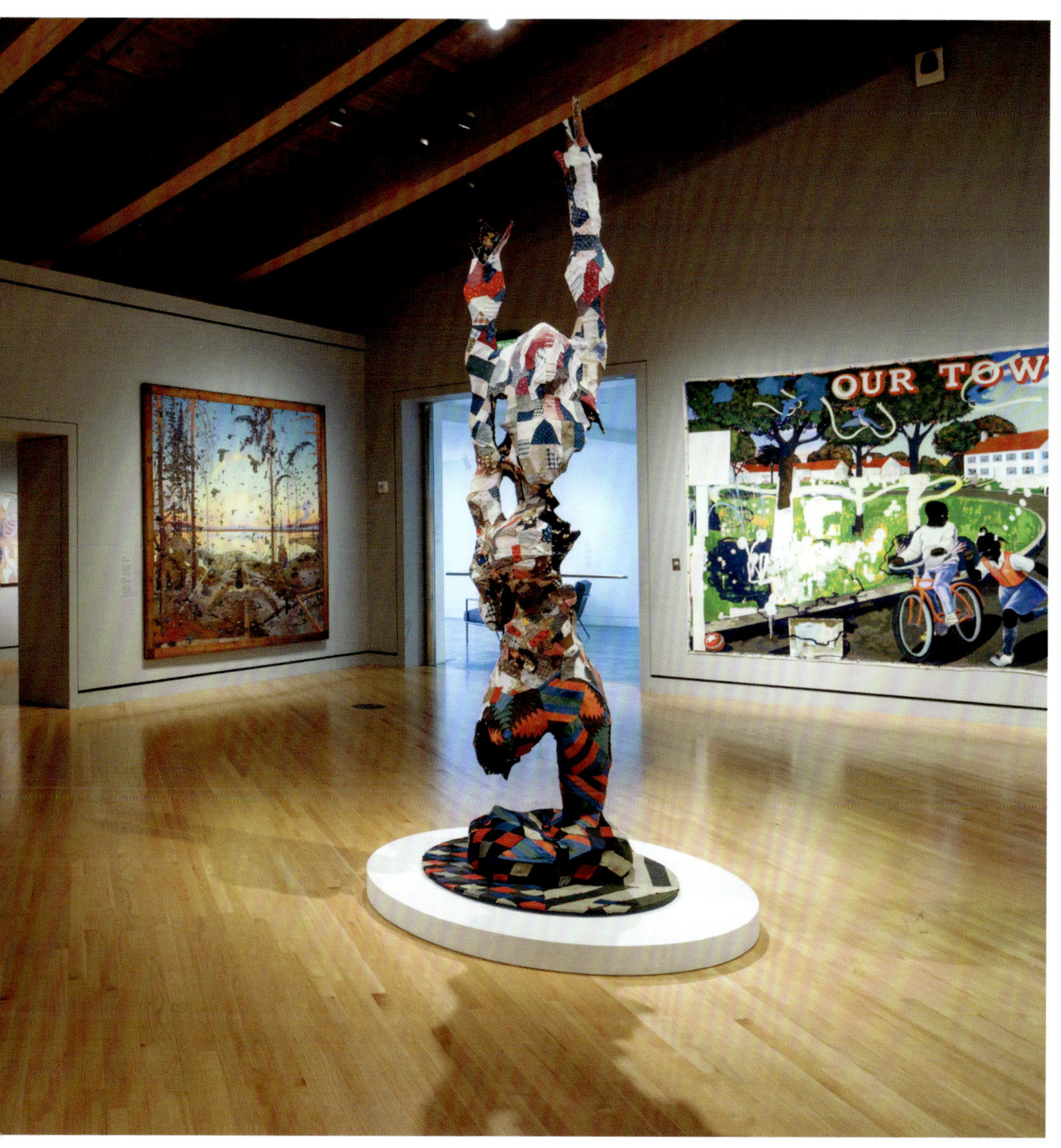

These galleries highlight Alice Walton's extraordinary collection of American art, and give Bentonville, Arkansas, a world-class art institution of its own.

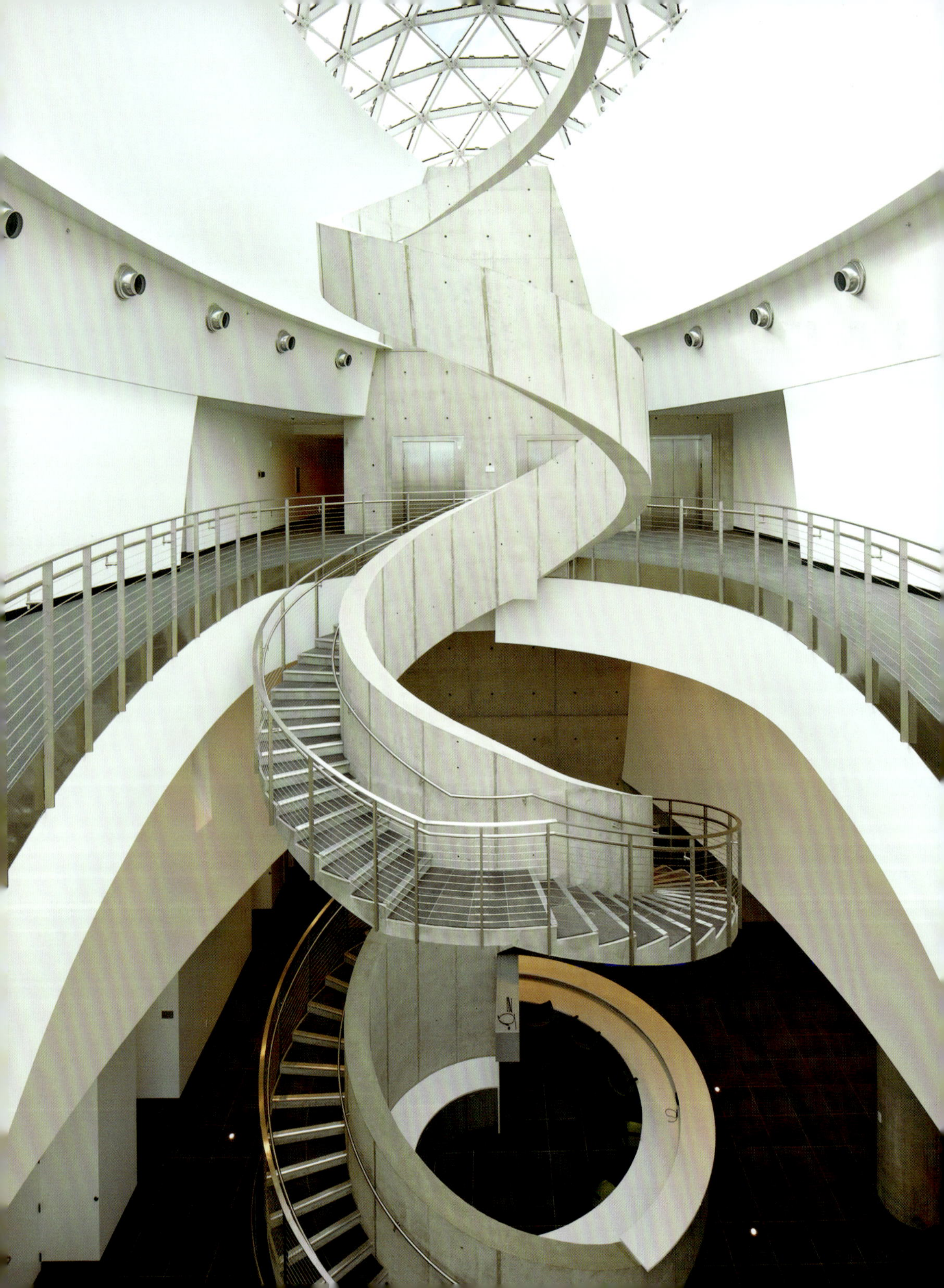

The Dalí Museum

It is hard to believe that the second largest collection of Salvador Dalí's works of art, drawings, paintings, and letters is in St. Petersburg, Florida.

THEDALI.ORG

WHO WOULD THINK that one of the greatest collections of Salvador Dalí works in the world would be in a museum in St. Petersburg, Florida?

The story starts in Ohio in 1942 when A. Reynolds Morse and his wife, Eleanor, visited the Cleveland Museum of Art to see a Salvador Dalí retrospective in a traveling exhibition from the Museum of Modern Art in New York. They fell in love with the work and bought their first painting, *Daddy Longlegs of the Evening—Hope!*, in 1943. When they met Dalí and his wife, Gala, soon after, it was the beginning of a lifelong friendship for the two couples and the beginning of the most significant collection of Dalí's work in America.

By the mid-seventies, the Morses decided to donate their entire collection to an institution with the stipulation that it had to be kept intact. Many were interested but would not or could not keep all the work together. After an official from St. Petersburg read about this intriguing story in the Wall Street Journal, he motivated the community to vie for the collection. St. Petersburg received the donation, renovations of a marine warehouse were begun, and The Dalí Museum opened in 1982.

More recently, a new building to house the museum was designed by Yann Weymouth of the architectural firm HOK. The award-winning new building opened in 2011 and is itself a

Below, a marine warehouse was transformed by an award-winning design to house the extensive collection of Dalí's works. Facing page, this dramatic and nearly surreal spiral staircase takes visitors between floors and out of the ordinary.

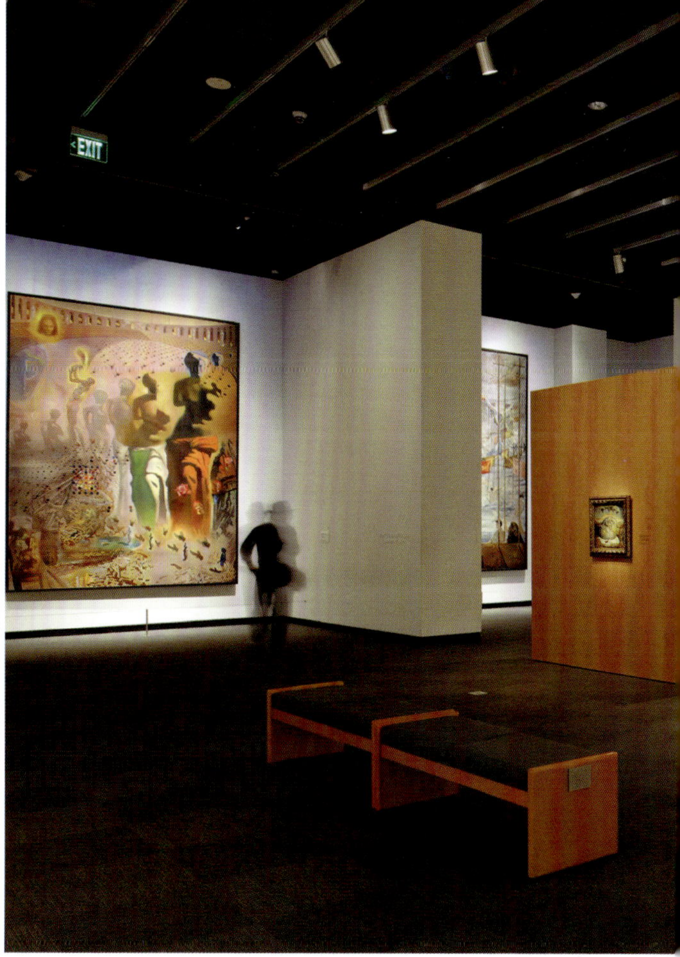

fascinating work of art from every angle. The design features a geodesic glass bubble, nicknamed the Enigma, which is an appropriate homage to Dalí's innovative and transformative artistic career.

The outstanding collection, remarkable in its depth, includes 96 oil paintings, more than 100 watercolors, and many drawings, photographs, and sculptures. On view in the main galleries are one masterpiece after another, including the first piece the Morses purchased in 1942. The museum also hosts traveling exhibits, perhaps in the spirit of the Morses' first introduction to Dalí.

When we visited, I was intrigued by a new exhibition named *Dalí Lives*. Using

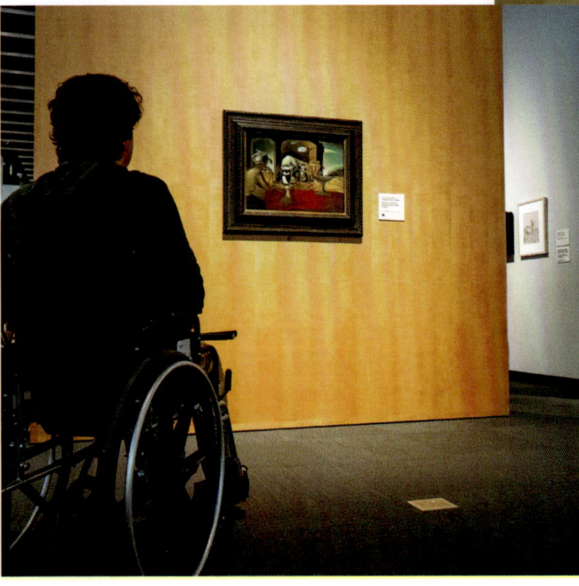

artificial intelligence, the curators created a modern-day Dalí. Reminding me of a hologram, the larger-than-life figure answered questions about his art and life. There was also a temporary installation by Sensory4 that projected Vincent van Gogh's art on the walls and floor of the gallery. Using 3D images and sound, the immersive experience allowed the viewer to feel like she was in a van Gogh painting. The experience was surreal and clearly appropriate given this museum's commitment to artistic innovation.

The large gift shop offers wonderful shopping opportunities at every price point, and the café serves Spanish food like tapas. The museum library contains more than 7,000 books, catalogues, and recordings.

The easily accessible galleries showcase many of Dalí's esoteric and fascinating works, while the delightful gift shop, at right, displays some of Dalí's artifacts, including his personal limousine.

Enjoy this cultural gift to Florida and reserve at least two hours to explore. Be sure to buy tickets beforehand on their easy-to-use ticket website. The day we were there, visitors were turned away because they had not previously purchased tickets.

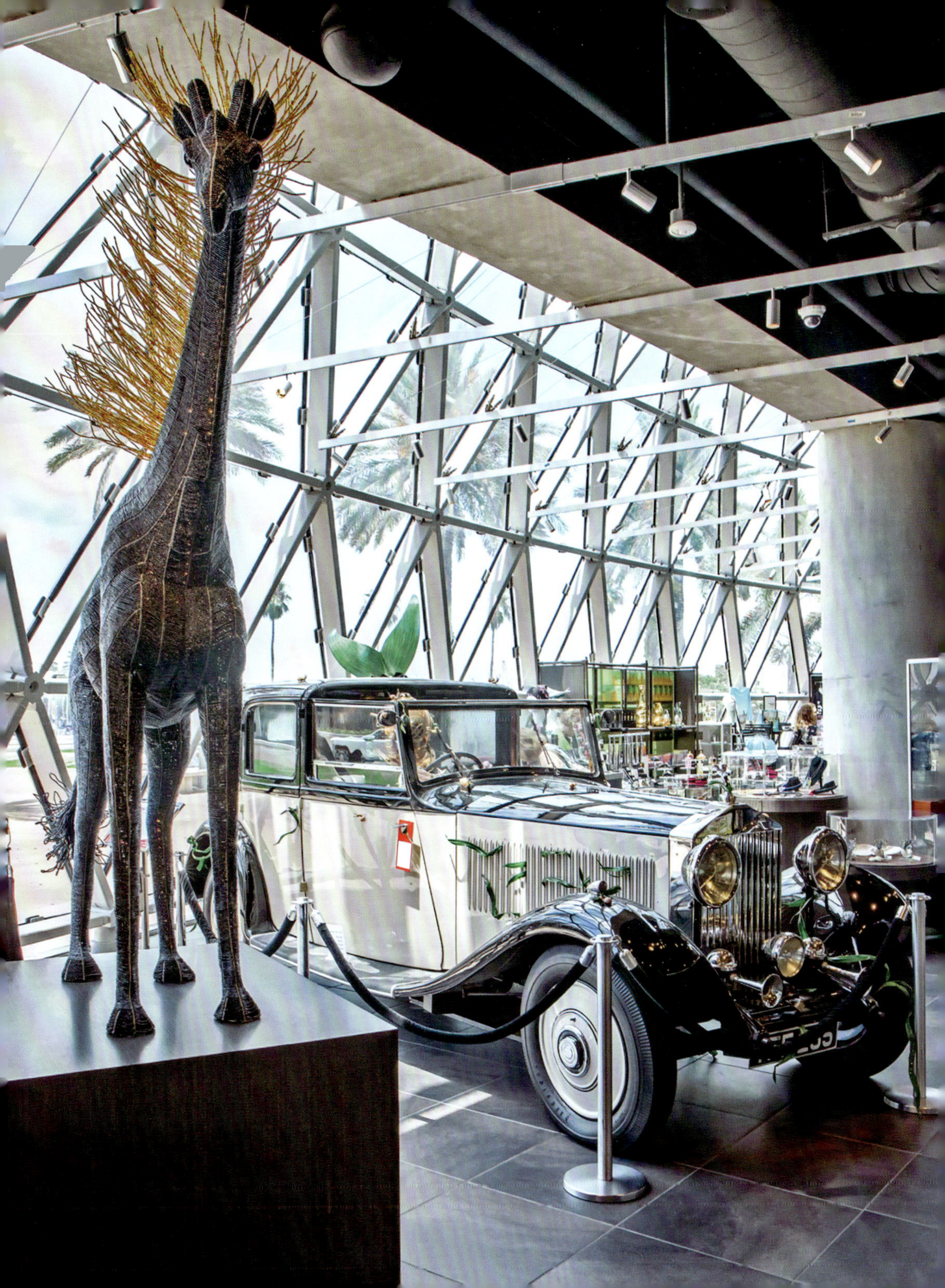

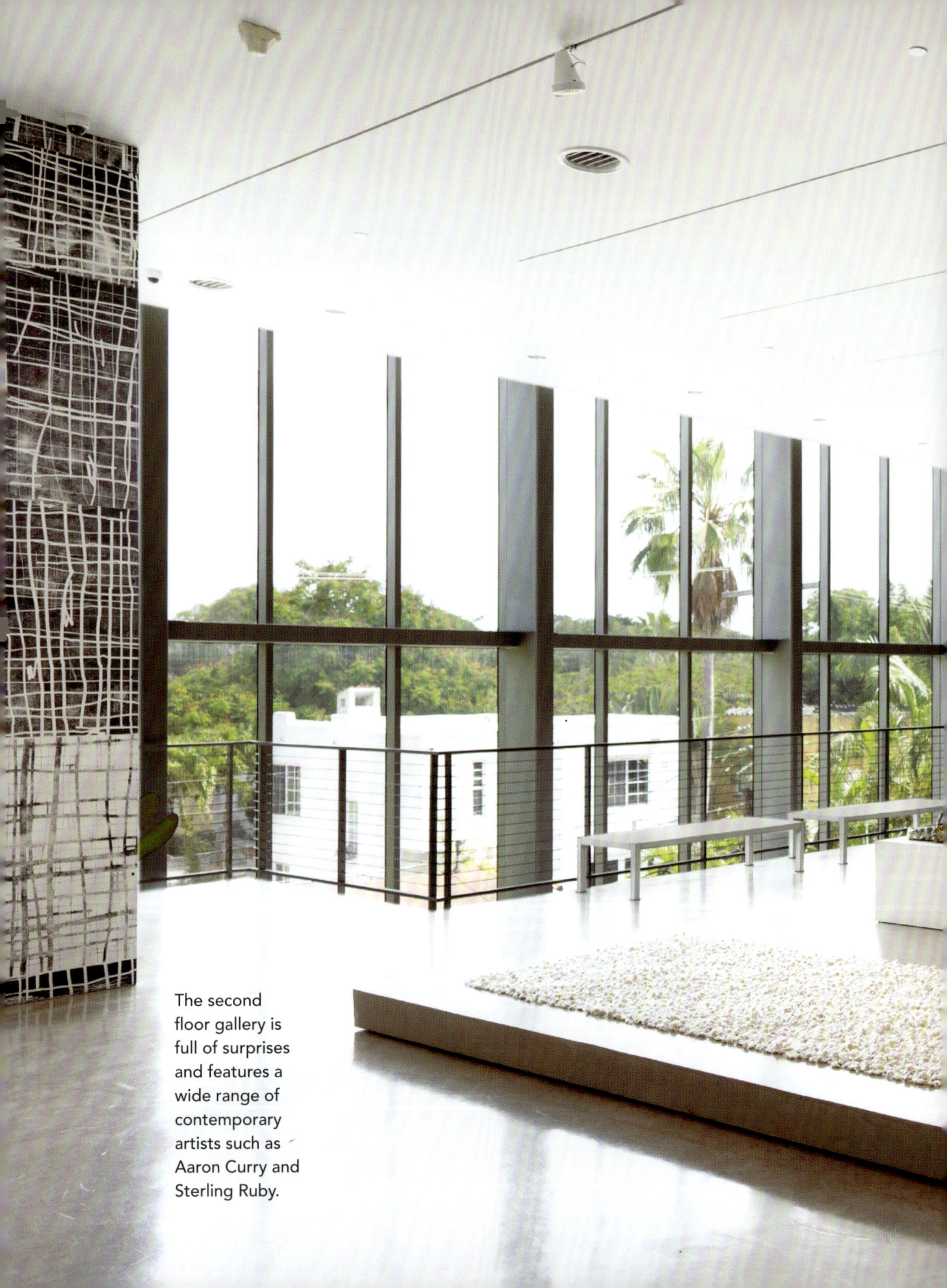

The second floor gallery is full of surprises and features a wide range of contemporary artists such as Aaron Curry and Sterling Ruby.

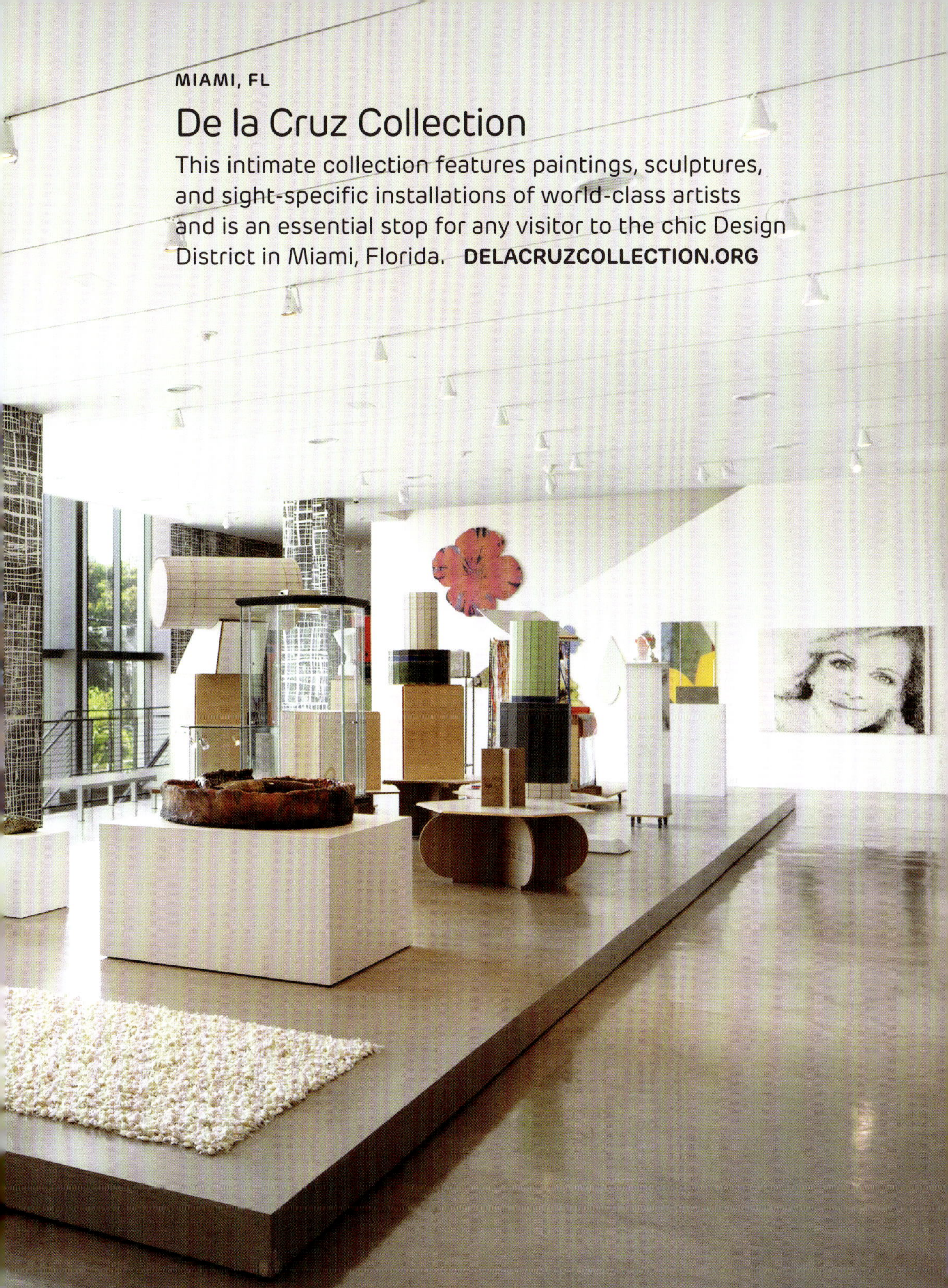

De la Cruz Collection

This intimate collection features paintings, sculptures, and sight-specific installations of world-class artists and is an essential stop for any visitor to the chic Design District in Miami, Florida. **DELACRUZCOLLECTION.ORG**

EVERY TIME I WALK INTO the de la Cruz Collection, I consider how lucky I am to visit this gem of a private art venue. In the 1980s, Rosa and Carlos de la Cruz, who are well known in Miami for their generosity and philanthropy, began opening their home by appointment for visitors to view their burgeoning collection of contemporary art. I remember being invited during the week of Art Basel in Miami. I was always astounded at the intimate setting, how lovingly the work was displayed and discussed by Rosa and Carlos, and how privileged I felt to be welcomed inside.

Over time, their collection grew and they needed more space if they were to continue to share their treasures with the community. In 2009, they opened the de la Cruz Collection in a building designed by local designer John Marquette in the Miami Design District. Comprising over thirty thousand square feet and spanning three levels, this museum remains private, accepts no government funding, and is open for the public to enjoy for free. Most fortunately, the building, while very large, has been designed to continue the feeling of intimacy they established with their original viewings and almost feels like an extension of their home.

Artists on view include Felix Gonzalez-Torres, Glenn Ligon, and Sterling Ruby. There are large installations by Aaron Curry. One of my favorite art experiences is to visit the side gallery on the third floor to see the brightly color-infused work of Alex Israel. Also on the third floor, be sure to see the photography and video installation by Ana Mendieta, who used her body as the focus for her work. A feminist visionary, she died too soon at thirty-seven.

The de la Cruzes' public programs are sensational and include lectures by famous artists from their collection posted on YouTube. One can also take advantage of their excellent

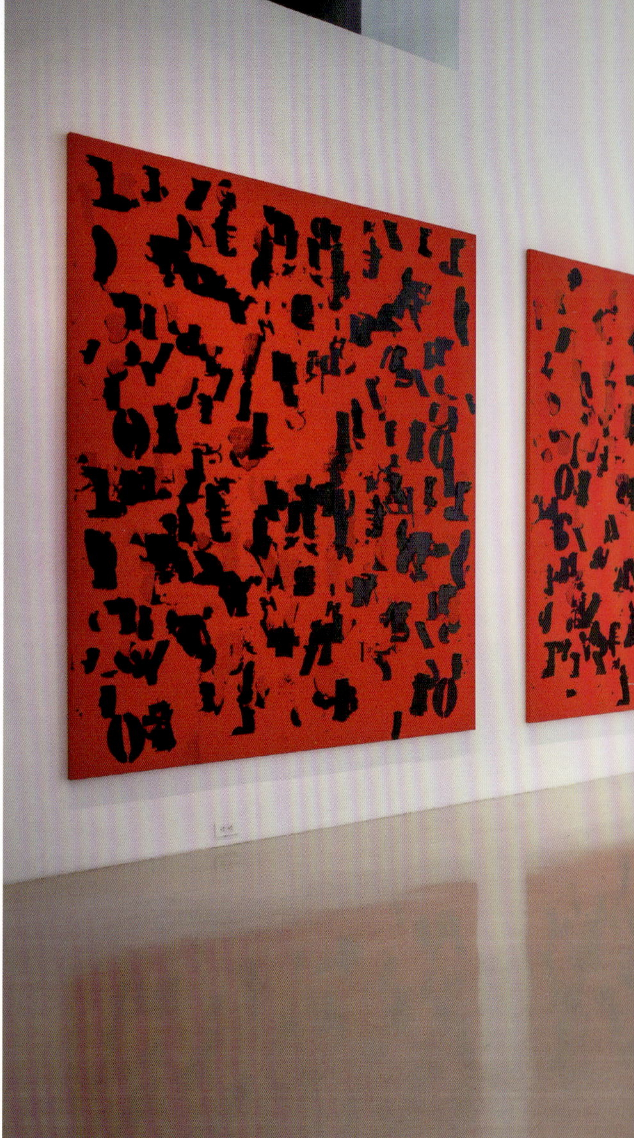

website, where they share past lectures and programming. Their scholarship program and support for young artists is renowned in the art world. As you enter the building, a sign reads: "Our exhibits are a collective effort to build new possibilities by creating a platform for the artists' vision. We have deliberately focused on art that questions issues relevant today."

If this is their mantra, it is certainly a good one.

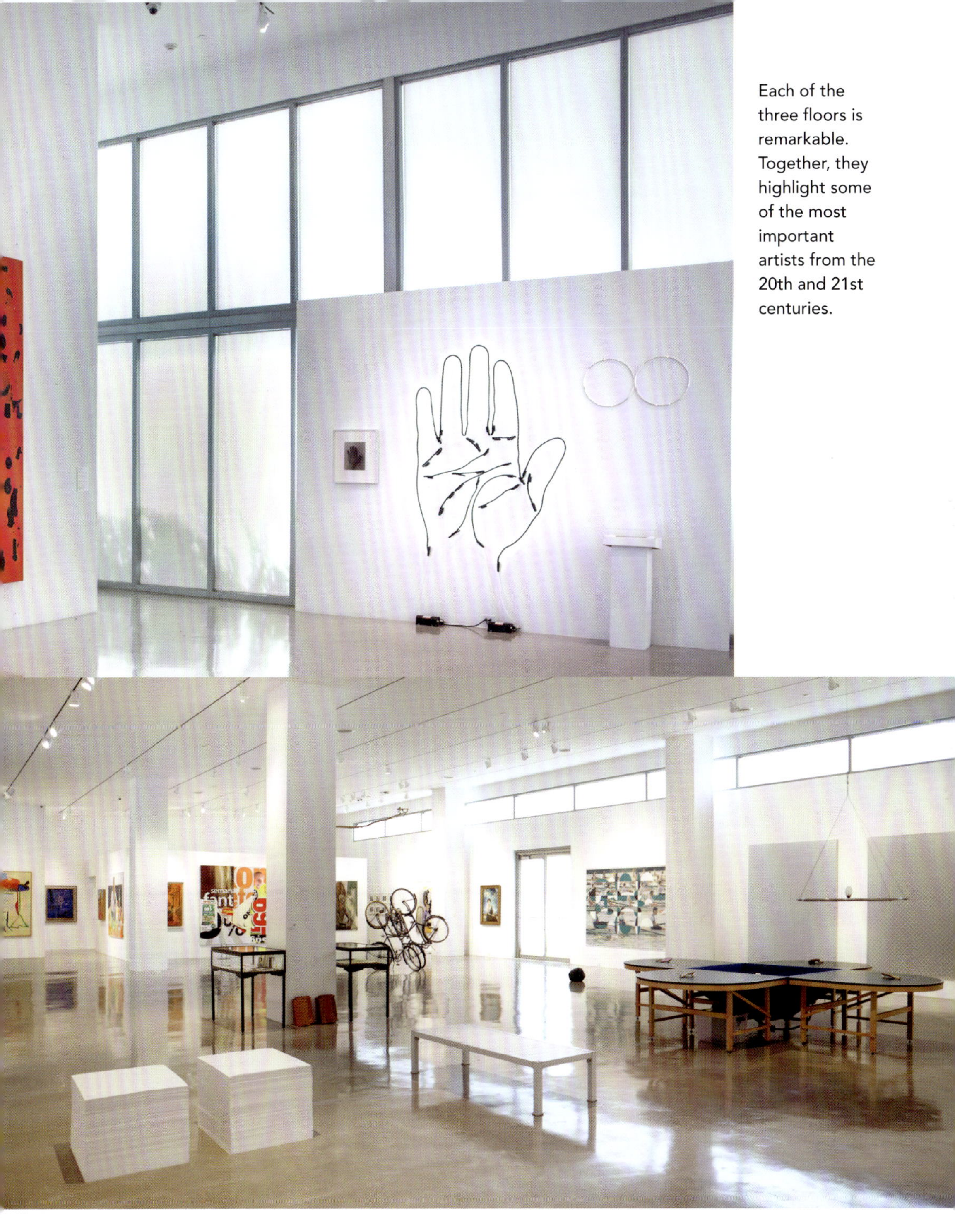

Each of the three floors is remarkable. Together, they highlight some of the most important artists from the 20th and 21st centuries.

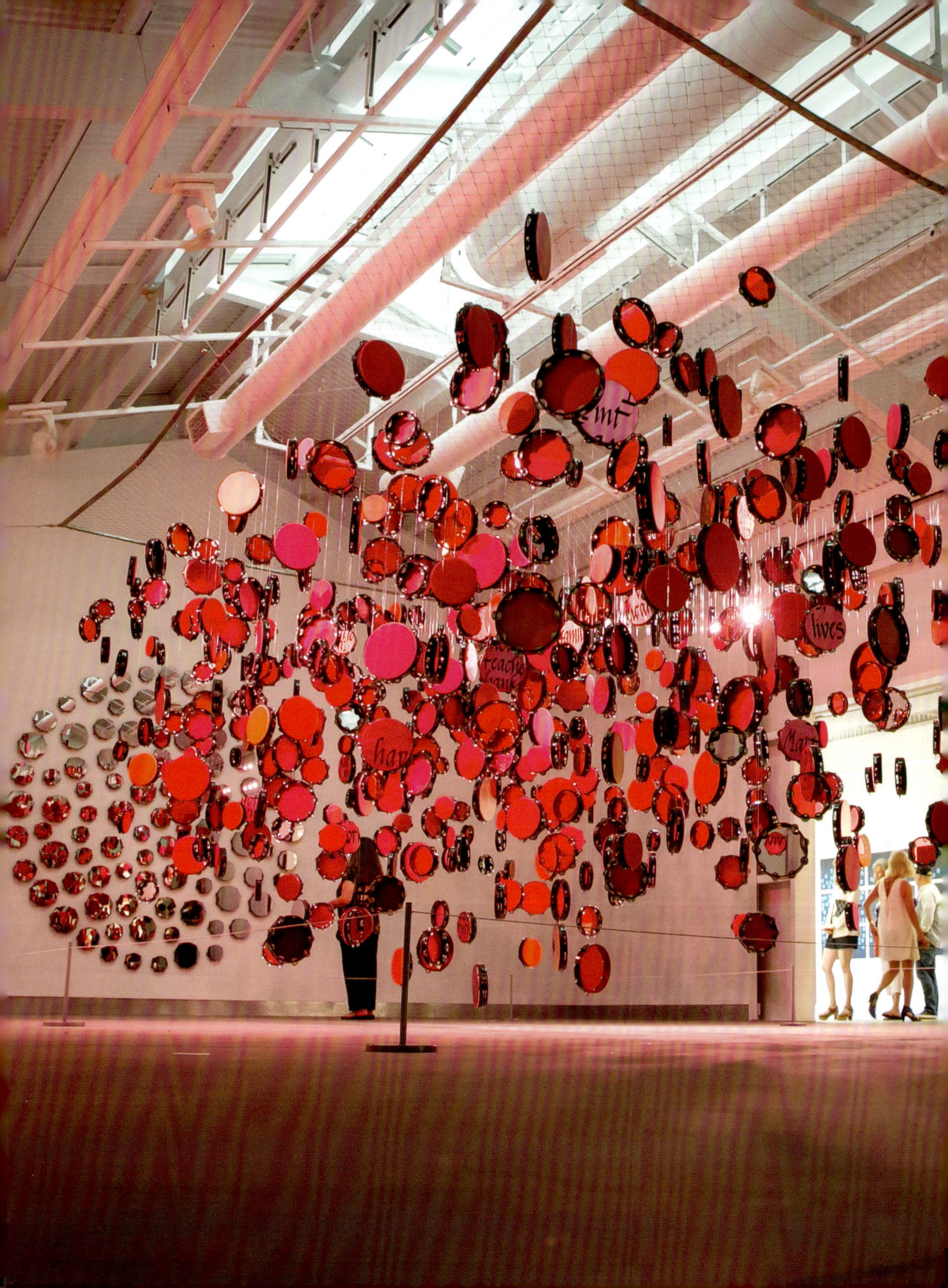

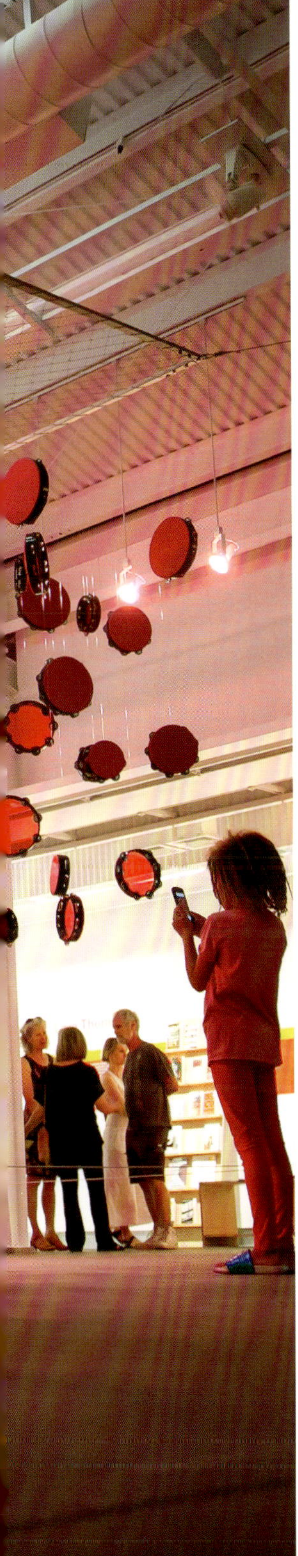

Di Rosa Center for Contemporary Art

Easy to access, and incredibly personal with a sixties vibe, this collection features the art of San Francisco Bay Area artists. Enjoy a fun day in the galleries and hiking through the nearby hills to see the sculptures. **DIROSAART.ORG**

Lava Thomas's light-filled but silent installation, featuring many red-hued tambourines, *Resistance Reverb: Movement 1*, 2018 is from Di Rosa's exhibition *Be Not Still: Living in Uncertain Times, Part II.*

LOCATED ON THE SOUTHERN END of Napa Valley in the Carneros region, the Di Rosa Center for Contemporary Art is an easy drive from San Francisco. About an hour north of the Golden Gate or the Bay Bridge, the collection of galleries and sculpture and the thirty-five-acre lake on the property are well worth a visit.

Rene di Rosa (1919–2010) was known as a quirky and prolific art collector who passionately supported many local and San Francisco Bay artists with whom he and his wife often became lifelong friends. A visionary, di Rosa was one of the first to grow grapes on his newly purchased property in Napa Valley in the 1960s. In 1986, the Seagram Company, owners of Sterling Vineyards, bought about 230 acres from him. The proceeds from that sale allowed di Rosa to create a public "art park" on the remaining 217 acres, which he filled with his collection of hundreds of California artists, showcasing more than 1,600 works of art. Today, the Di Rosa Center continues his mission with contemporary exhibitions as well as an outstanding permanent collection of work from the mid-twentieth century to the present day.

As we drove into the parking lot, we were welcomed by a huge Mark di Suvero red sculpture—a harbinger of great things to come. We were not disappointed when we encountered the first gallery, which featured a show of contemporary ceramics as well as a highlight of the collection: a 1985 work by David Best, one of the masters of assemblage. Titled *Rhinocar*, Best decorated a 1976 Oldsmobile with found objects to create one of his mobile works of art.

To reach the other galleries, one can take a tram, but we chose to walk and enjoy the magical scenery. On the left

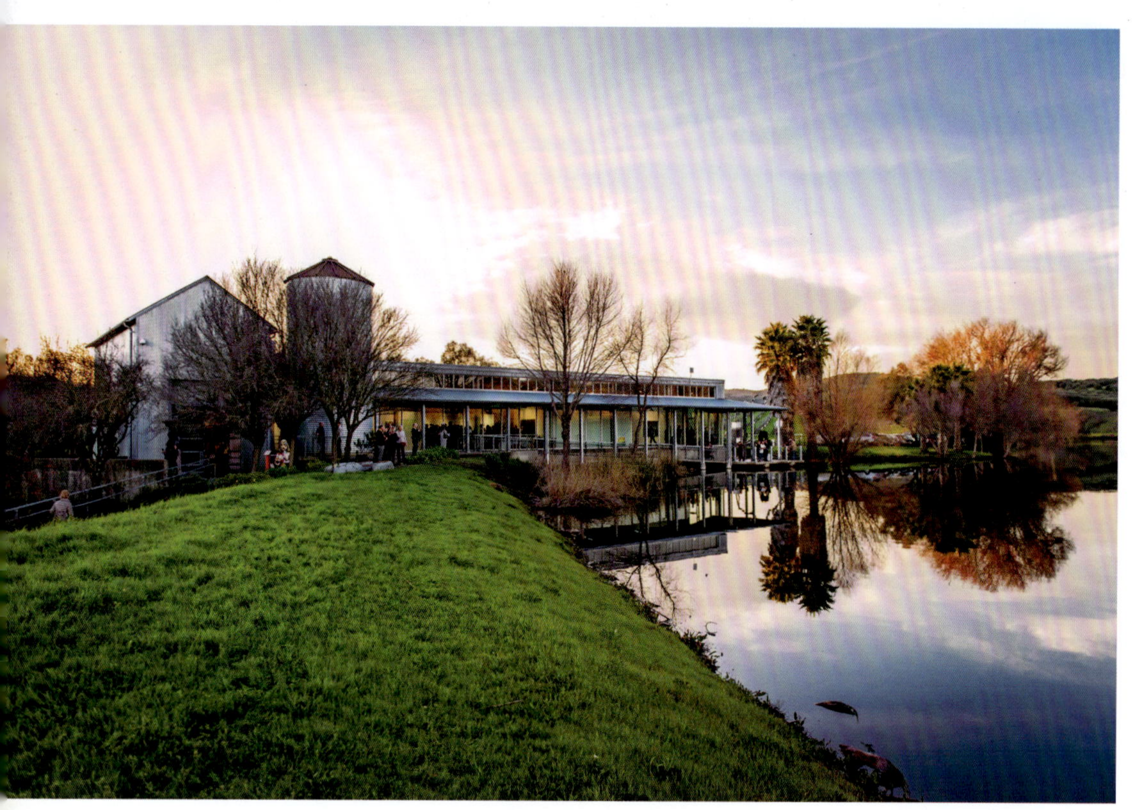

were acres of grape vines, and to the right was the lake with sculptures dotting the perimeter. Upon reaching our destination, we were met by a giant sleeping nude ceramic sculpture by Viola Frey.

The galleries were jam-packed with work by San Francisco Bay artists, and I must admit I was delighted to discover work by artists whose works I had never seen before.

For me, the jewel in the crown is *Chartres Bleu* (1986/1996) by Paul Kos. Hos created an installation of twenty-seven television monitors, laser disc players, and electronics to replicate the stained-glass windows in Chartres Cathedral. The installation truly feels like being in a sacred chapel. Placed a little outside of the galleries, it may be difficult to locate, but it is the "must-see" artwork in the collection.

Give yourself a lot of time to enjoy this curated collection and the very special park. Be sure to walk the rolling hills amid the vines and to visit the site-specific sculptures and architectural remnants that di Rosa found interesting. The Di Rosa is an extraordinary art experience and one that I can guarantee you will always remember.

The beautiful grounds surrounding di Rosa's Gallery 1. The open galleries exhibit many new and exciting Bay Area artists that are just now getting exposure, in addition to an outstanding permanent collection. Facing page, Mark di Suvero's sculpture, *For Veronica*, anchors the entrance to the Center's 217-acre art park.

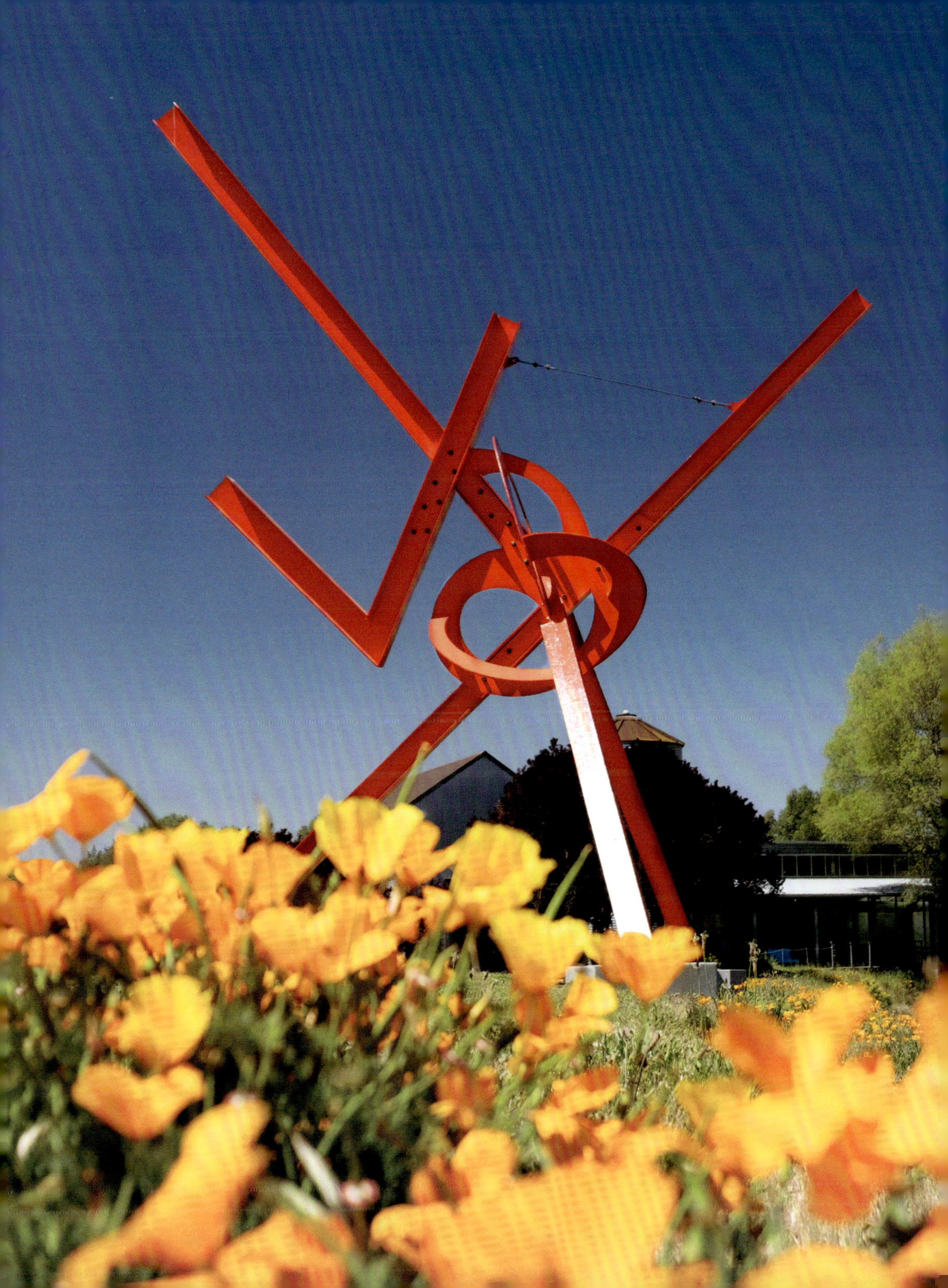

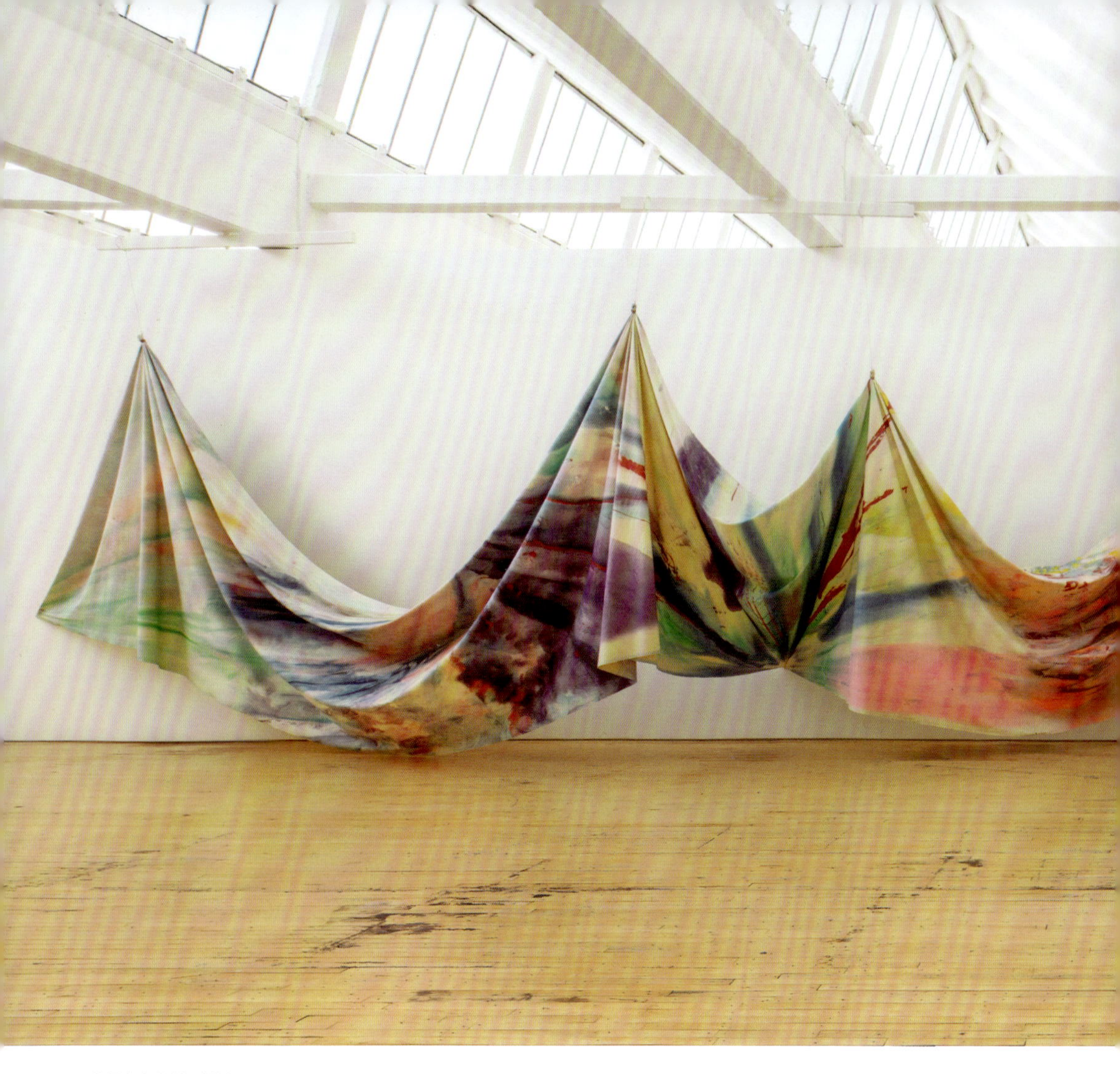

Dia Beacon

One of the first and most important sites in the Hudson Valley Area for viewing and experiencing immense installations by twenty and twenty-first century artists.

DIAART.ORG

The enormous former factory space that is now Dia Beacon easily accommodates this overscaled work by Sam Gilliam.

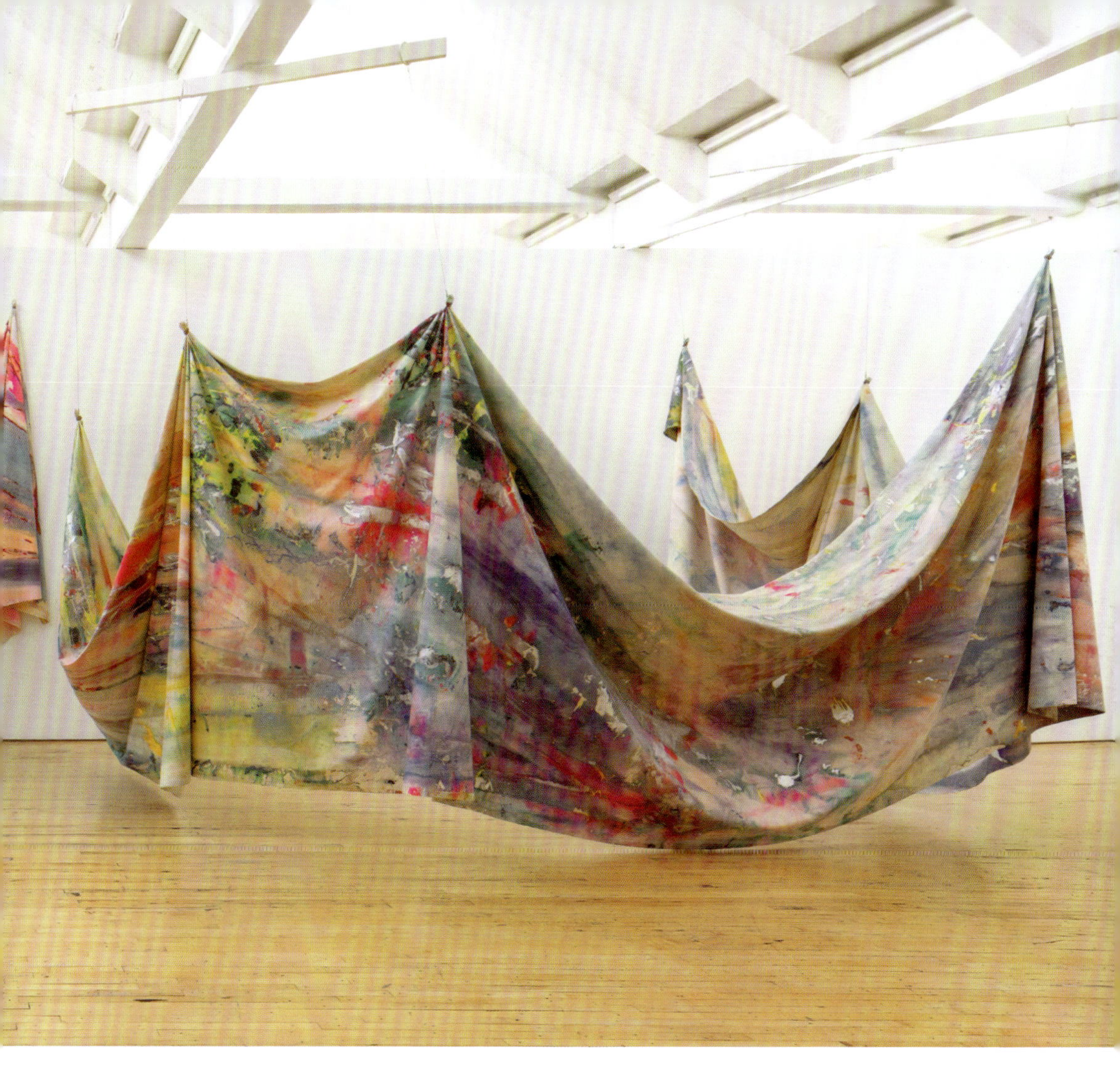

N 2003, the Dia Art Foundation opened Dia Beacon in New York's Hudson Valley. Housed in a former Nabisco box-printing factory in Beacon, New York, the museum encompasses nearly 300,000 square feet of loft-like space. The original construction materials of brick, steel, concrete, and glass are the backdrop to art from Dia's collection dating from the sixties to the present, as well as current exhibitions, commissions, and public programming.

The building's enormous unbroken spaces between the supporting columns combined with the never-ending skylights and clerestory windows are the ideal setting for seeing and experiencing contemporary art in its true colors. The overscale sculptures and room-sized installations seem to float in the enormous rooms, which are flooded with natural light from the skylights overhead. In fact, the only light here is provided by nature, and the museum closes at dusk. At Dia Beacon, the enormous football field–sized, art-filled rooms begin to feel like meditation as you proceed through the spaces and become more and more removed from the hustle and bustle of the very busy outside world.

By design, each vast room is dedicated to the work of only one artist, which allows for a unique experience and understanding of the artist and their work. To name just a few, there are serene white enamel works by Robert Ryman, an exhibition of steel and Plexiglass boxes by Donald Judd, twisted metal sculptures by Richard Chamberlain, jaw-dropping Richard Serra pieces lined up in a row, and a stunning collection of Louise Bourgeois sculptures, including her room-sized bronze spider. Immense and unstretched canvases by Sam Gilliam are an undulating riot of wild color, while the multiple canvases of *Shadows* by Andy Warhol are installed edge-to-edge around the perimeter of a tremendous room, surrounding the viewer while adhering to his original and precise vision.

After a few hours looking at art, instead of rushing home, don't hesitate to drive or walk over to the town of Beacon, NY, located just a few minutes away. Walk up and down the main street, enjoy a meal at one of the many cafés, and poke around the stores and galleries. Dia's visitors have ensured that this charming town in the Hudson Valley continues to thrive.

In addition to Dia Beacon and Dia Bridgehampton and Dia Chelsea, Dia maintains and operates a constellation of commissions, long-term installations, site-specific projects, and Land Art, nationally and internationally. Dia's locations and sites in NYC are always free. Some of my favorite locations from past visits are by Walter De Maria, who has created *The Broken Kilometer* and *The New York Earth Room*, both located in Manhattan. Be sure to check them out if you have the chance to visit.

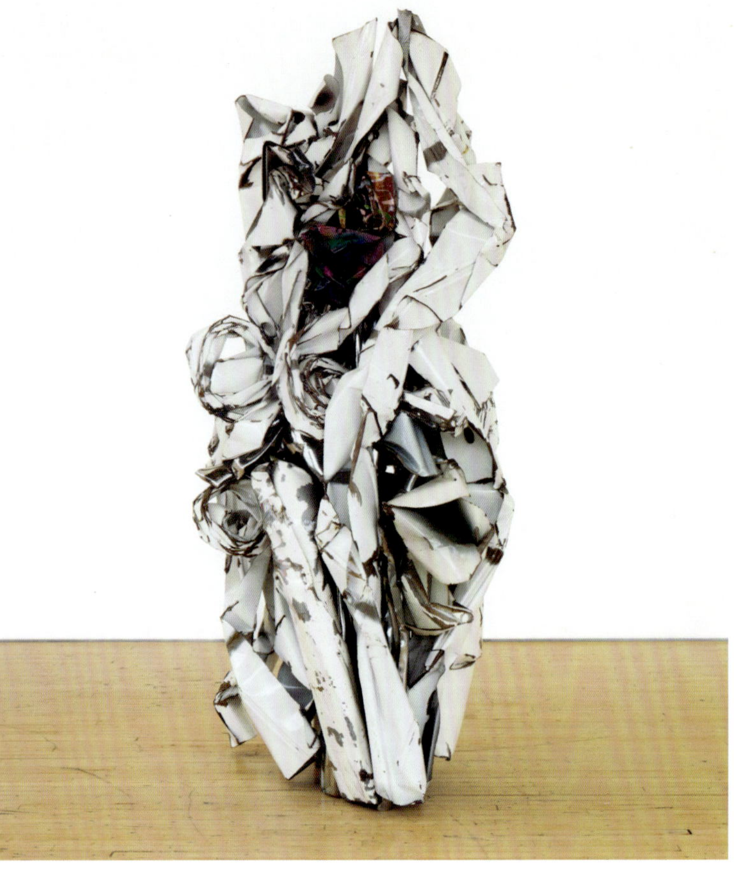

A striking assemblage of automotive chrome by John Chamberlain.
Facing page, Bruce Nauman's *Left or Standing, Standing or Left Standing*, 1971, always provokes.

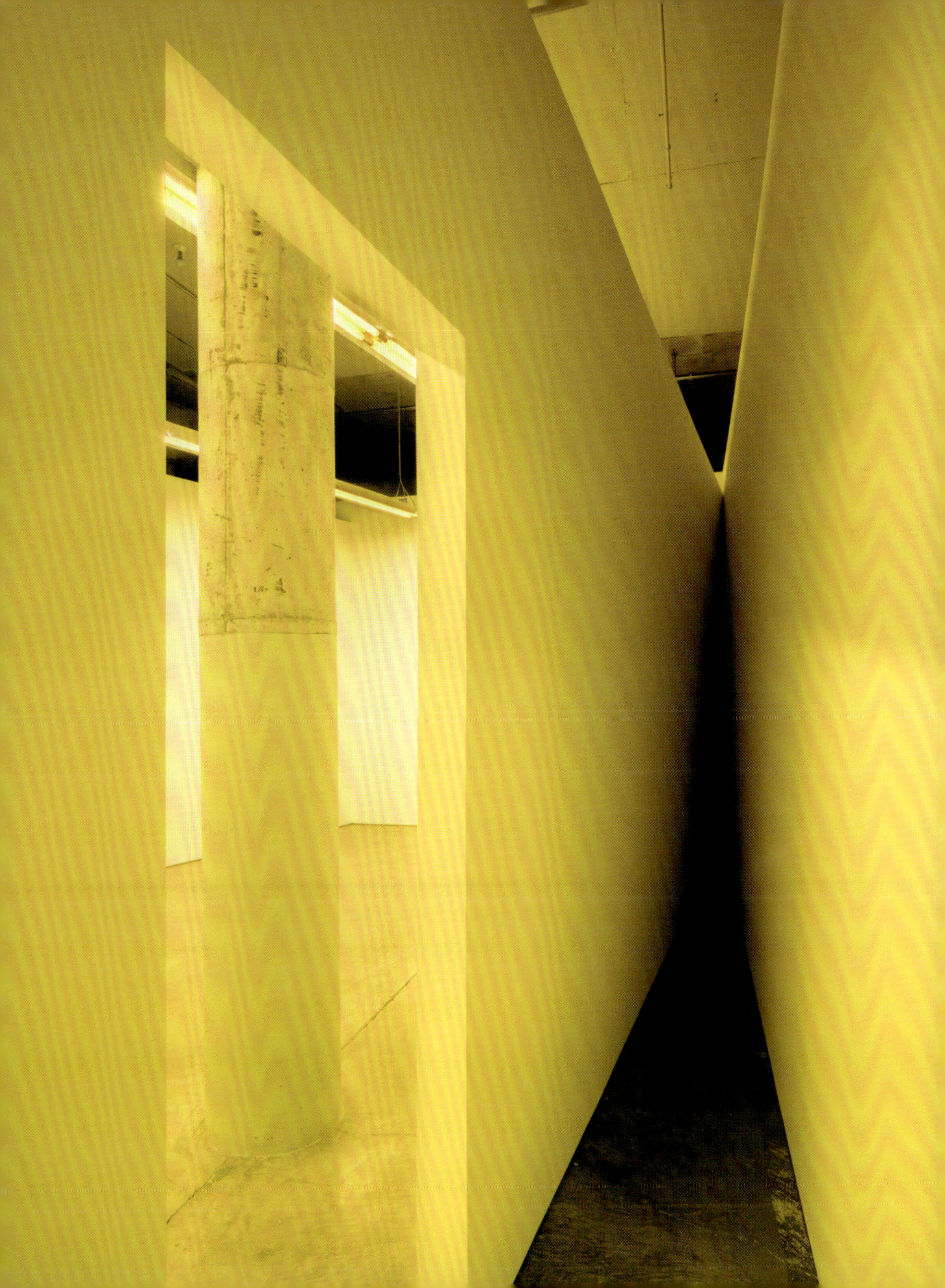

Dia Bridgehampton And the Dan Flavin Art Institute

The interiors of this easy-to-miss humble structure on a side street in Bridgehampton pack a lot of power with their marvelous Dan Flavin fluorescent light works.

DIAART.ORG

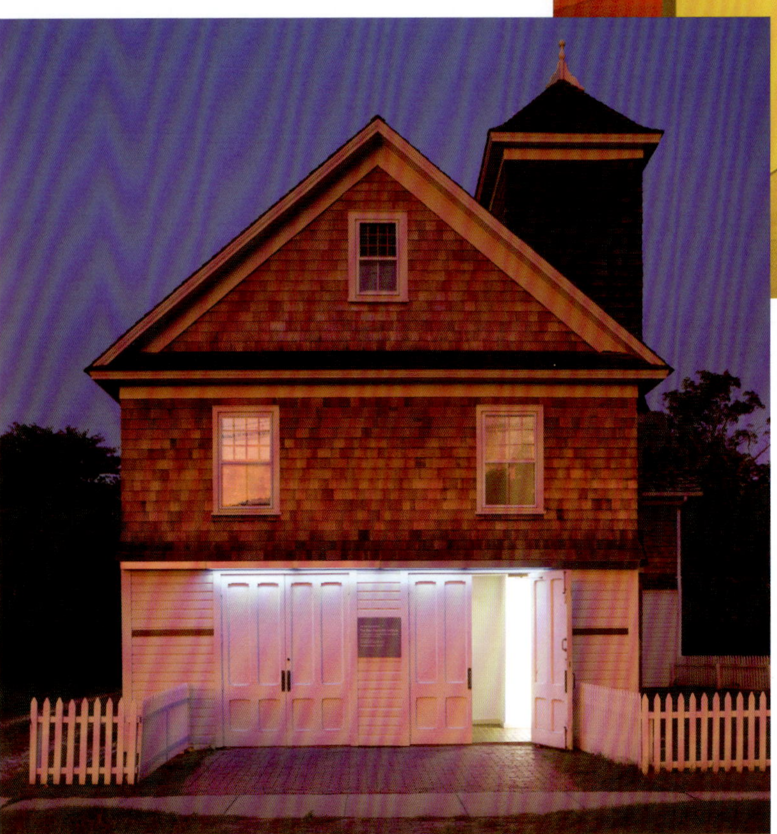

The immersive experience of Dan Flavin's mesmerizing light installation illustrates its power to enthrall.
Dia Bridgehampton, at left, a storied building that was once a firehouse and later a Baptist church, practically glows in the early evening.

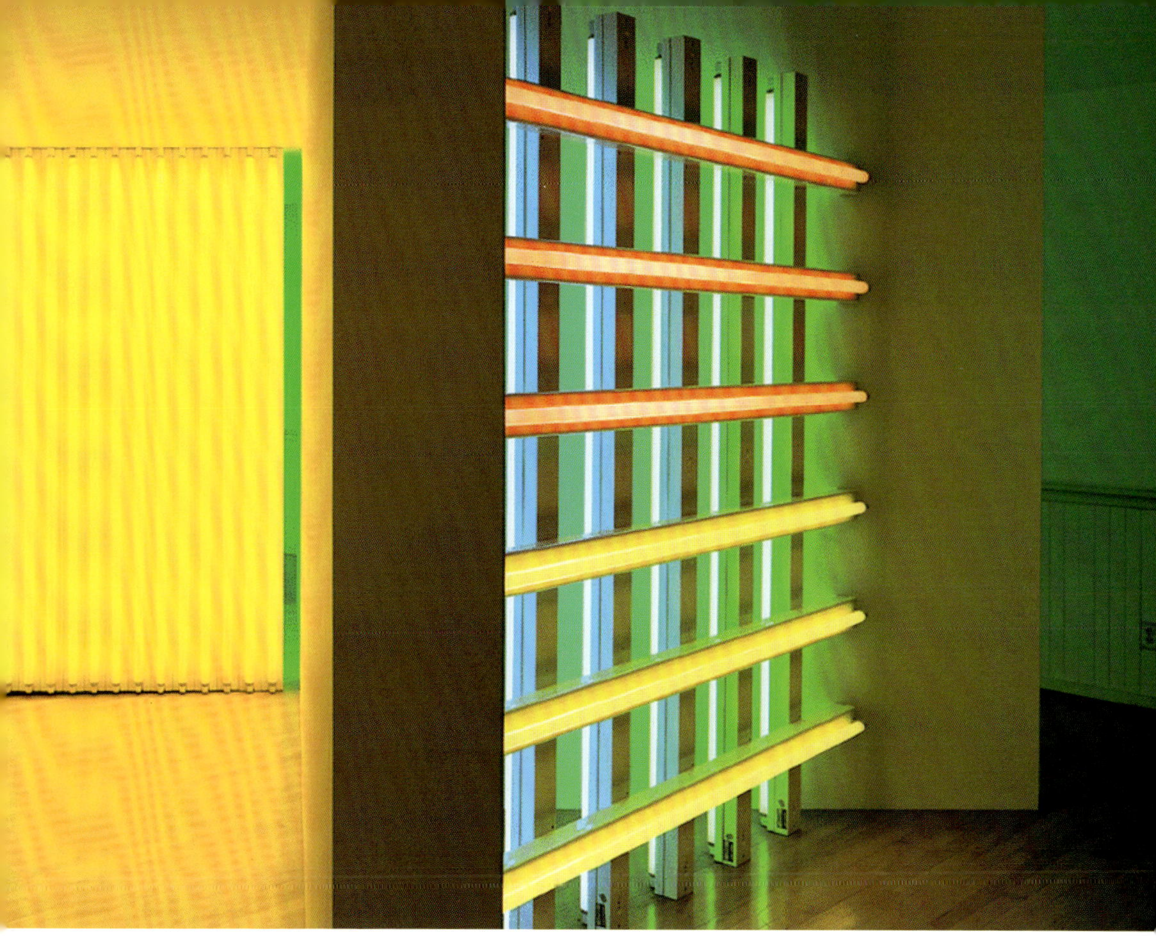

IT IS EASY TO MISS the Dan Flavin Art Institute in the charming town of Bridgehampton, New York. It is located on a side street in a discreet structure that once housed a firehouse, then a Baptist church in the early twentieth century, and is now home to Dia Bridgehampton. With Dia's support, Flavin renovated the building to create a home for nine of his signature fluorescent light works, in addition to a gallery for Dia to feature changing exhibitions of their own.

Head up to the second floor to see the dazzling colors created by Flavin's permanent installation. The viewer, absorbed in the colored light, becomes transfixed on how these works are created. Where is the source of the color? How is the color generated with fluorescent tubes? Viewing his works, one is transported by the intense colored light and in awe of his genius.

A small first-floor gallery exhibits rotating programming for individual artists. The day I visited, Jill Magid's photographs were on view. Her photographs captured how light fell on Josef Albers's iconic series *Homage to a Square* that was in the home of architect Luis Barragán in Mexico.

There is also a room off the second-floor gallery that pays tribute to the former First Baptist Church of Bridgehampton with artifacts such as a stained-glass window, a cross, a bible, and vintage photographs. One leaves the Dia Bridgehampton and the Dan Flavin Art Institute thinking about light, color, and even spirituality.

The Donum Estate

While the wine is the main event, the magnificent sculptures by world-renowned artists are the very best addition to this otherworldly vineyard experience.
THEDONUMESTATE.COM

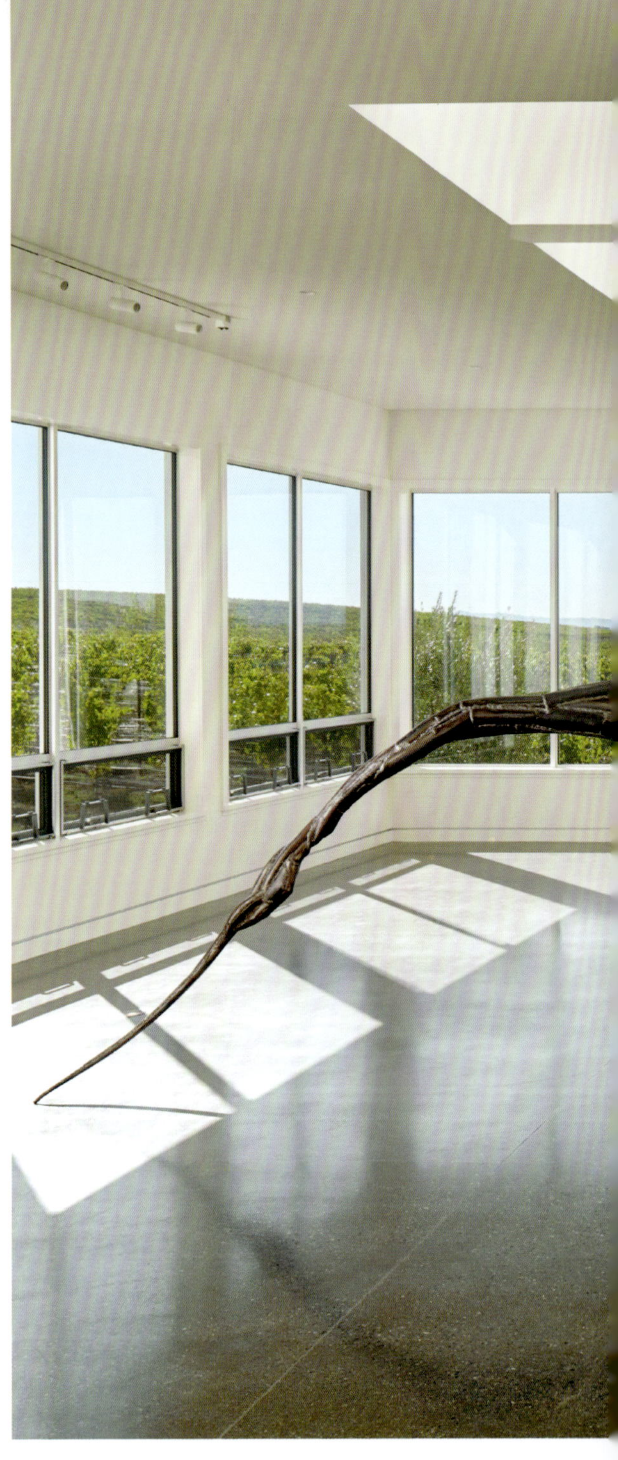

WHEN YOU ARE IN the Napa and Sonoma Valley area, there is a little-known art experience at a vineyard called The Donum Estate that I highly recommend. There is a fee, and you must book a spot in advance, but it is well worth the price and the planning to taste the wines and to see museum-quality art.

In the foreword of their gorgeous Donum catalogue, Mei and Allan Warburg state, "Often good things in life come by coincidence." The Warburgs have lived in Hong Kong for many years, where they have been collecting Chinese paintings. In the early 2000s, by chance, they heard that the Donum winery in northern California was for sale and purchased the vineyard. They started to collect sculpture with an eye toward their newly acquired winery.

A friend of theirs introduced them to Ai Weiwei. A phone call with the artist enabled them to directly acquire his bronze *Circle of Animals/Zodiac Heads*. All twelve animal heads that represent the signs of the zodiac were installed at the winery and today are one of the great focal points of the collection. As a special commission, the artist also designed their wine labels so that

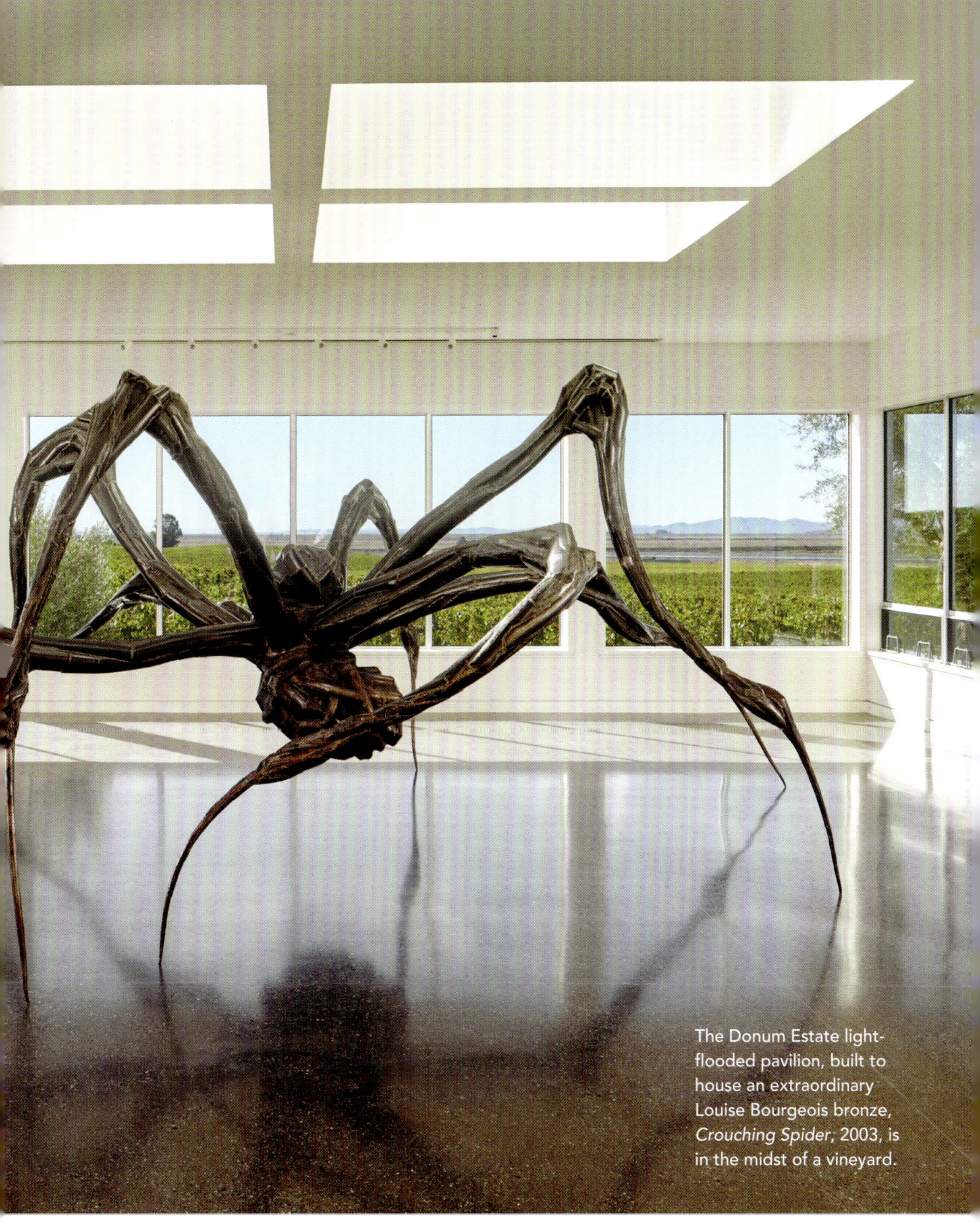

The Donum Estate light-flooded pavilion, built to house an extraordinary Louise Bourgeois bronze, *Crouching Spider*, 2003, is in the midst of a vineyard.

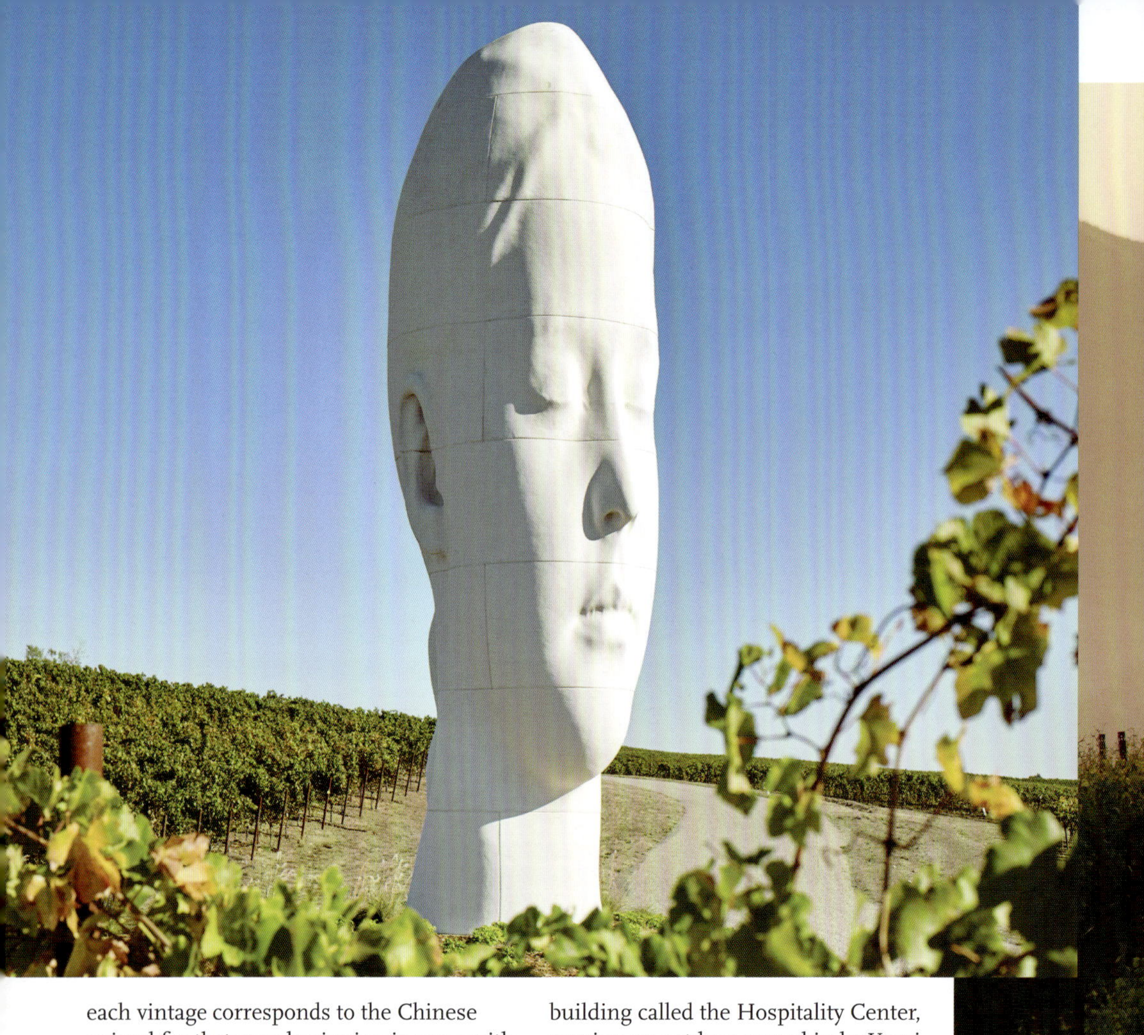

each vintage corresponds to the Chinese animal for that year, beginning in 2014 with the Year of the Horse.

Their commitment to collecting sculpture has taken them around the world to meet artists, often in their studios, from Subodh Gupta in New Delhi to Doug Aitken in Los Angeles. Today their outstanding collection is unique and very personal. One of my favorite moments on the day we visited was entering their custom-built pavilion to see the enormous bronze and steel *Crouching Spider* by Louise Bourgeois.

A visit to Donum is an extraordinary experience visually and taste-wise. We met our art/wine guide in a beautiful modern building called the Hospitality Center, passing an outdoor pumpkin by Yayoi Kusama as we entered. The guide poured glasses of Donum wine to enjoy as we walked the property and interacted with the many sculptures. It was exciting to see the works up close and to see the sculpture across the rolling hills of vines. The scale and commanding presence of the sculptures from a distance was incredible, especially while drinking the delicious wine.

Mei and Allan Warburg's sophistication and dedication to collecting the best names and the best pieces of sculptures cannot be overstated.

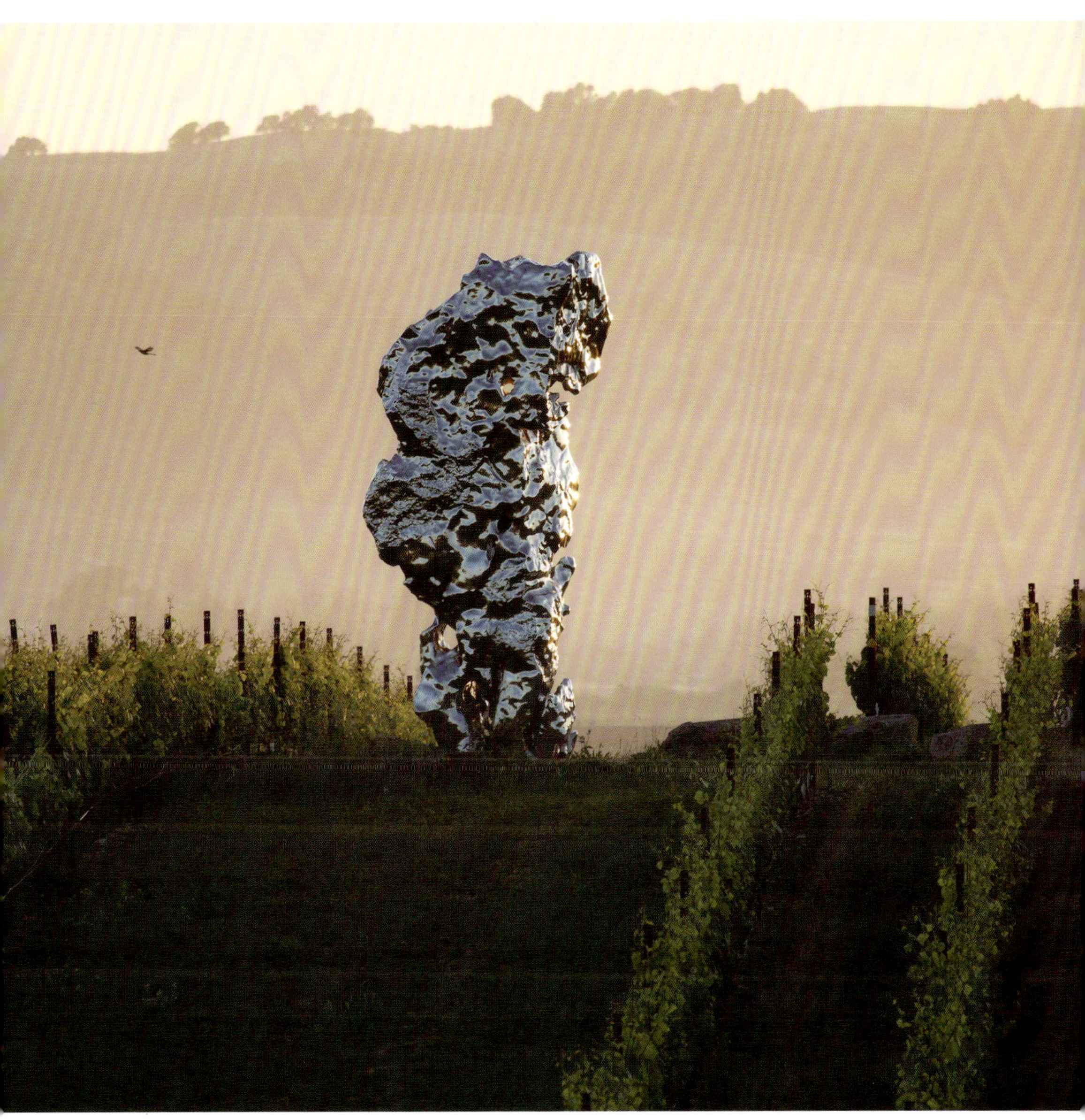

Facing page,
Jaume Plensa's
sculpture, *Sanna*,
2015, set amid the
vines and hills of
the winery.

Artificial Rock no. 126,
by Chinese artist Zhan
Wang is a contemporary
reference to the eroded
rocks long revered by
Chinese scholars.

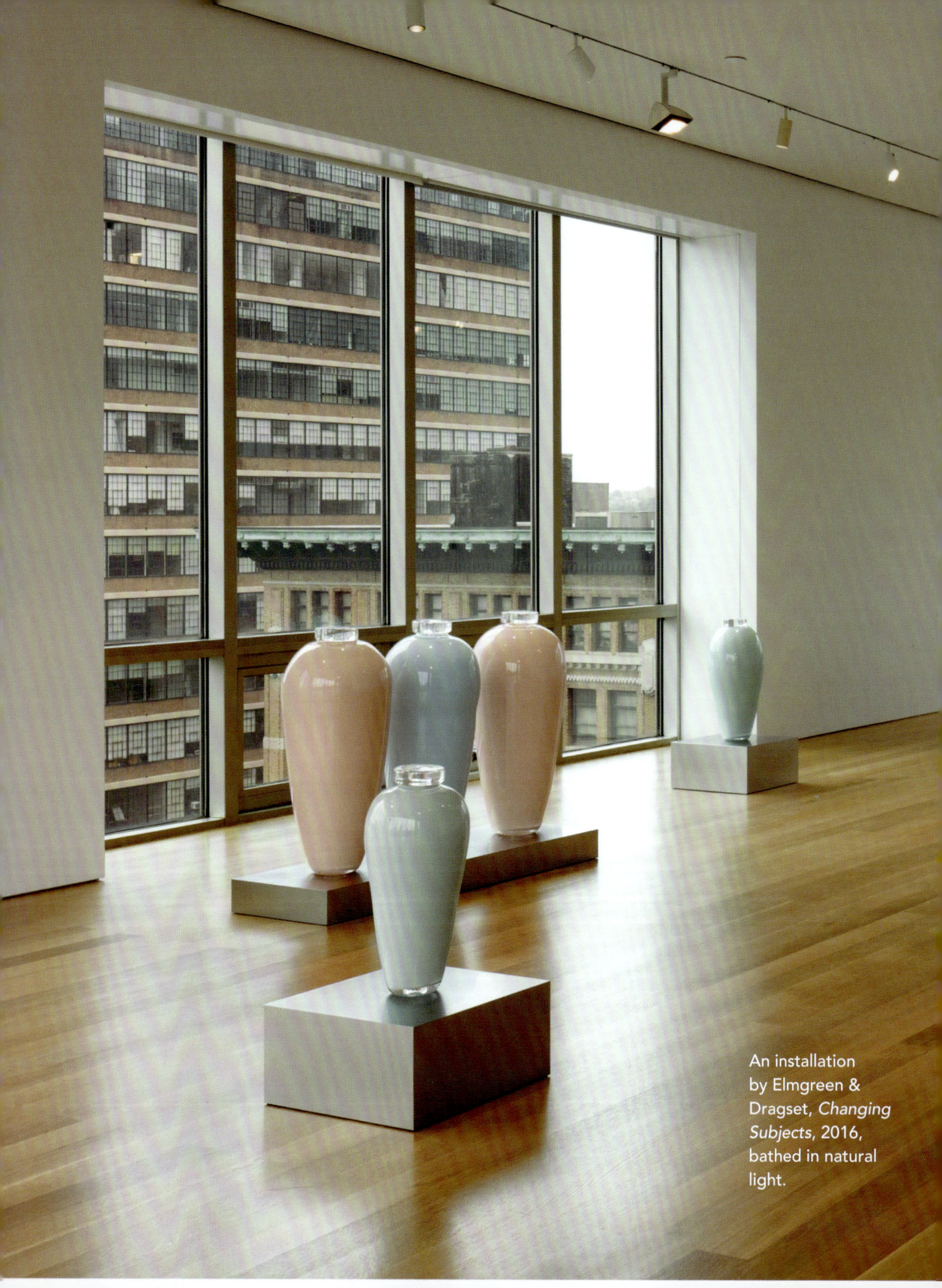

An installation by Elmgreen & Dragset, *Changing Subjects*, 2016, bathed in natural light.

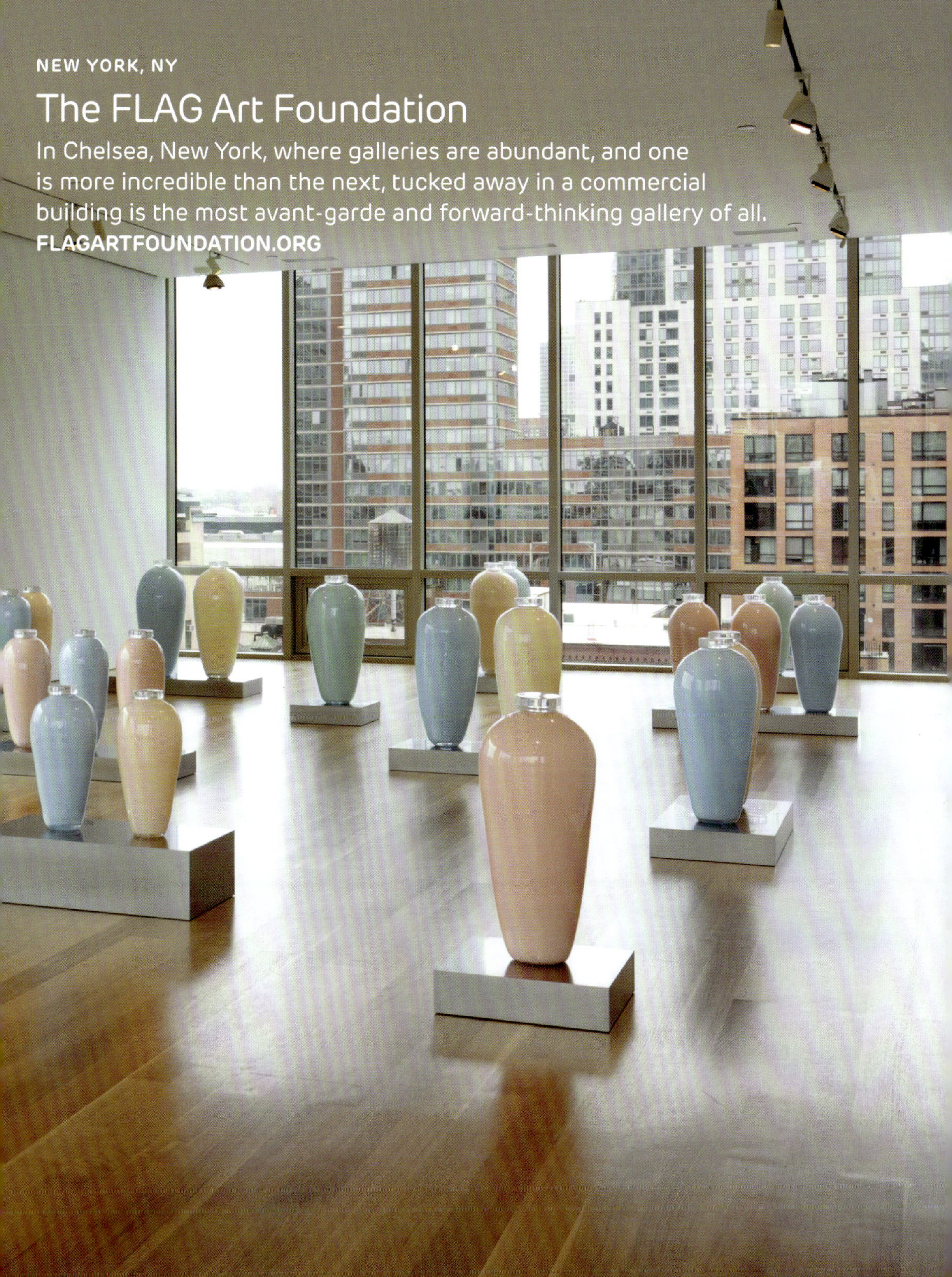
NEW YORK, NY
The FLAG Art Foundation
In Chelsea, New York, where galleries are abundant, and one
is more incredible than the next, tucked away in a commercial
building is the most avant-garde and forward-thinking gallery of all.
FLAGARTFOUNDATION.ORG

E STABLISHED IN 2008, The FLAG Art Foundation is high up on the ninth and tenth floors of a commercial building on West Twenty-Fifth Street in New York City. If someone didn't tell you about it, you would never know it was there. In it's own subtle way, this jewel of a museum is an epicenter of exciting and creative contemporary art programs, as well as a platform for contemporary artists to show their work and find support from world-class curators.

The founder, Glenn Fuhrman, is an outstanding art philanthropist who has been involved with contemporary art for many years. We were both members of the Contemporary Art Council at MoMA where I loved attending his artist lunch time events. Glenn would invite a guest artist to lunch and treat us to a Power Point presentation, which always led to a meaningful dialogue discussing their work and their intent. Interacting with artists such as Alex Katz and Tom Sachs were just a few of the highlights. These events reflected his desire to fully examine an artist's process alongside their work and to show us that understanding how an artist manifests their inspiration with their process is the best way to learn.

I think that these lunches are worth mentioning, as they speak to Fuhrman's overarching goal to create a space of dialogue, exhibitions, and workshops and to work closely with emerging artists at the start of their careers. I always look forward to the next installation at the FLAG. One of my past favorites was an installation by Nicholas Party who completely transformed the space by painting the walls in chalky pastel shades and hanging artwork from various centuries created almost exclusively with pastels.

In sharp contrast to the ethereal soft colors of Party's work was a photography show by Awol Erizku of odalisque-centered paintings like those romanticized and made popular by artists such as Ingres and Manet. Erizku's photos show these sex workers, the *Olympias of Nigeria* as he calls them, in anonymous hotel rooms without the opulence and idealized settings of the historic paintings. They were a powerful reminder of an artist's ability to make us reconsider what we are looking at when we view classic masterpieces hanging in a museum and what we take for granted about the subjects portrayed.

Always an exciting place to visit, The FLAG Art Foundation is well worth an afternoon of discovery.

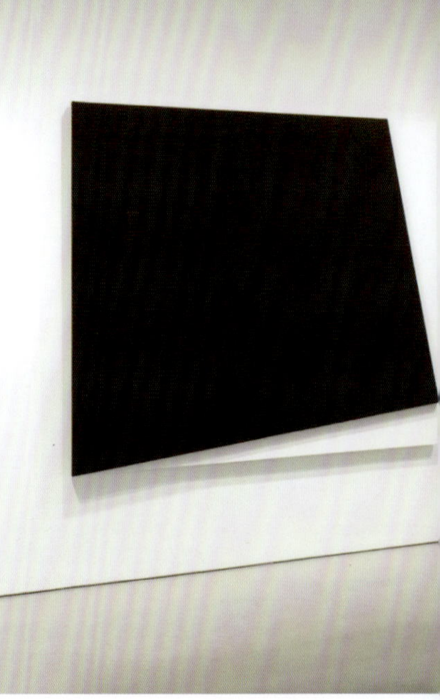

At right above, Ellsworth Kelly's crisp dialogues in black and white are given plenty of space to assert themselves.

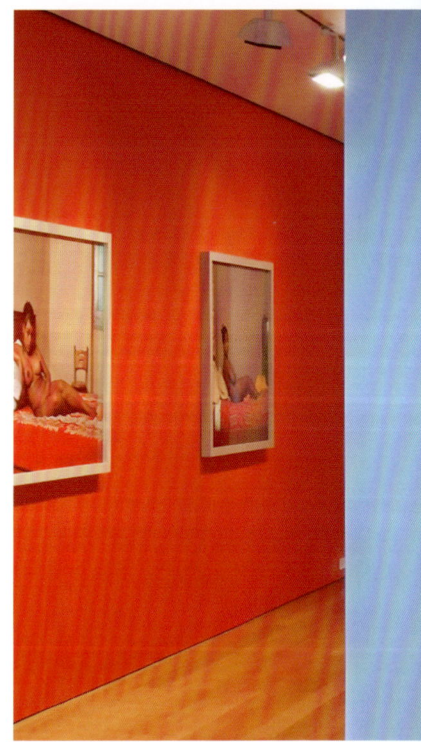

Below, Awol Erizku's photo-based work uses classical references to initiate conversations of sex and power.

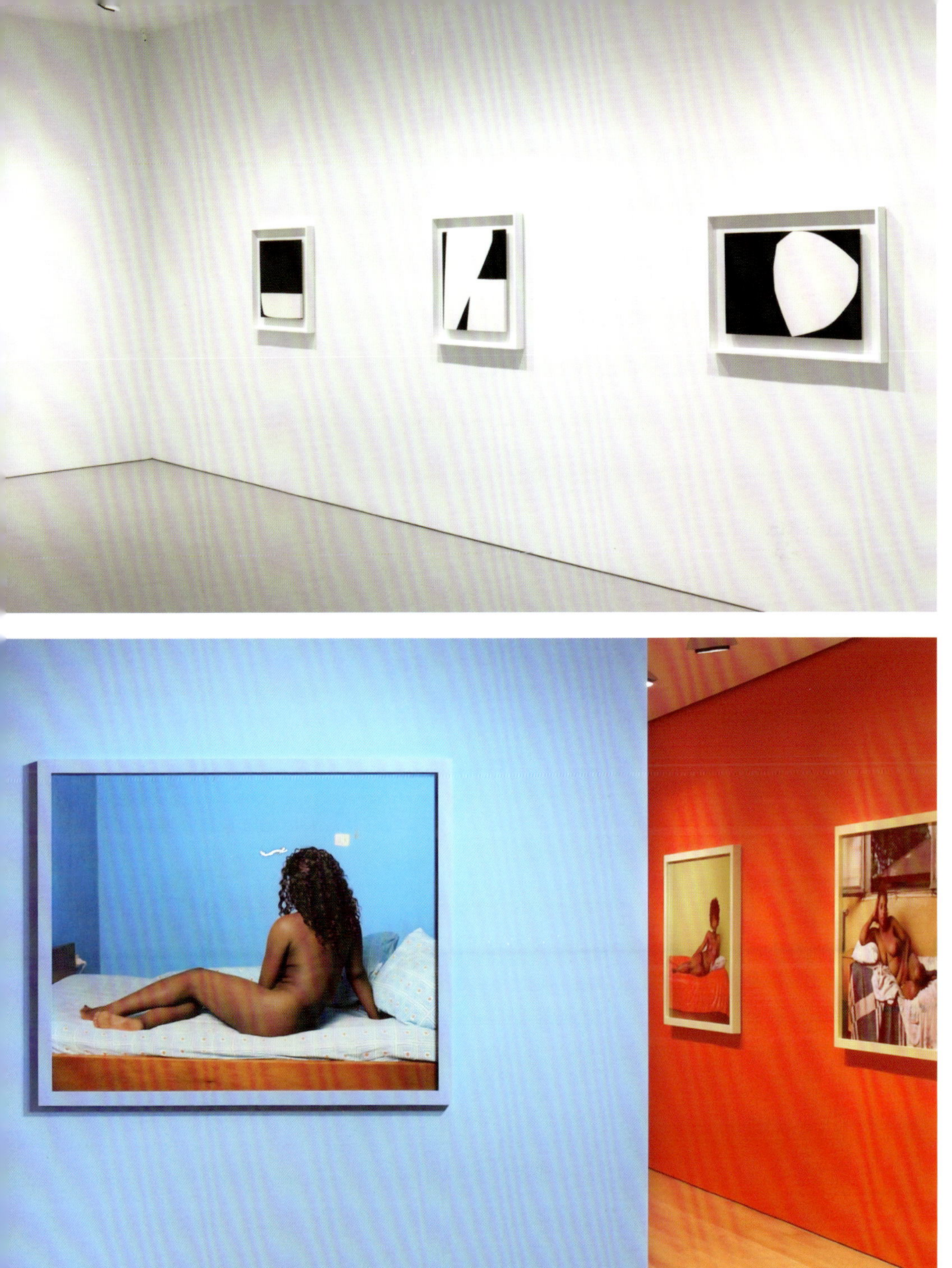

Frederick R. Weisman Art Foundation

Visitors to this intact home museum in Southern California will feel as if time stands still and they are enjoying a friend's personal collection of twentieth-century art. **WEISMANFOUNDATION.ORG**

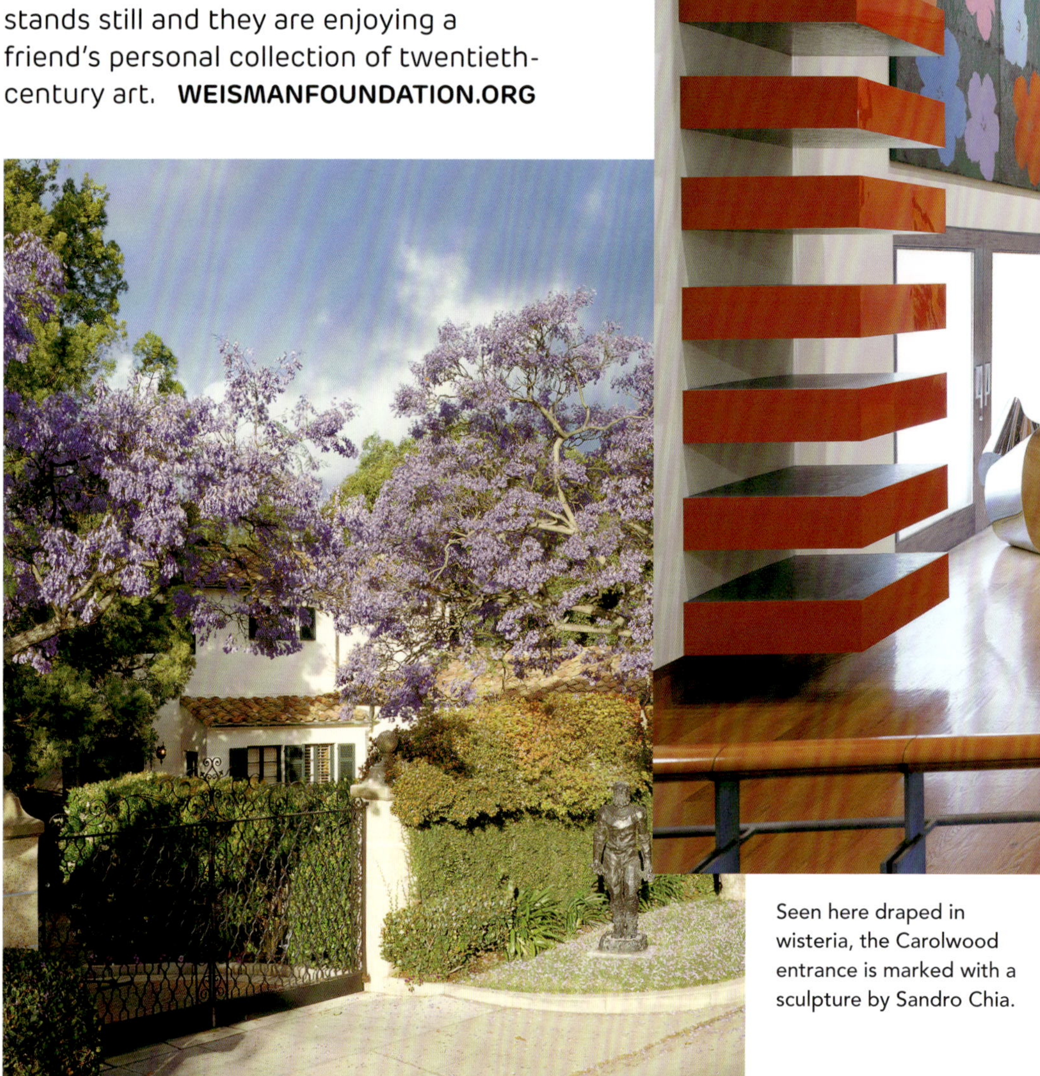

Seen here draped in wisteria, the Carolwood entrance is marked with a sculpture by Sandro Chia.

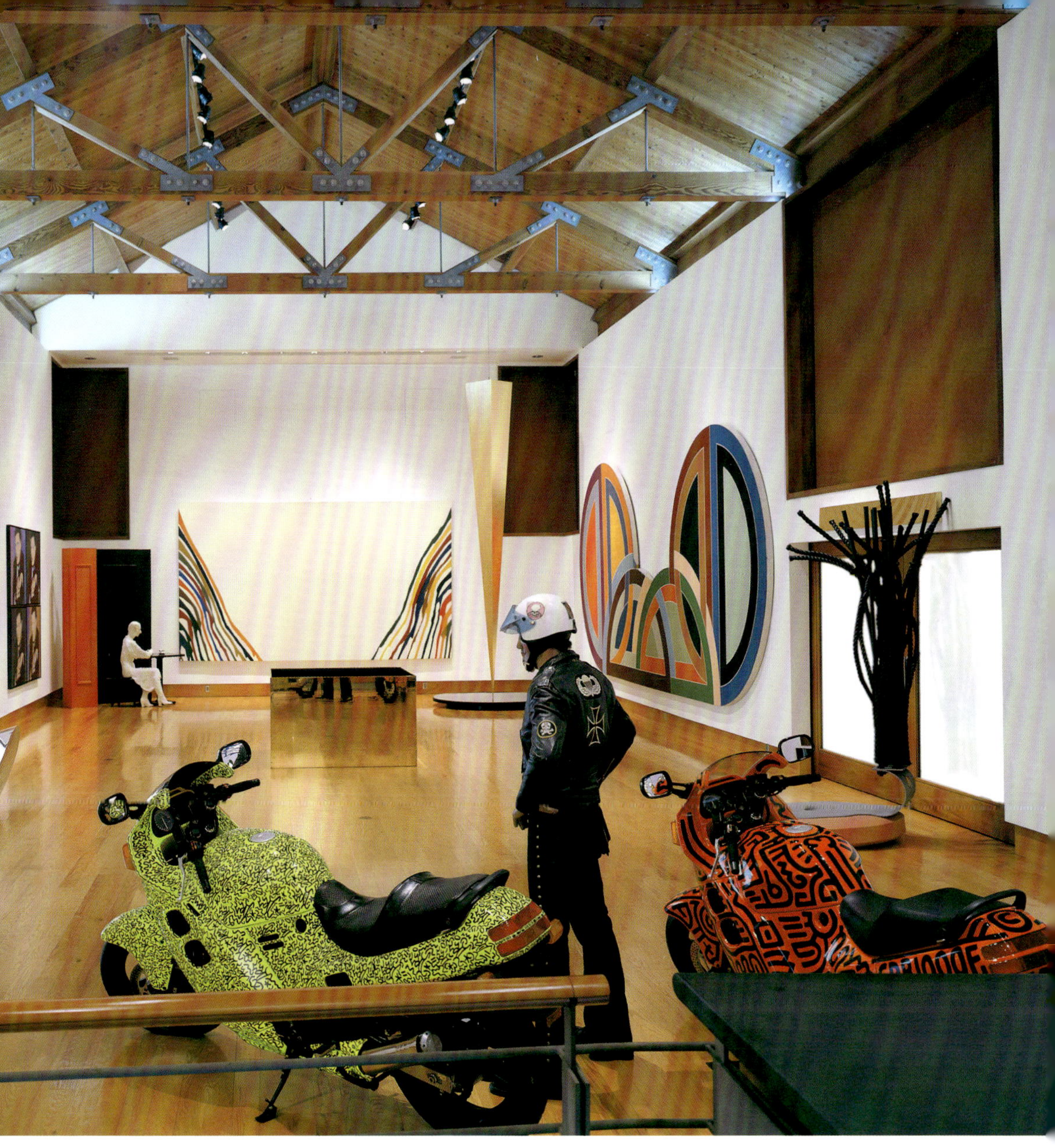

Imagine living with all this art! This beautiful annex gallery designed by Franklin D. Israel is filled with the work of some of the most outstanding twentieth-century artists, clockwise from left: Donald Judd, Andy Warhol, Ron Arad (bench), James Rosenquist, Andy Warhol, George Segal, Morris Louis, Lita Albuquerque, Frank Stella, Peter Erskine (over door), Claes Oldenburg, Keith Haring, Duane Hanson, LA II, Donald Judd, (in center of room).

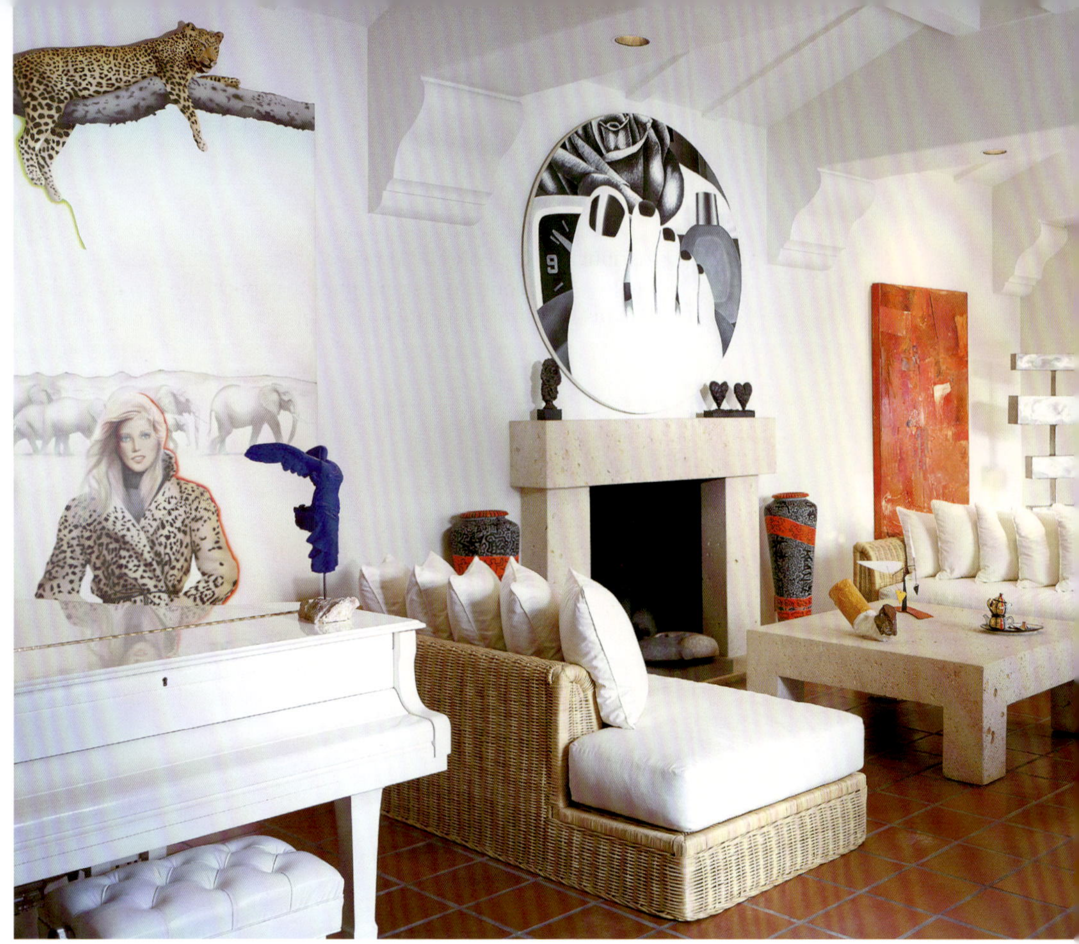

Artworks in the music room, above, by (clockwise from left): Larry Rivers, Yves Klein, Keith Haring, Jean Dubuffet, Tom Wesselmann, Jim Dine, Keith Haring, Robert Rauschenberg, David Smith, Ronald Davis (above), Lita Albuquerque, John Buck (reflected in mirror), Ray Howlett, Alan Siegel, and (on tables left to right) Claes Oldenburg, Alexander Calder, Roy Lichtenstein, Andrzej Lemiszewski, Lucas Samaras.

Rauschenberg, Picasso, Noguchi, Kenneth Noland, and Ed Ruscha, to name just a few. Seeing how Weisman and his wife, Billie, created a domestic setting with this art is a very personal and unique experience. The Foundation's goal to preserve the collection and make it publicly accessible strengthens and contributes to our collective intellectual and artistic lives.

The Foundation continues to support the arts through loans to museums, public art exhibitions, and in many other ways. But perhaps most notable is the funding of several art museums including the Frederick R. Weisman Museum of Art at Pepperdine University in Malibu and the Weisman Art Museum at the University of Minnesota, which was designed by Frank Gehry. The existence and continued support for the estate in Holmby Hills is a testament to the Weismans' desire to affirm that art is meant to be lived with and enjoyed just as much as it is meant to hang in a museum.

"I don't think there is anything that communicates better than art—it is quicker than language and clearer than philosophy" is a statement from the foreword of Weisman's own catalogue about his Foundation.

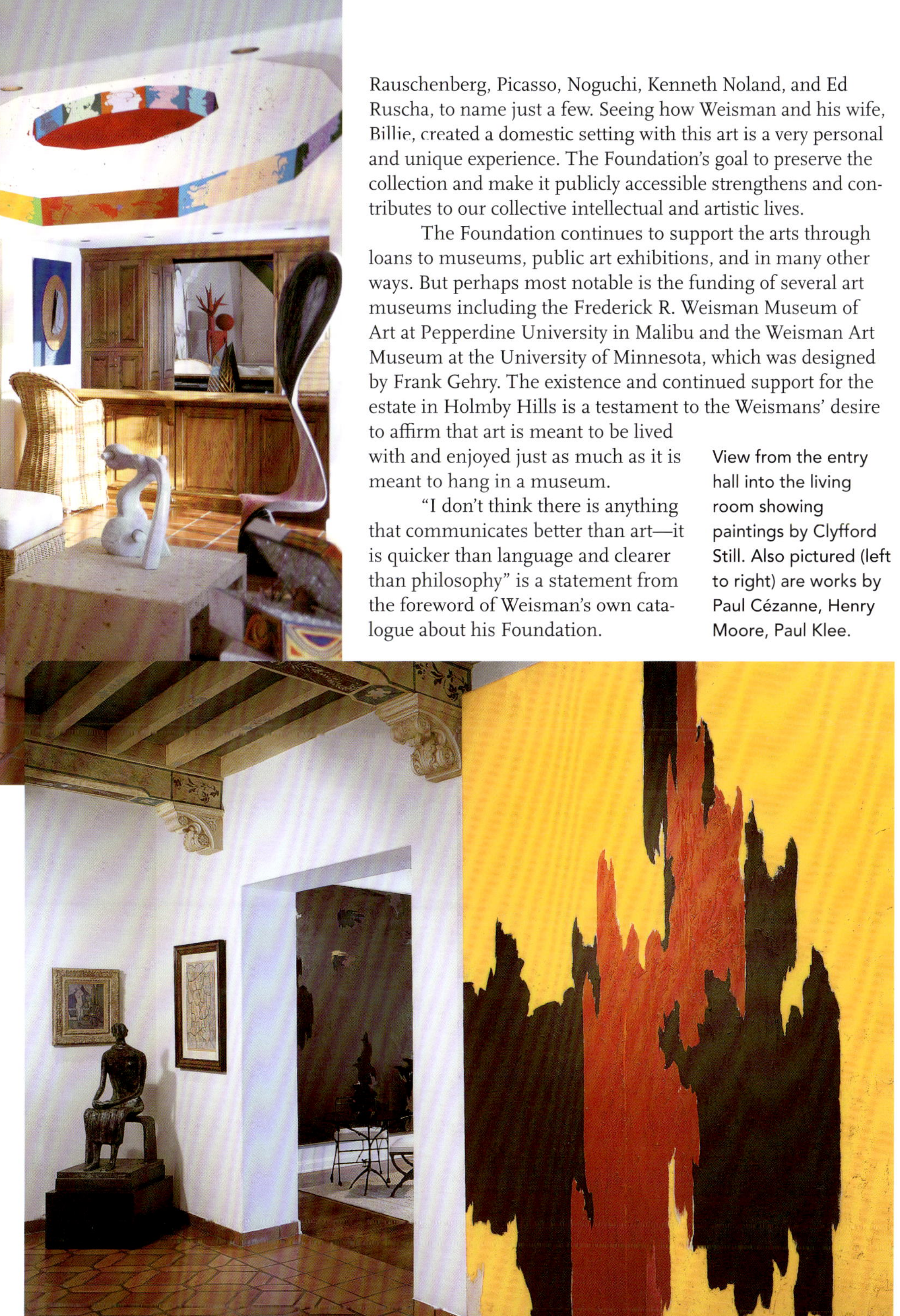
View from the entry hall into the living room showing paintings by Clyfford Still. Also pictured (left to right) are works by Paul Cézanne, Henry Moore, Paul Klee.

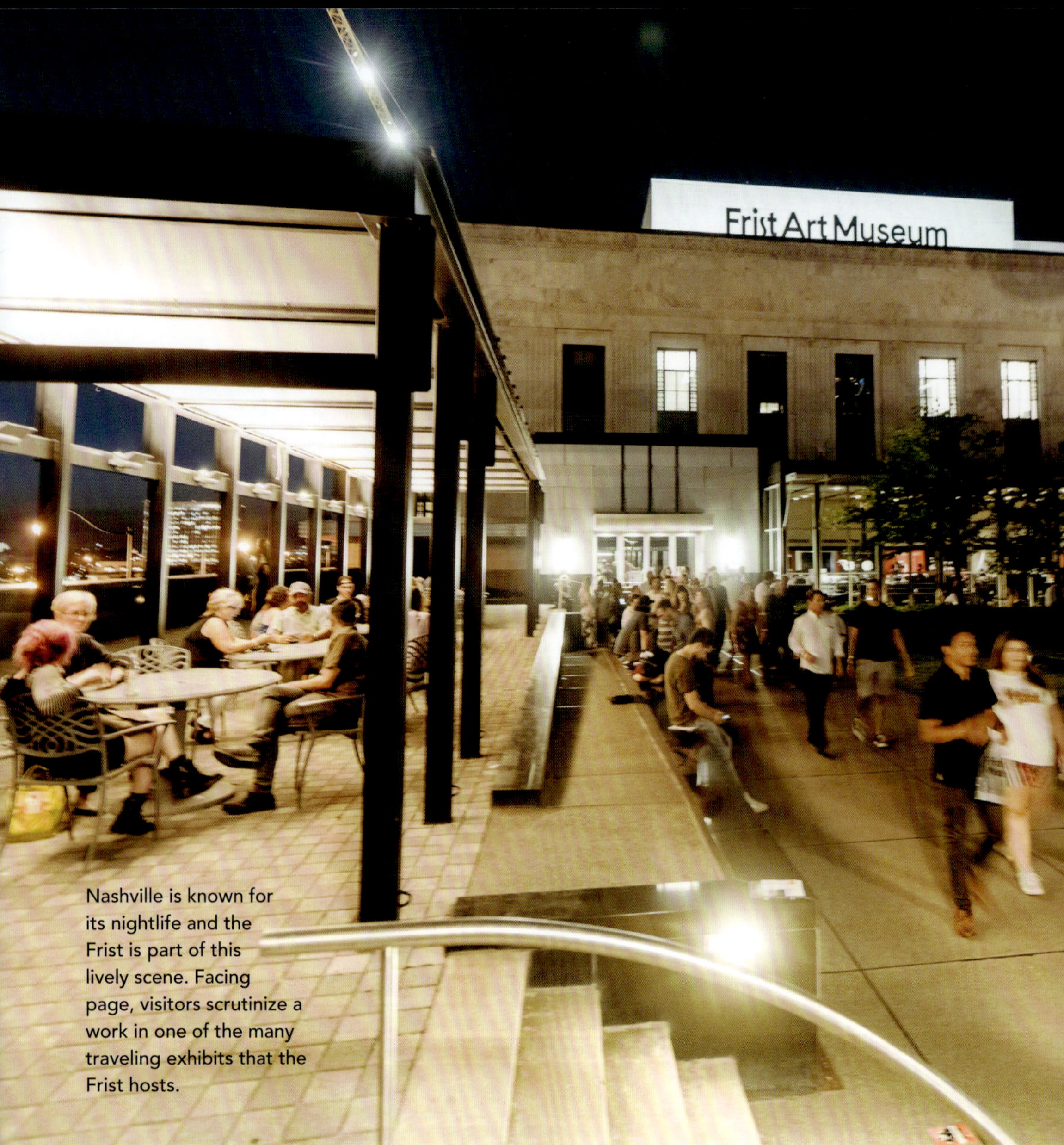

Nashville is known for its nightlife and the Frist is part of this lively scene. Facing page, visitors scrutinize a work in one of the many traveling exhibits that the Frist hosts.

Frist Art Museum

Art Deco interiors are the backdrop for ever-changing traveling exhibitions. The Frist is an opportunity for visual enrichment in a city known for its music and songwriting. **FRISTARTMUSEUM.ORG**

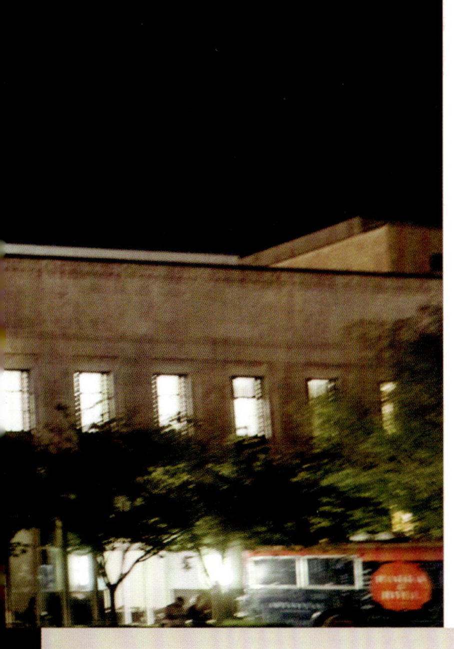

O**N MY FIRST TRIP** to Nashville, I was excited just to see the charming streets where country music flourished. I wanted to visit the Country Music Hall of Fame and Museum, taste the world-famous barbecue cuisine, and experience the honkytonk bars for which this city is world-renowned. I never realized that Nashville is also home to the Frist Art Museum.

Located in a former post office building, the Frist could stand alone without any art. The art deco interiors and classic details of the exterior are breathtaking. The Frist family formed a public/private venture with the city of Nashville to renovate the building and create a visual arts center that was opened to the public in 2001. The name was changed to the Frist Art Museum in 2018.

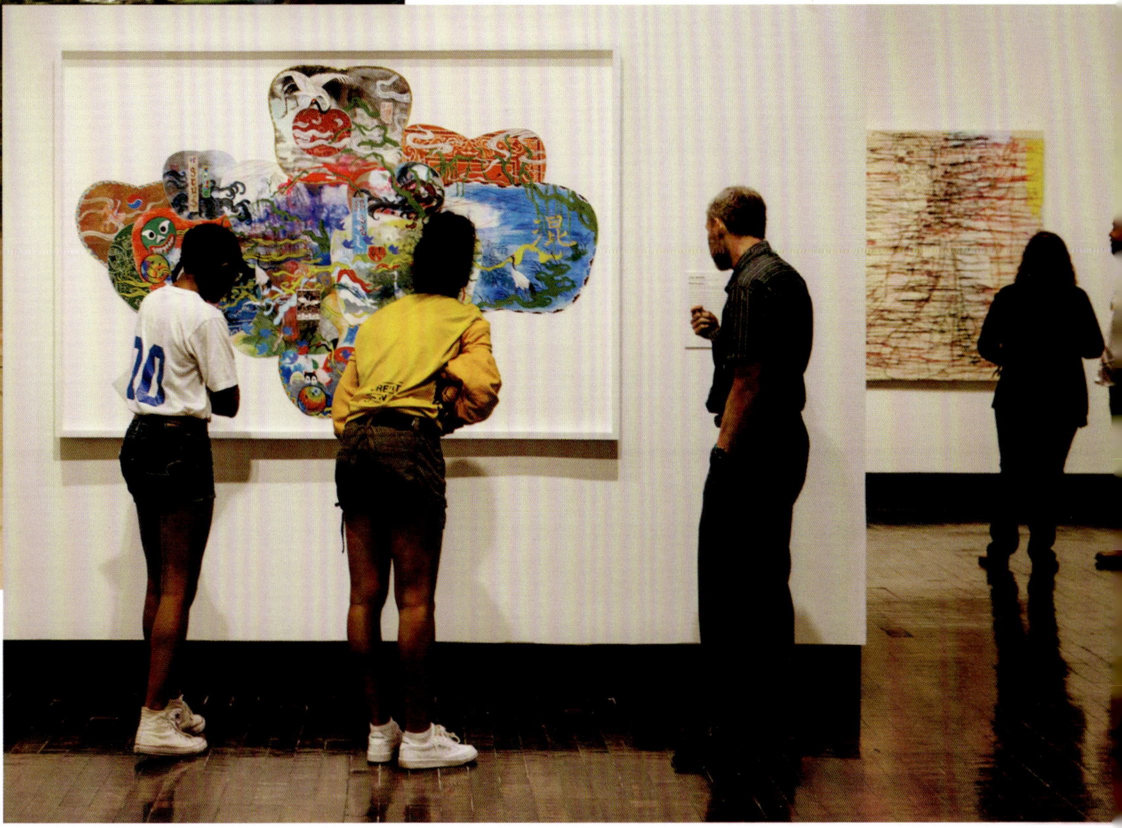

The Frist is not a typical museum with a permanent collection but instead shows traveling exhibitions that change frequently. The day we visited, there was a large and impressive retrospective of famed documentary photographer Dorothea Lange. Her well-known image of a poor mother and her three children, *Migrant Mother*, was included, showing the hardship many Americans endured during the Great Depression. I read the gallery guide about what Lange said about this iconic image: "It doesn't belong to me anymore. It belongs to the world." The statement resonated for me and felt like the connective tissue that runs through all museums, large or small.

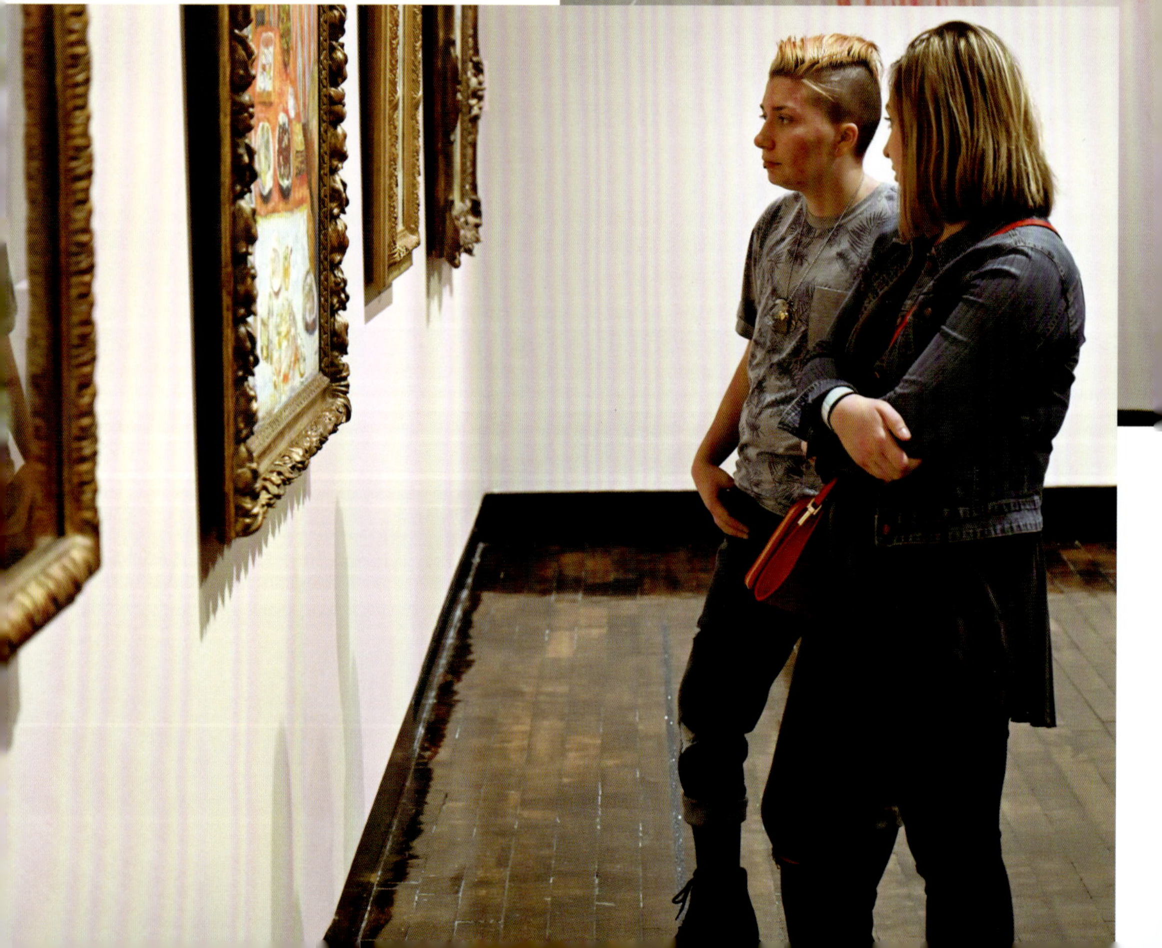

The biggest surprise in the retrospective was her photo documentation of the Japanese internment camps on the West Coast after the bombing of Pearl Harbor. Lange's images were shocking. I had not seen these images prior to the show. Issues that Lange documented such as extreme

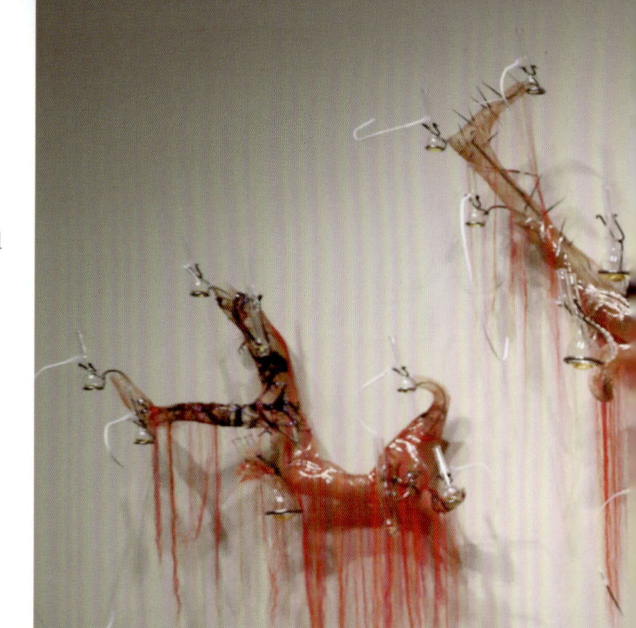

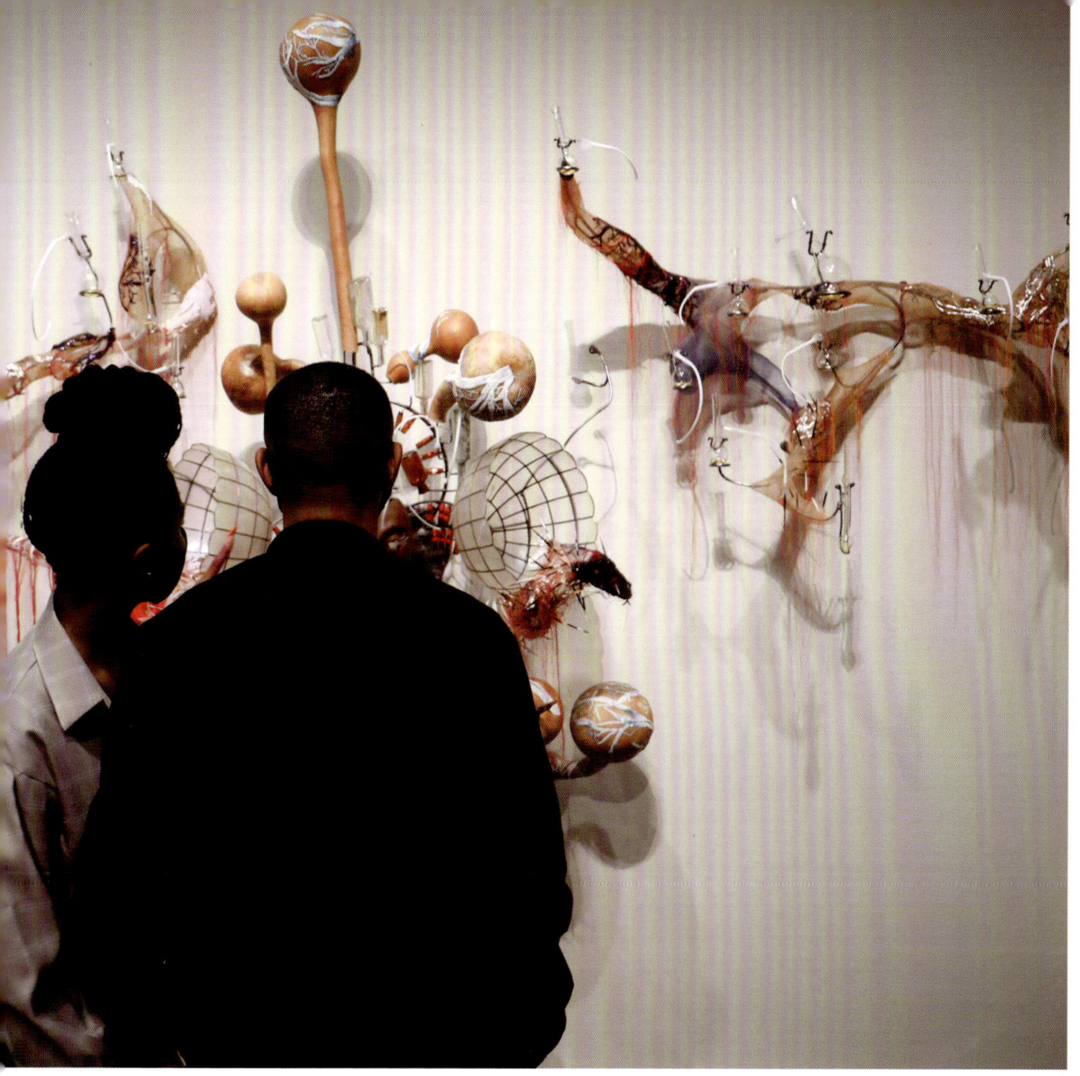

poverty, racism, and criminal injustice are still relevant today. Again, I was struck by the universality and timelessness of her art, and I am reminded that all art has the potential to unite us across generations and experience.

When in Nashville, this is one museum you must make time to visit. If you want to be surrounded by more art, visit or stay at the 21C Museum Hotel. The hotel has 10,500 square feet of public display space for contemporary art as well as art in every guest room.

Exhibits at the Frist can range from conceptual to classical, attracting a wide cross-section of patrons. Regularly changing exhibitions make this a lively community resource as well as an arts destination.

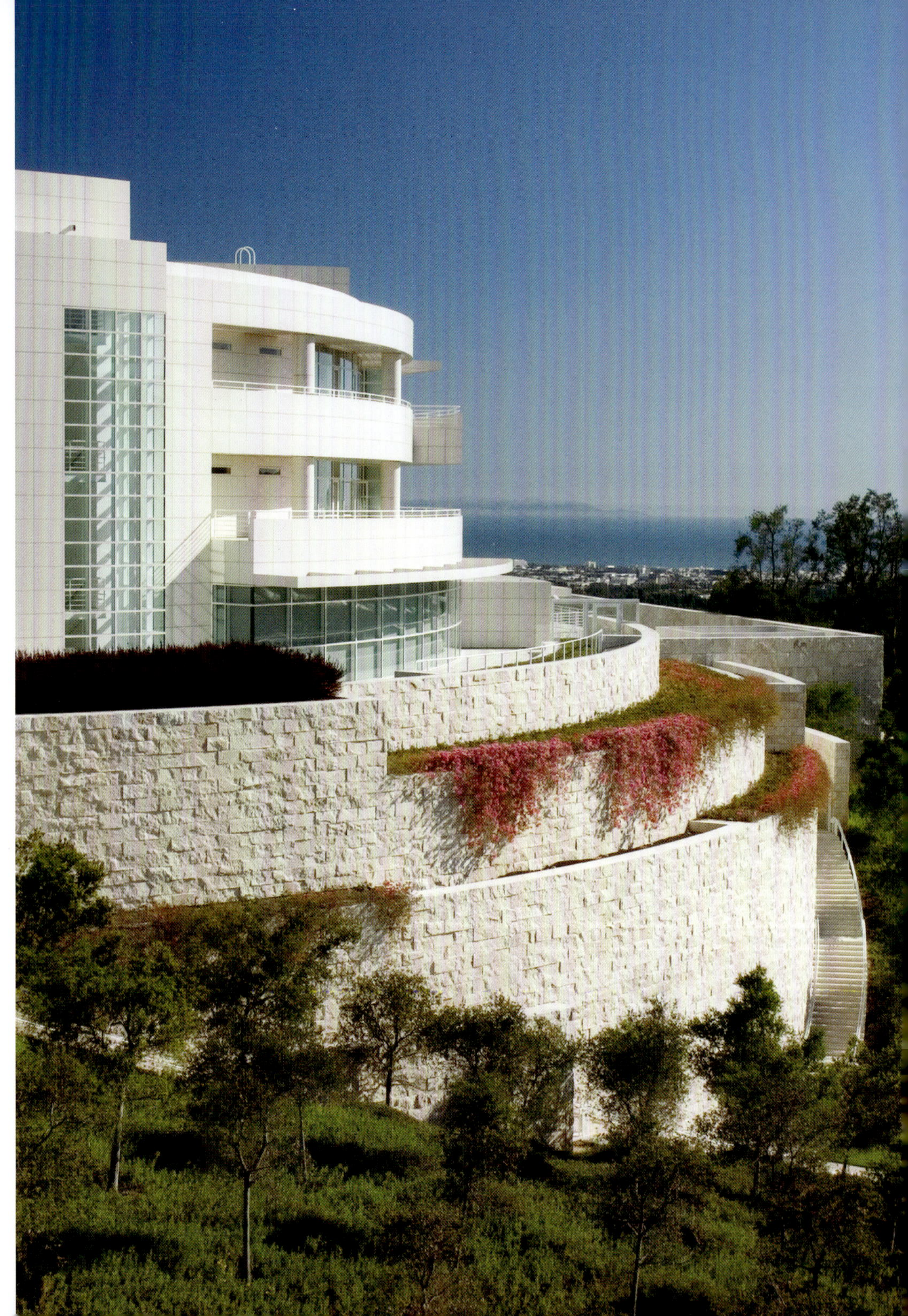

Getty Center and Getty Villa

It is well worth a day's excursion to absorb the wide range of diverse art, gardens, and antiquities at the Getty Center and the Getty Villa. **GETTY.EDU**

Not only is the architecture breathtaking, but one must also explore the gardens to fully comprehend this gift to Los Angeles.

THE GETTY CENTER is a major contribution to the landscape of the art world. The J. Paul Getty Museum at the Getty Center is home to European paintings, drawings and sculpture, and decorative arts. Of particular interest is the Center's comprehensive collection of international photography from its invention in England and France in the mid-nineteenth century to the present day. With a fabulous campus in the Brentwood neighborhood of Los Angeles designed by Richard Meier and extensive gardens planned by Robert Irwin, a day at the Getty is an immersive and visually stimulating experience.

When you arrive, I suggest taking the automated hover train, the Getty Center Tram, from the 1,200-space underground parking garage to the museum, which sits high up in the hills. In the Entrance Hall, be sure to start a self-guided tour or join one of the tours or lectures always offered. It is best to have a guided experience here, as there is simply too much to see, and it is such a diverse collection that one could never be an expert in all the areas.

When we visited, there was an architecture tour, a garden tour, and a collection tour—all for the taking. We were so fortunate to see the main exhibition at that time, *Manet and Modern Beauty*, that highlighted works from the last decade of Manet's life. While many of the gorgeous paintings and pastels were from the Getty collection, other works were borrowed from museums and collections all over the world. I noticed a beautiful pastel was from the Jeff Koons Collection, which reminded me that even bold contemporary artists such as Jeff

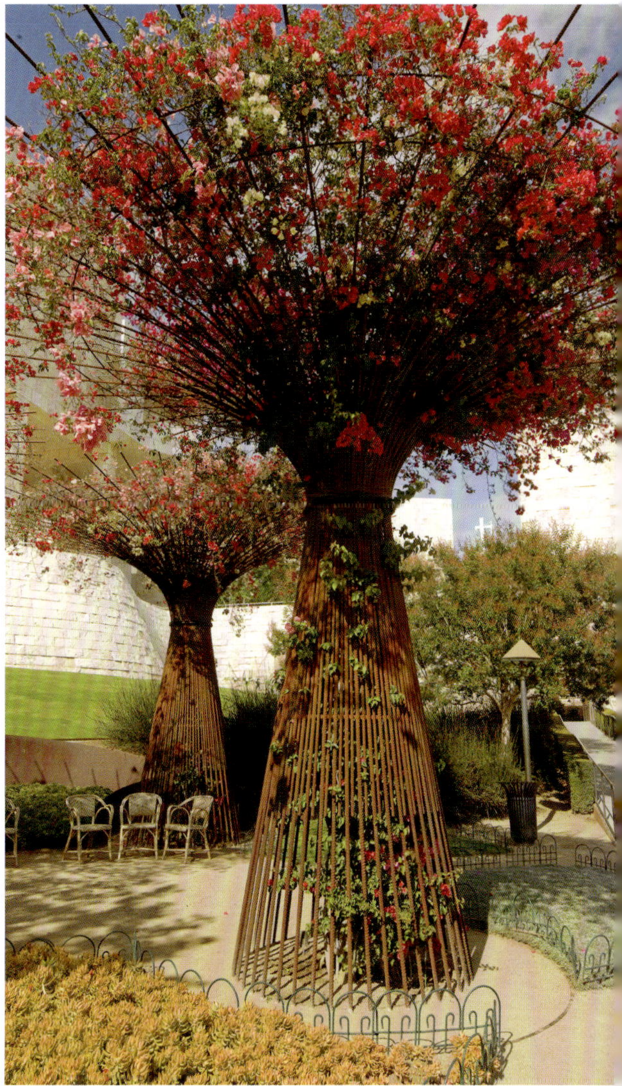

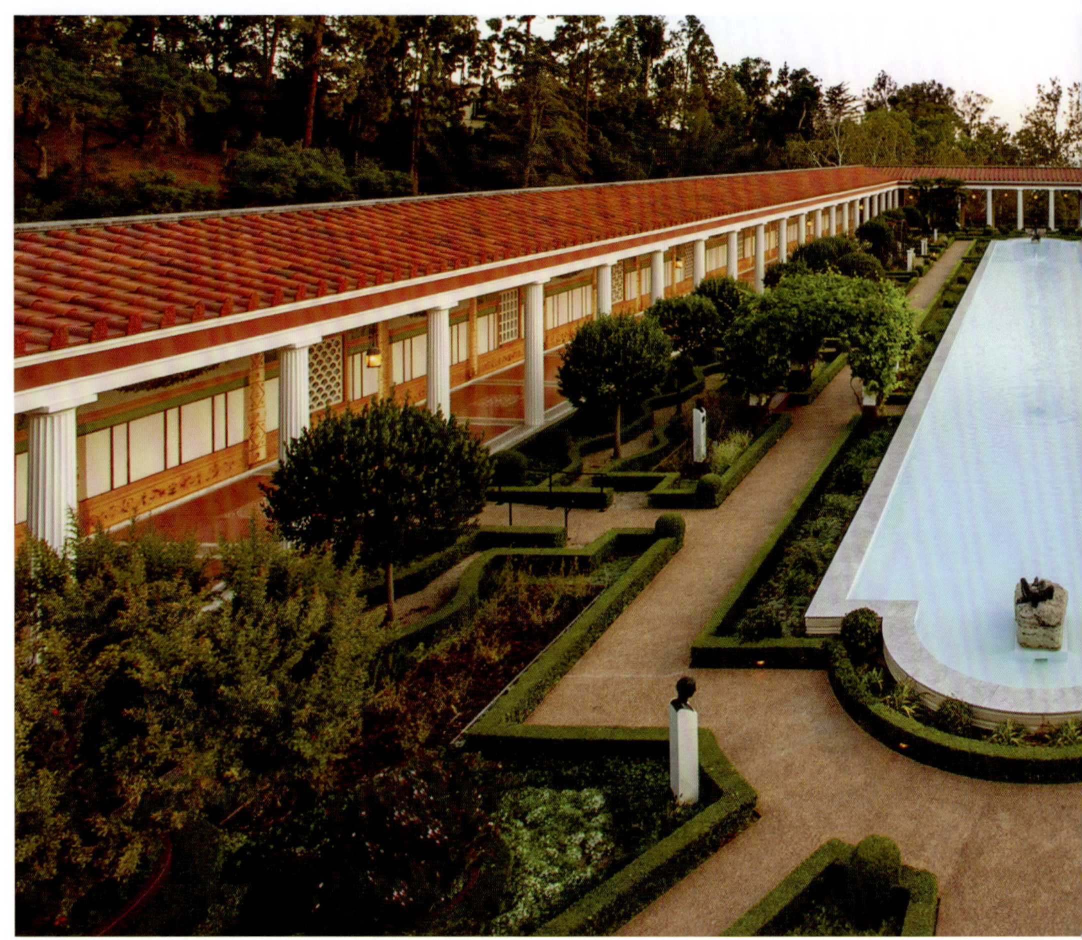

Koons are inspired by the great masterworks of art.

After journeying up the hill, exploring the gardens, admiring the architecture, and enjoying the Manet show, we simply ran out of time and never made it to the permanent collection. I recommend you reserve a full afternoon for the Getty, as it is one of my favorite places to visit when I am in LA.

On another day in Los Angeles, you must visit the other campus of the J. Paul Getty Museum, the Getty Villa. Located only twenty minutes away (depending on the traffic, of course) from the Getty Center, the Villa is in the Pacific Palisades. When you leave the Center, drive down Sunset to the Pacific Coast Highway. Turn right onto the highway, and before you get to Malibu, you'll find the parking lot of the Villa. The views from the Villa are spectacular, and the collection of antiquities is extraordinary. On display is a wide range of Greek, Roman, and Etruscan art from the Neolithic to late antiquity. Getty wanted the public to experience how an authentic Roman villa, surrounded by beautiful gardens, would look and feel. There is even an amphitheater on site. When you visit the second floor, be sure to find the balcony that provides a breathtaking view of the gardens and the Pacific Ocean across the highway.

There is a parking fee, and buses bring guests from the parking lot to the Villa, or you can walk.

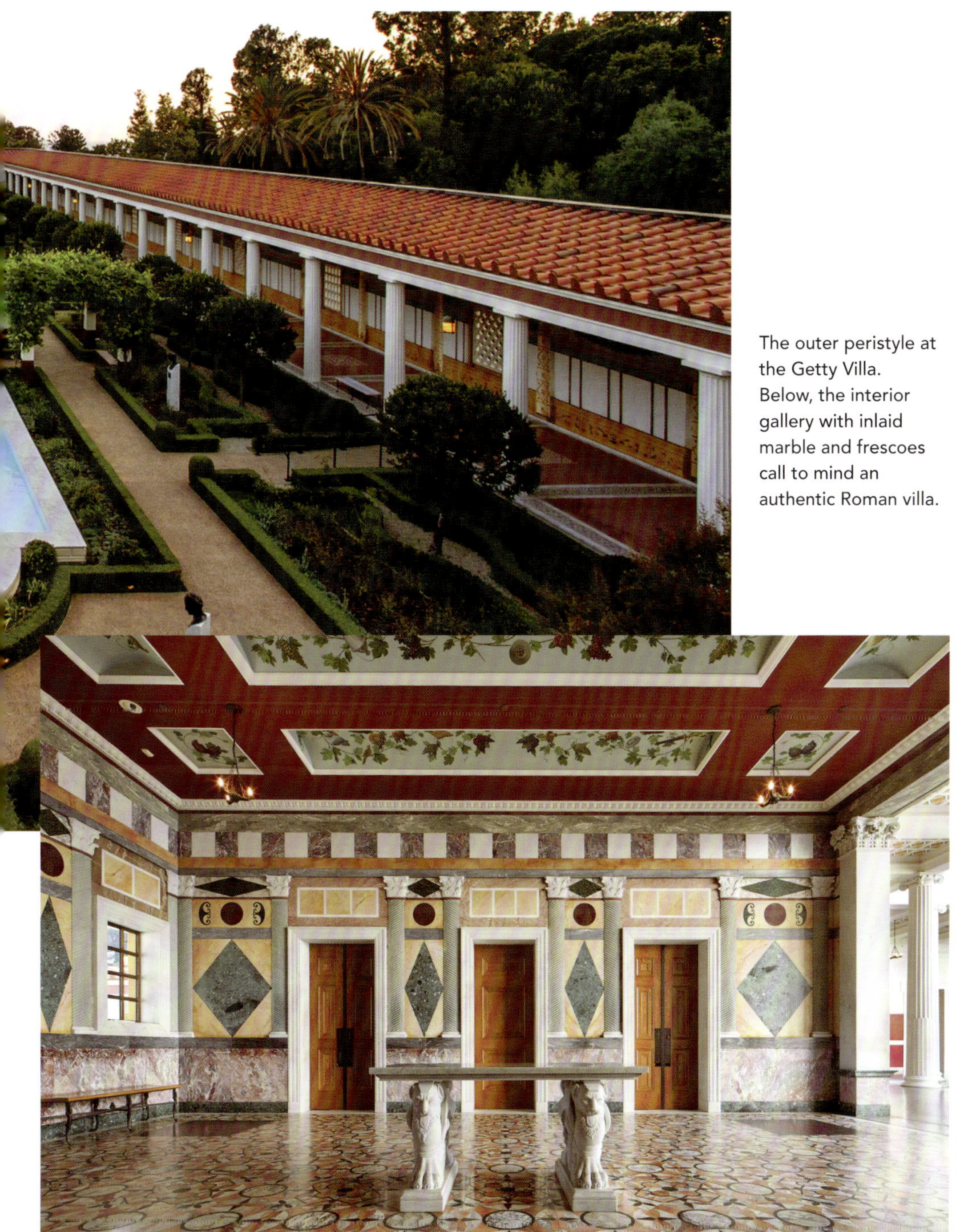

The outer peristyle at the Getty Villa. Below, the interior gallery with inlaid marble and frescoes call to mind an authentic Roman villa.

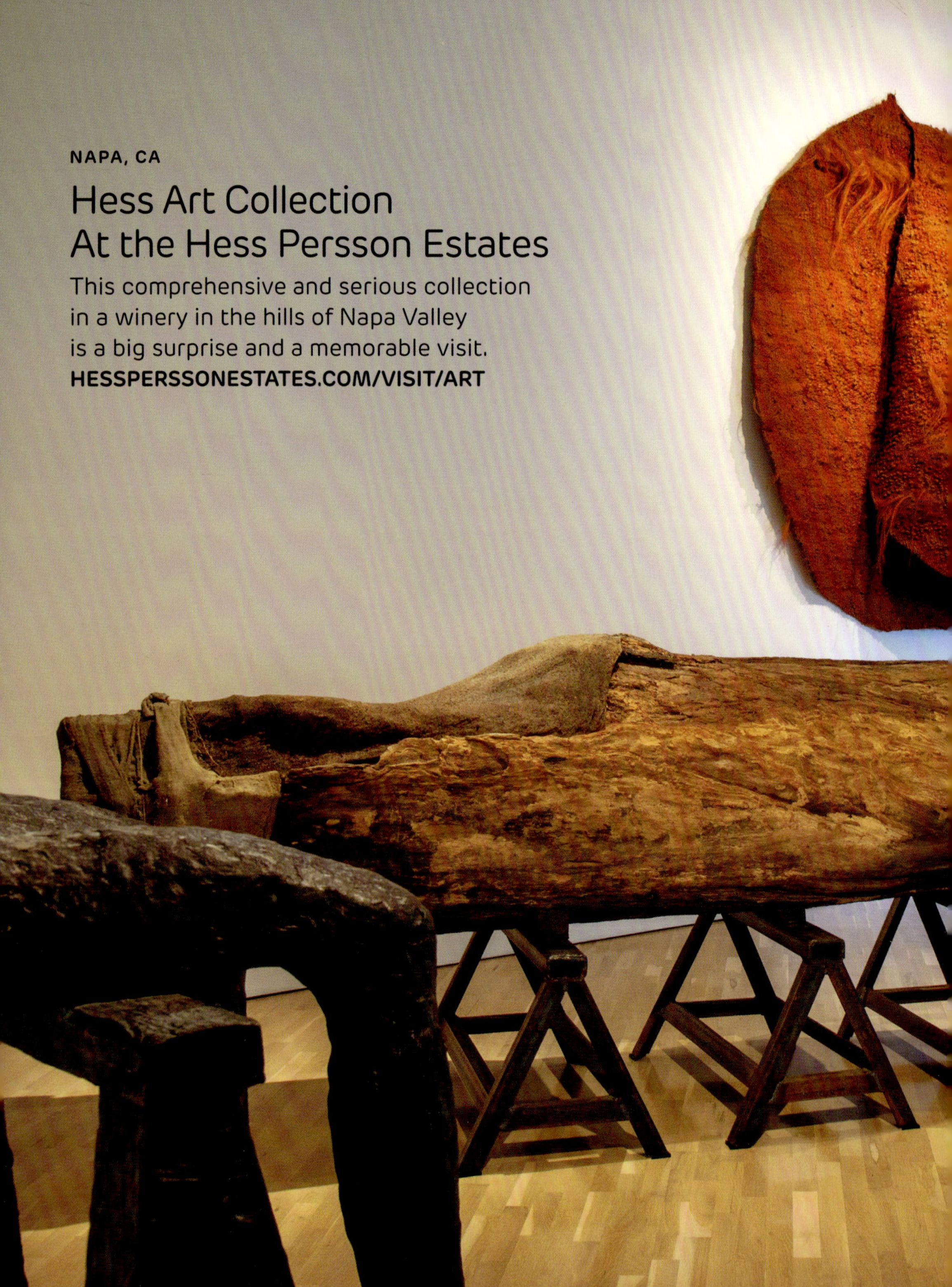

NAPA, CA

Hess Art Collection
At the Hess Persson Estates
This comprehensive and serious collection
in a winery in the hills of Napa Valley
is a big surprise and a memorable visit.
HESSPERSSONESTATES.COM/VISIT/ART

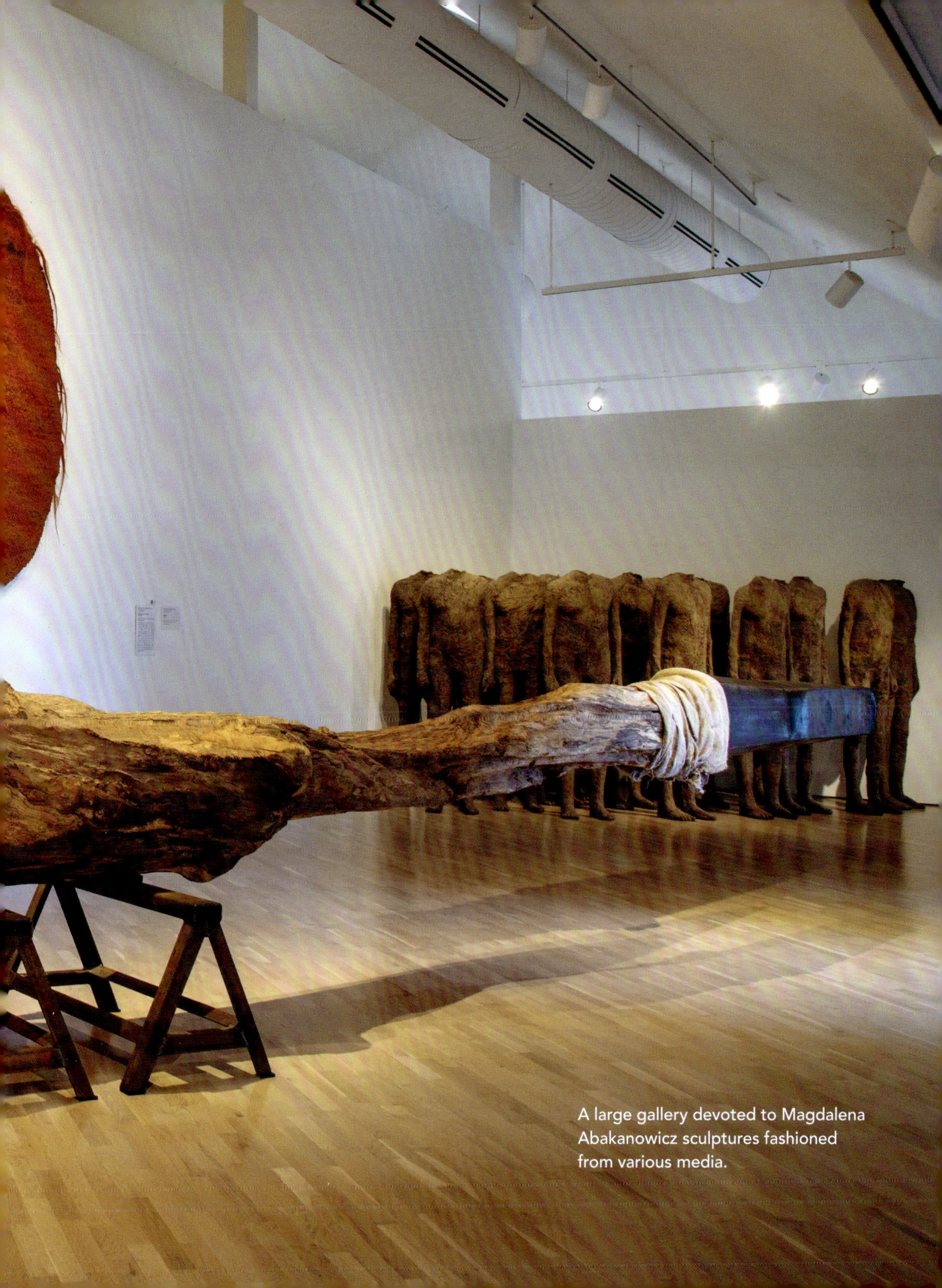

A large gallery devoted to Magdalena Abakanowicz sculptures fashioned from various media.

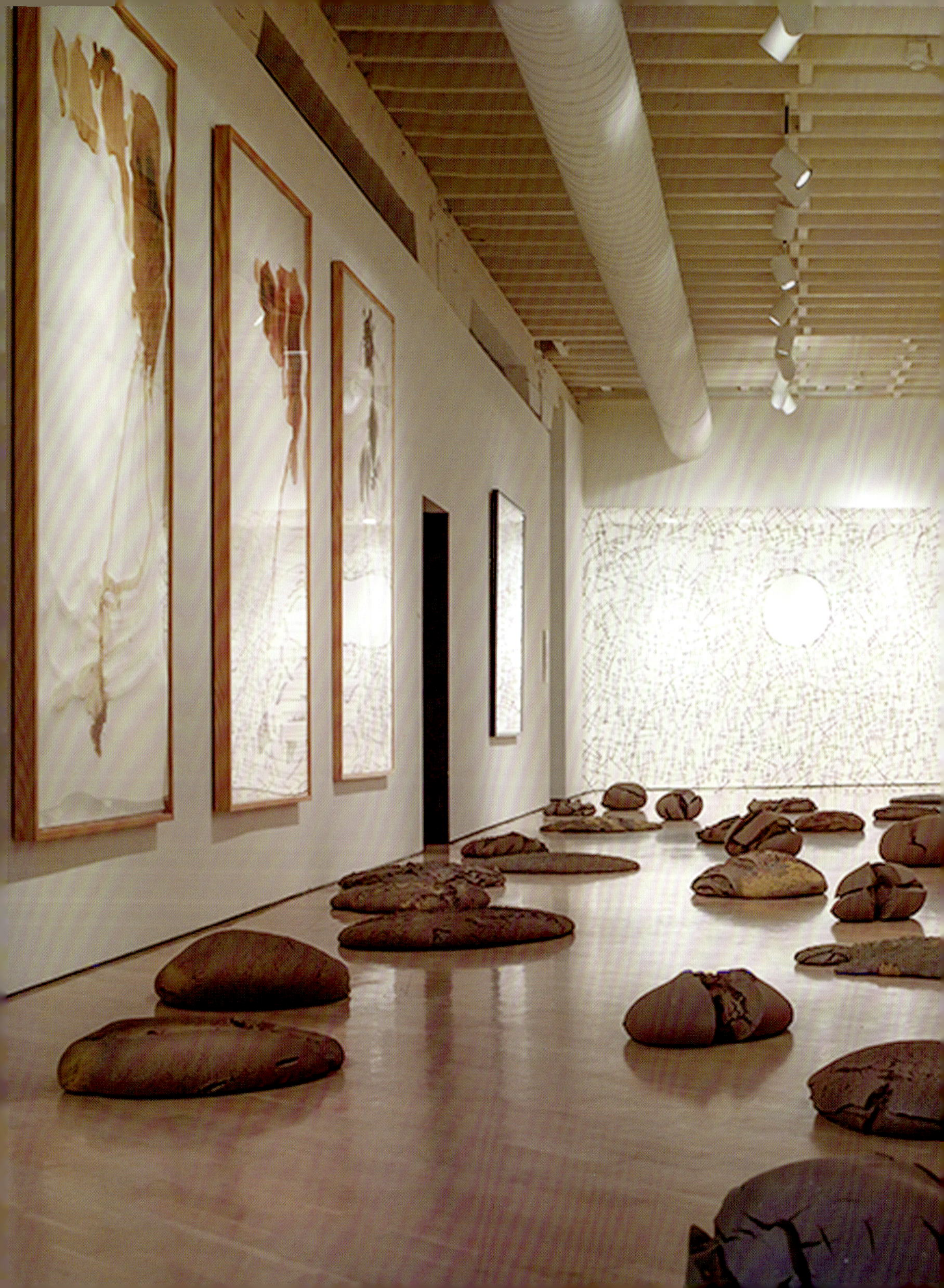

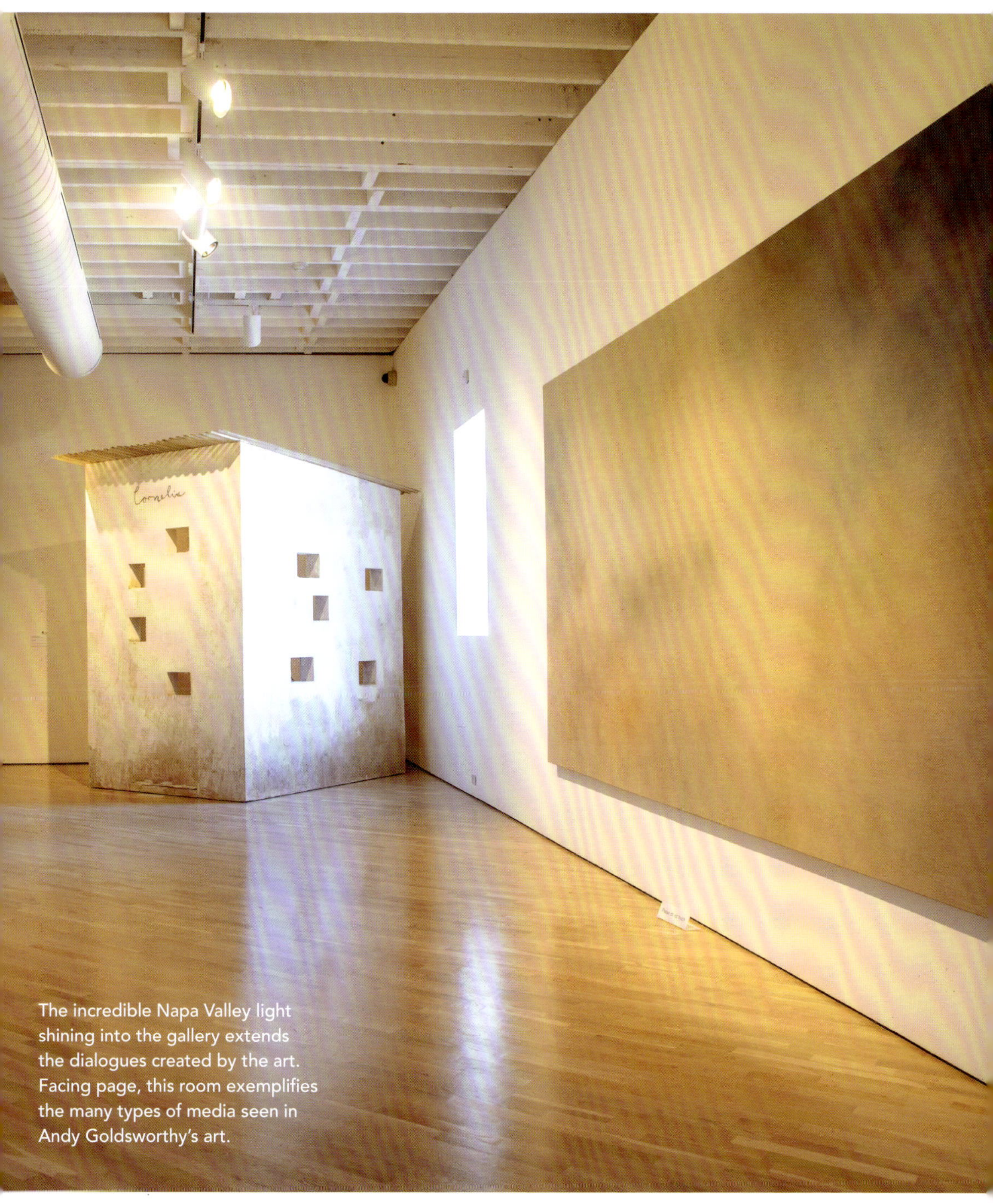

The incredible Napa Valley light shining into the gallery extends the dialogues created by the art. Facing page, this room exemplifies the many types of media seen in Andy Goldsworthy's art.

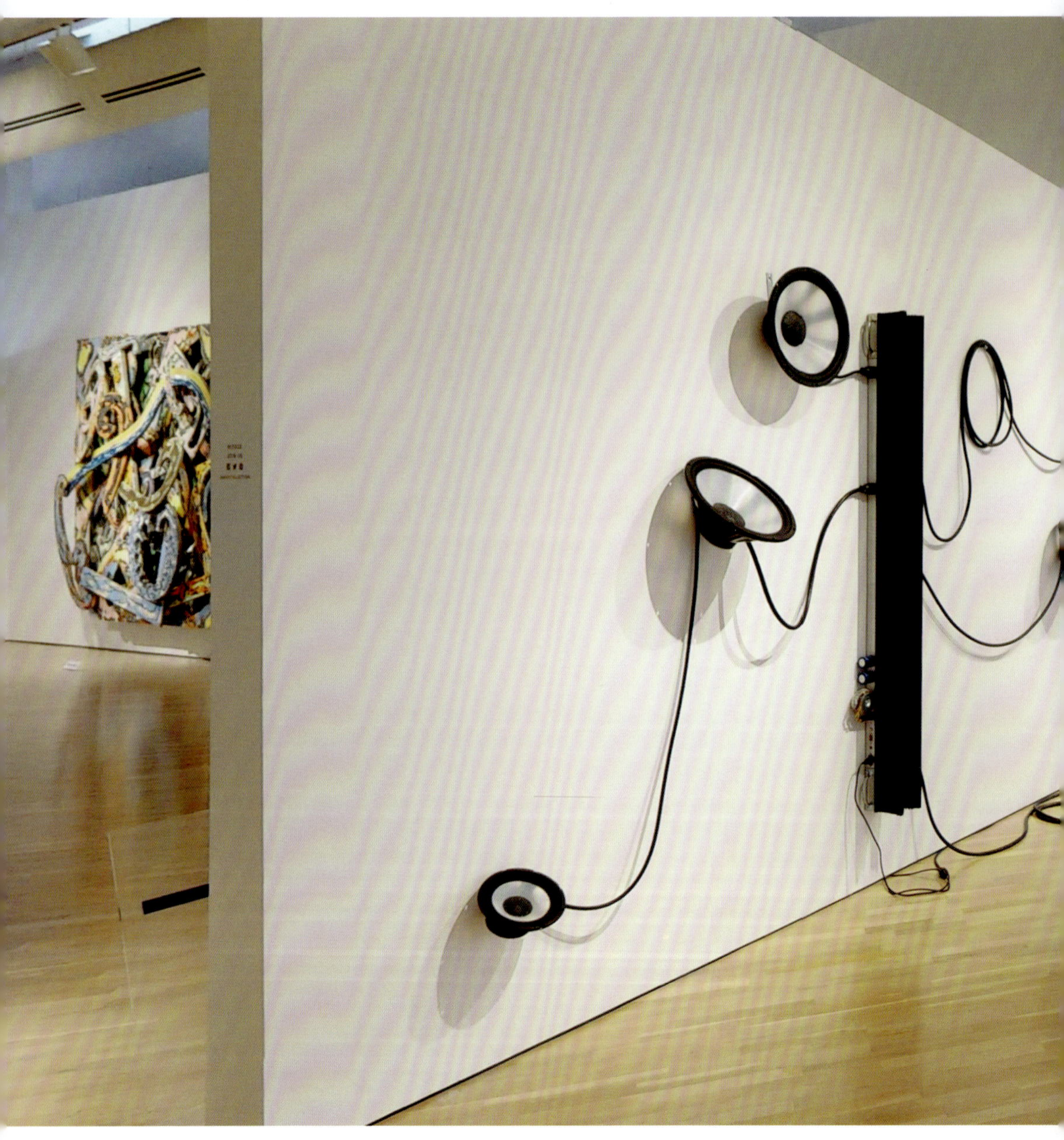

Super Wall Flower, by Alan Rath, is a newer acquisition to the collection.
Inset at right, the showstopper piece in the Hess Persson collection, *Homage*, 1974, by Leopoldo Maler.

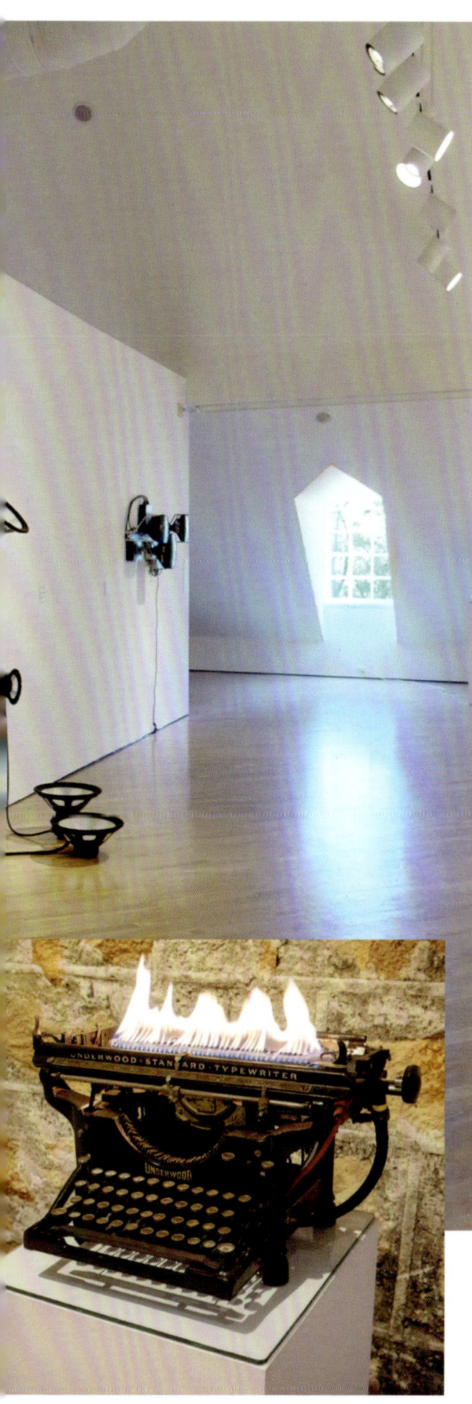

THE HESS ART COLLECTION at the Hess Persson Estates in Napa Valley is one of the most impressive and important private collections of contemporary art in America. In addition, this premier winery is a family owned and family run company that is highly regarded in the world of California wines.

Swiss businessman and wine producer Donald M. Hess, now retired, had been collecting art for more than forty years with an intensely personal philosophy about collecting. Recently, Sabrina and Timothy Persson, Hess's daughter and son-in-law, have taken over the business of creating top quality wines and have brought a new point of view to the art collection. The galleries show familiar artists from the original collection, as well as exciting new works of art that reflect their younger taste and personalities.

The point of view here is that contemporary art should be made available to the widest possible audience, and that collectors have a responsibility to make their collections accessible to the public to the best of their abilities.

They further say that too often in the art world, and in the wine world, people gravitate to what they feel they should like, going to exhibitions that others have defined "worthy." Many admire the art or drink the wine that they have been told is good art or good wine. But here they emphasize that you should find out what is good and true for you, not follow blindly what you are told, trusting what resonates with you, and that art must personally "touch" the viewer.

As we walked through the galleries with the director we were amazed at the quality of the art, much of it worthy of the finest museum. The over one thousand works in the collection are by internationally known artists including Anselm Kiefer and Magdalena Abakanowicz, art stars such as Robert Rauschenberg, and extensive earth works by Andy Goldsworthy that fill their own galleries. There were many impressive works on display including work by Georg Baselitz, Frank Stella, Franz Gertsch, Alan Roth, and John Connell.

In 2021, the Hess Collection embraced a new name, the Hess Persson Estate. The new name reflects the next vibrant generation of family stewardship. Not many people are aware that this gift of art is in the mountains of Napa Valley and easily accessible to all. Make your reservations in advance to enjoy a wonderful day in the magic of Napa looking at their world-class art and enjoying their wine.

Isabella Stewart Gardner Museum

Visit the Gardner to take in the history, the art, and the contemporary energy added by an artist-in-residence program, among other cultural events, for the public.
GARDNERMUSEUM.ORG

A SHORT WALK FROM the Boston Museum of Fine Art, one can experience an authentic Italian Palazzo at the Isabella Stewart Gardner Museum. In the late 1800s, the Gardners lived in Venice, spending time at the Palazzo Barbaro, a Venetian palace owned by Mr. and Mrs. Daniel Curtis from Boston. At the palazzo, the Gardners mingled with a group of American expats, including John Singer Sargent, James McNeil Whistler, and art connoisseur Bernard Berenson. Both Berenson and the Palazzo Barbaro itself inspired Isabella to create her own art museum in Boston. In the summer of 1897, Isabella and her husband, Jack, traveled through Italy collecting architectural fragments from doorways to balustrades, from Roman to Renaissance, for the construction of their proposed new home.

In 1899, Mrs. Gardner purchased land and selected Willard T. Sears to draw plans for a Venetian style palazzo-like building to house all of the art she had collected and continued to collect in the years to come. By 1902, she was living in the fourth-floor quarters while her extraordinary collection of paintings, sculptures, tapestries, furniture, manuscripts, rare books, and decorative arts, personally arranged by her, were installed on the first three floors.

Over the next twenty years, she continued to acquire works and change

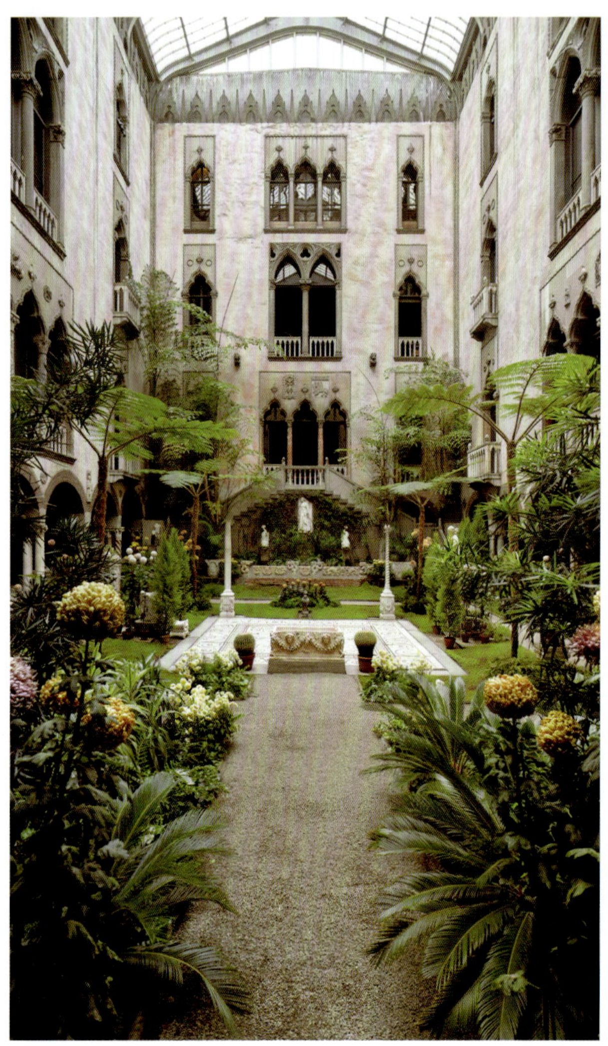

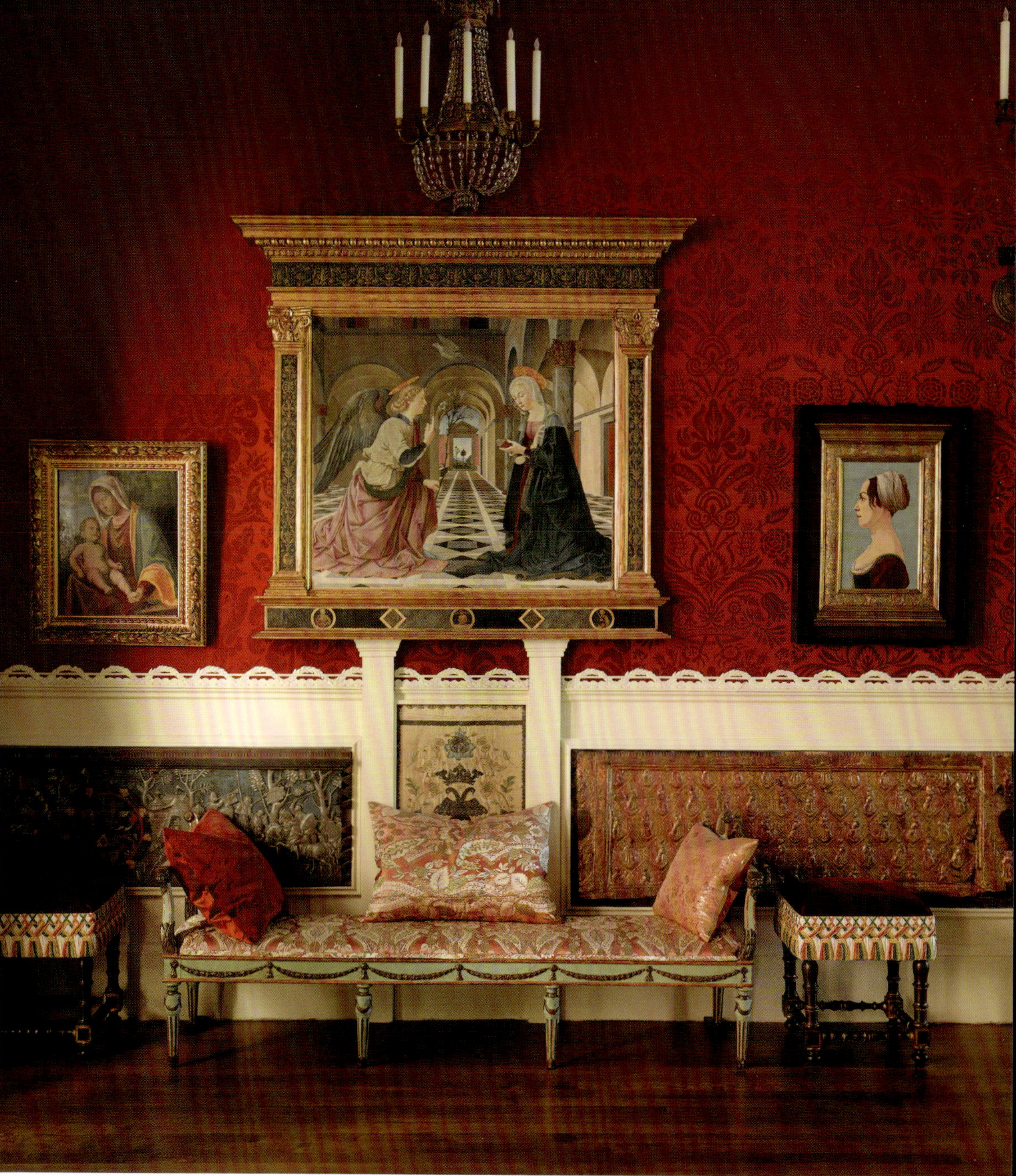

Facing page, the magnificent world-famous garden of the Palazzo.

The sumptuous Raphael room with its richly detailed décor, luxurious wall coverings, and the artist's masterworks invites the visitor to linger.

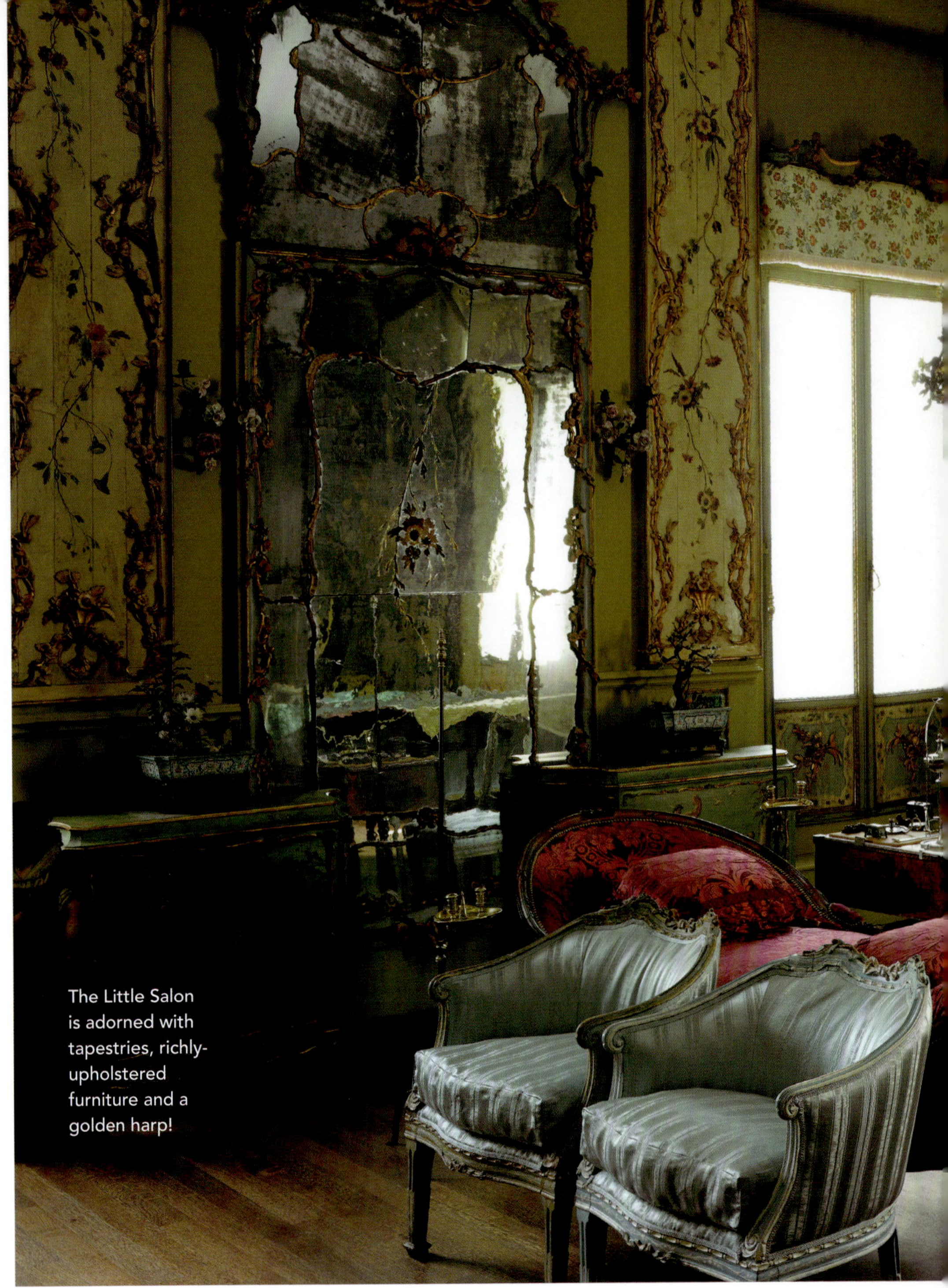

The Little Salon is adorned with tapestries, richly-upholstered furniture and a golden harp!

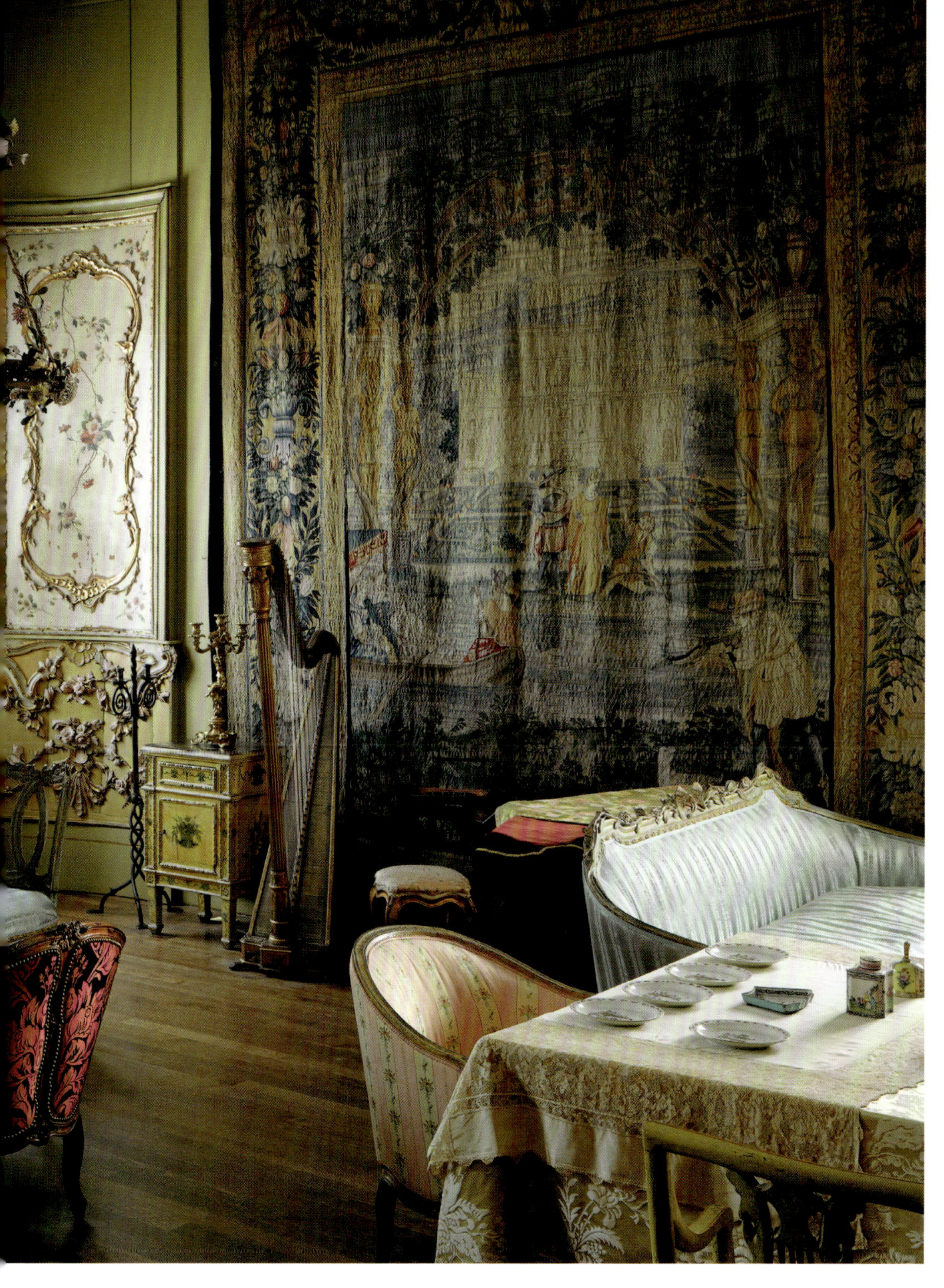

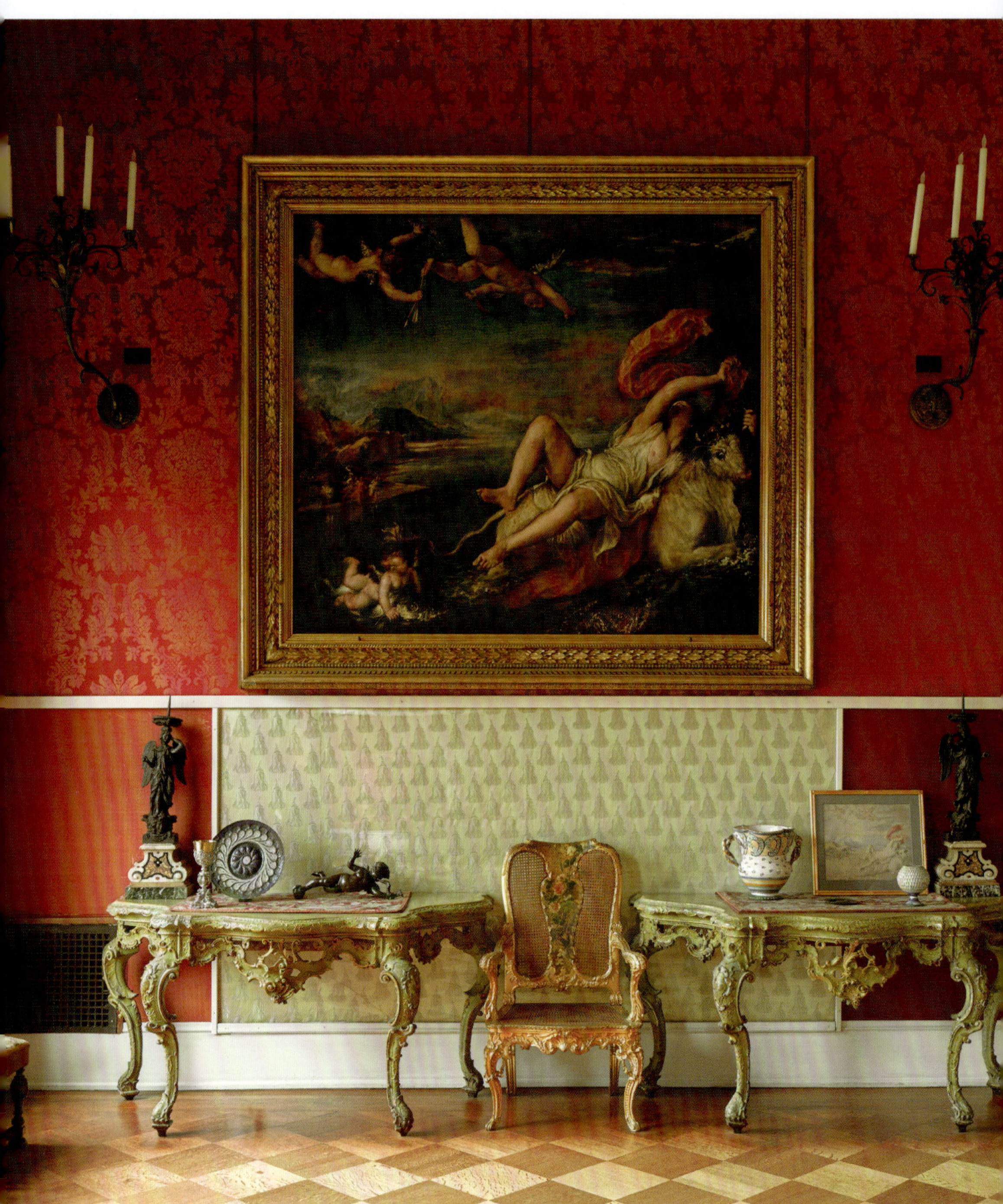

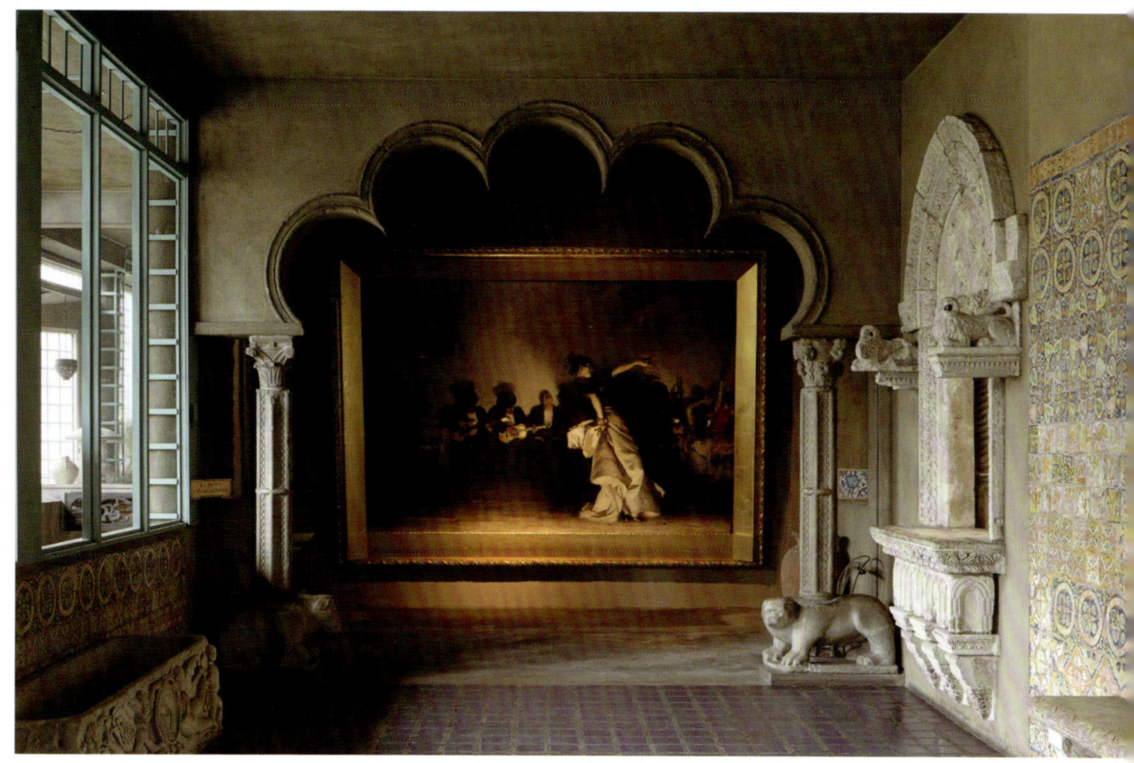

the installations. Performing artists were also invited to the Palazzo. Sargent painted in the Gothic Room, Ruth St. Denis danced on the premises, and operas were sung from the balcony of the Dutch Room.

From 2010 to 2012, the building was renovated by Renzo Piano, who created a see-through glass extension. As you enter the villa and look to your left, you will be in awe of the courtyard, which is defined by the architectural elements and columns that the Gardners collected in Italy. The landscaping is extraordinary, and the lush gardens create a true focal point. But when you enter the room on your right, there is a larger-than-life John Singer Sargent painting, *El Jaleo*, from 1882, that will stop you in your tracks. At the Renzo Piano–designed restaurant, Café G, you can sit and enjoy views of the gardens.

Isabella Stewart Gardner was a brilliant collector and an exemplary socialite. Her legacy lives on not only in the rooms filled with art and in her commitment to keeping her home open to the public as a museum, but in the museum's expanded artist-in-residency programs for visual artists, musicians, and dancers. Be sure to visit their website to take advantage of their community programming and family-focused resources.

On March 18, 1990, thirteen works of art were stolen from the Gardner Museum, including an oil by Johannes Vermeer and three pieces by Rembrandt, that have never been recovered. While the theft continues to be an unsolved mystery of the art world, the empty frames remain on view in their original locations.

The Spanish Cloister room, with *El Jaleo* by John Singer Sargent is surrounded by tile and stonework.
Facing page, this fantastic painting dominates in the richly embellished Titian Room.

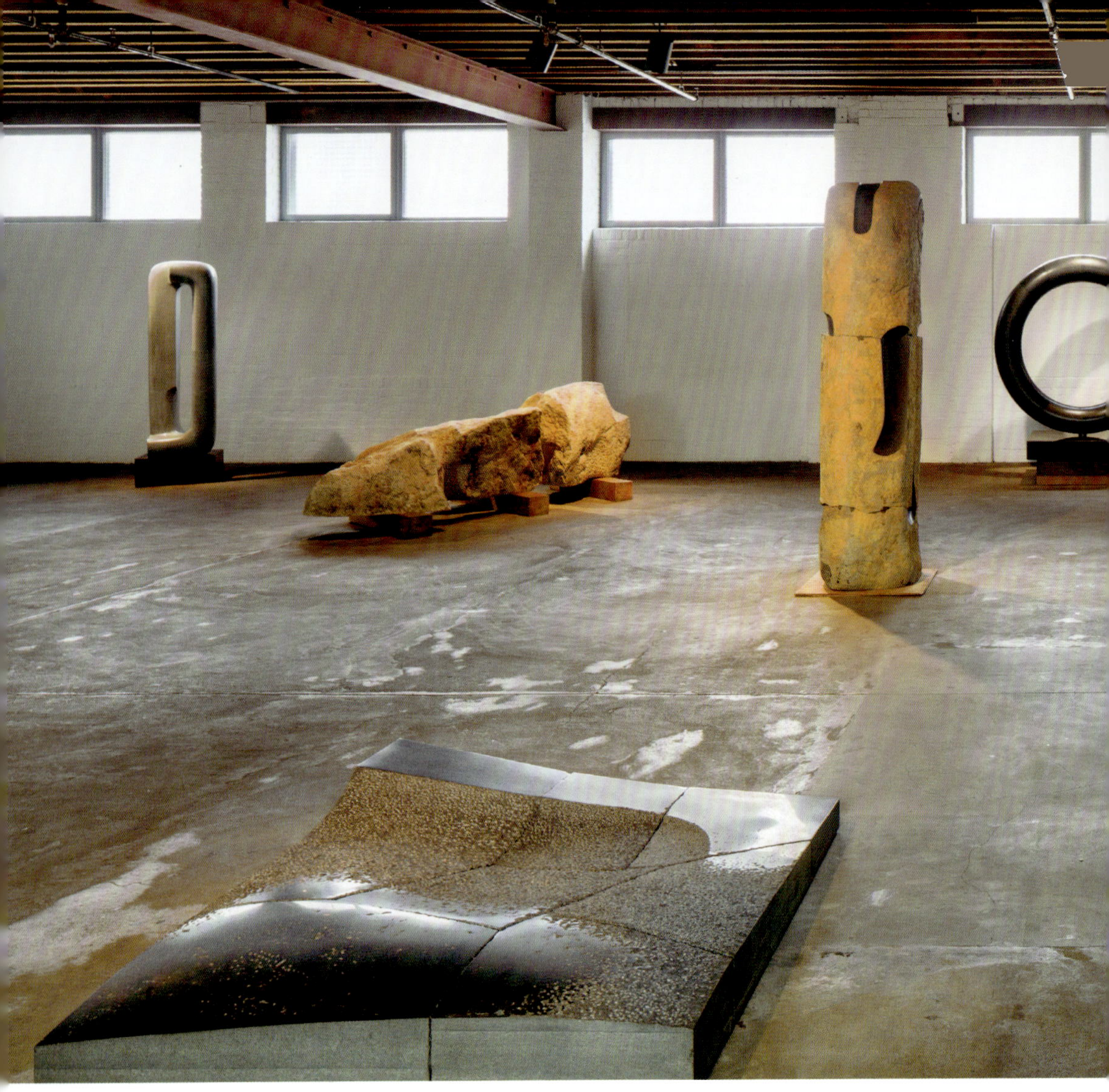

The Isamu Noguchi Foundation And Garden Museum

The Zen gardens and interior installations of brilliantly simple sculptures by this singular artist are to be savored. **NOGUCHI.ORG**

The contrast between the formal sculptures, the exterior gardens, and the industrial architecture of the building is evident. At right, *Ding Dong Bat*, 1968.

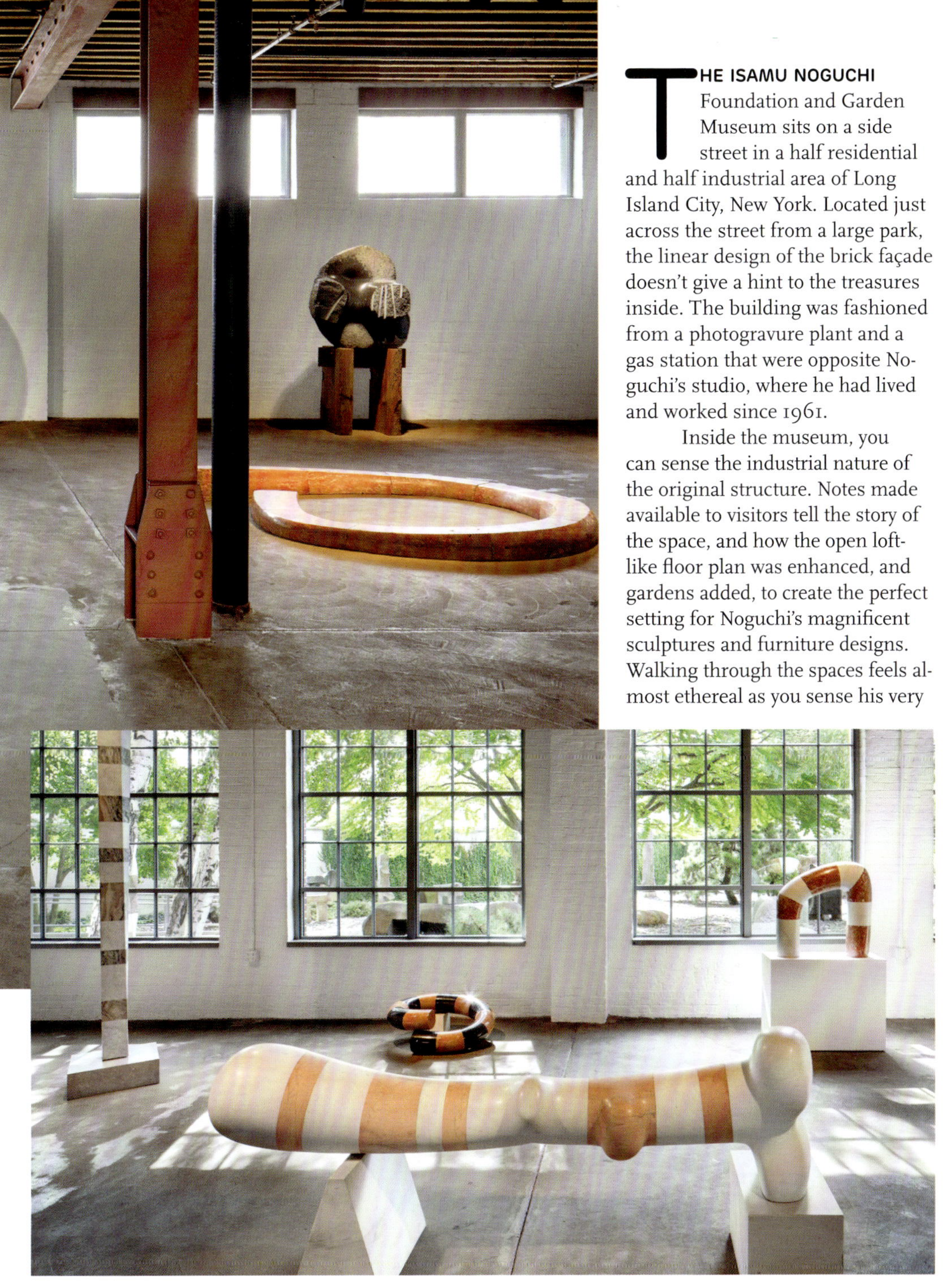

THE ISAMU NOGUCHI Foundation and Garden Museum sits on a side street in a half residential and half industrial area of Long Island City, New York. Located just across the street from a large park, the linear design of the brick façade doesn't give a hint to the treasures inside. The building was fashioned from a photogravure plant and a gas station that were opposite Noguchi's studio, where he had lived and worked since 1961.

Inside the museum, you can sense the industrial nature of the original structure. Notes made available to visitors tell the story of the space, and how the open loft-like floor plan was enhanced, and gardens added, to create the perfect setting for Noguchi's magnificent sculptures and furniture designs. Walking through the spaces feels almost ethereal as you sense his very

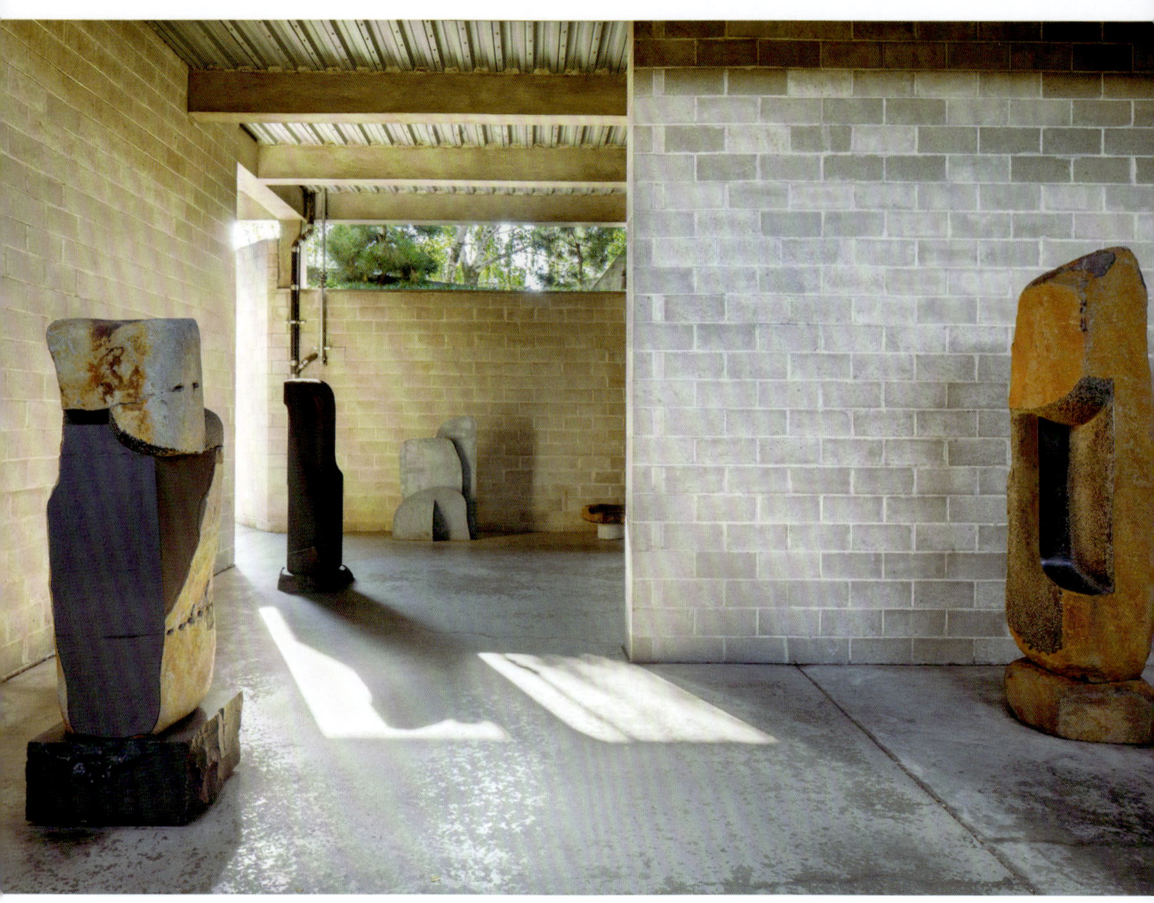

strong ties to the natural world through his choices of oversized stone and the wide variety of textures he employs.

Most importantly, and unique to this museum, is that it was created by Noguchi to preserve and display his own work. While the museum does regularly feature the work of other artists that share a connection to Noguchi in some capacity, as well as a gallery of rotating Noguchi pieces, he actually placed the one-of-a-kind sculptures in the main spaces. Between the monolithic stone creations, and the fountains and benches and sculptures in the garden, one really gets a sense of the scope of his work and the sheer abundance of his creative genius.

The other major sources of constant revenue for the foundation are Noguchi's product designs, and especially his famous Akari lights of parchment and bamboo. All of his products can be purchased at the wonderful shop on premises. Evan runs the store and is the most helpful resource for all-things Noguchi. The store tries to channel Noguchi's spirit in the way all of the objects are arranged and by selling only objects created by hand by artists and craftspeople. Speaking with Evan at length at the end of our visit left us feeling as though we'd had a very personal tour of this world-class museum in the heart of Long Island City.

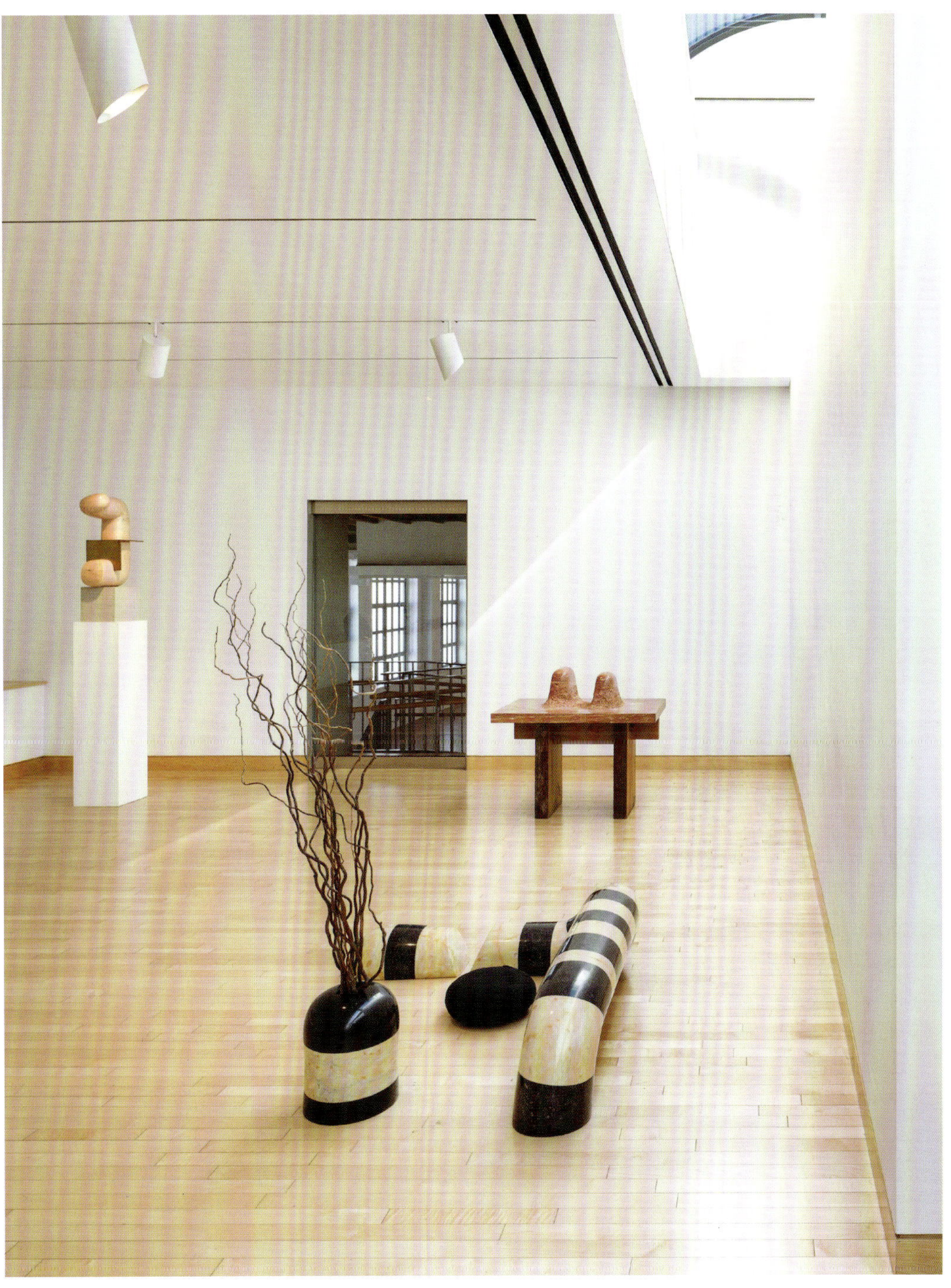

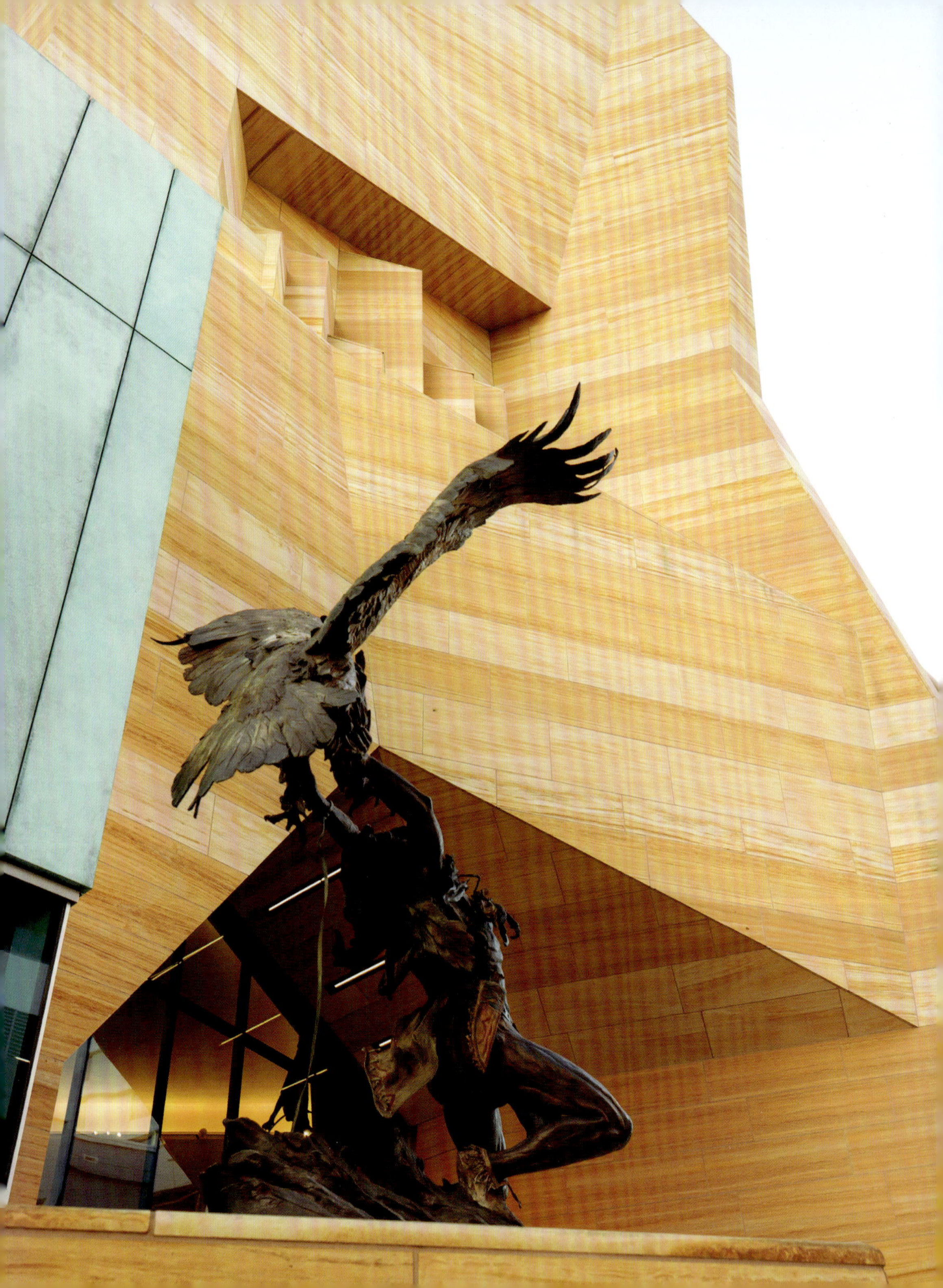

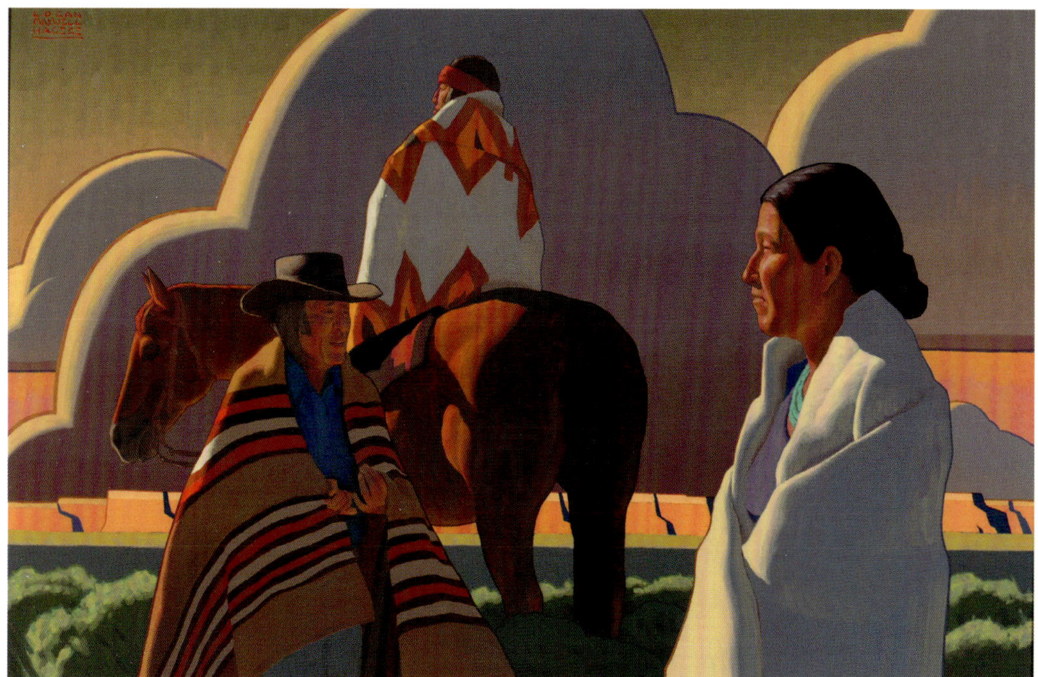

The James Museum Of Western & Wildlife Art

This museum highlights the full panorama of Western, wildlife, and Native American art and cements St. Petersburg, Florida, as an art destination. **THEJAMESMUSEUM.ORG**

Light on the Round Clouds, by Logan Maxwell Hagege, recalls the quintessential light of the Western sunset. Facing page, the building was designed to evoke the aesthetic of the American Southwest.

NO MATTER WHERE you live, it's worth a visit to St. Petersburg, Florida, to visit The James Museum of Western & Wildlife Art. Established in 2018, The James is a relatively new museum that houses the collection of Mary and Tom James.

As a young married couple attending college in the Boston area, Mary and Tom began a lifelong love of collecting art with an emphasis on emerging local artists in the Massachusetts area. By speaking with gallery owners, museum staff, and artists, they educated themselves as they purchased paintings and sculptures, and at the same time, they helped the artists to earn a living.

After moving to St. Petersburg, the couple continued to collect and support local artists in the Gulf Coast area. Years had passed when Mary convinced Tom to go on a skiing trip to Aspen. On a day when a blizzard prevented them from

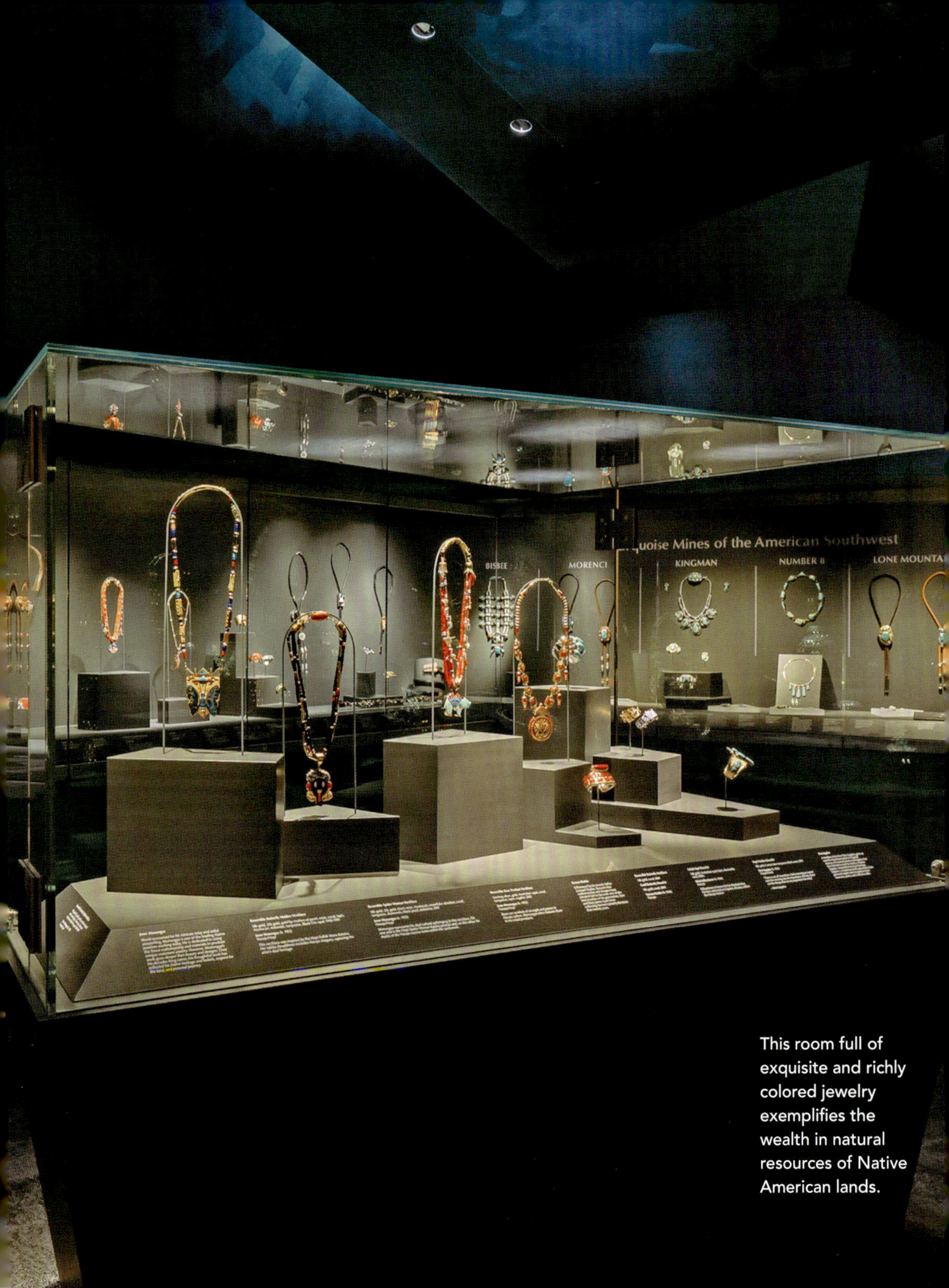

This room full of exquisite and richly colored jewelry exemplifies the wealth in natural resources of Native American lands.

skiing, they decided to visit the local galleries filled with work by artists of the American West. Incredibly inspired by what they saw, they changed their focus to collecting and championing Western Native American art.

The James' first purchase was a very large oil, a masterpiece by Earl Biss, *Winter Sunrise Circle of the Big Sky People.* At the time, Earl Biss was a well-known Crow Native American painter from Montana and Washington State. Mary and Tom met with Earl and were fortunate to purchase more of his works prior to his death in 1998. This was the seed for The James Museum, which they established in 2018. Ever since, they have been collecting the paintings, stone sculptures, ink drawings, and jewelry created by artists of the twentieth and twenty-first centuries who highlight the narrative of the Western theme.

The museum is arranged in different sections from the Early West to Native Life, Native Artists, Frontier, and Wildlife. Walking into the museum and seeing formidable bronze sculptures of Native Americans in different poses is a breathtaking experience. This unique—and unexpected in its location—museum sheds light on a geographical and stylistic area of art that has not been highlighted in the mainstream canon of the contemporary art community. With The James Museum, Mary and Tom James have fulfilled their vision to share their passion for the art, traditions, and culture of the West with all who visit St. Petersburg.

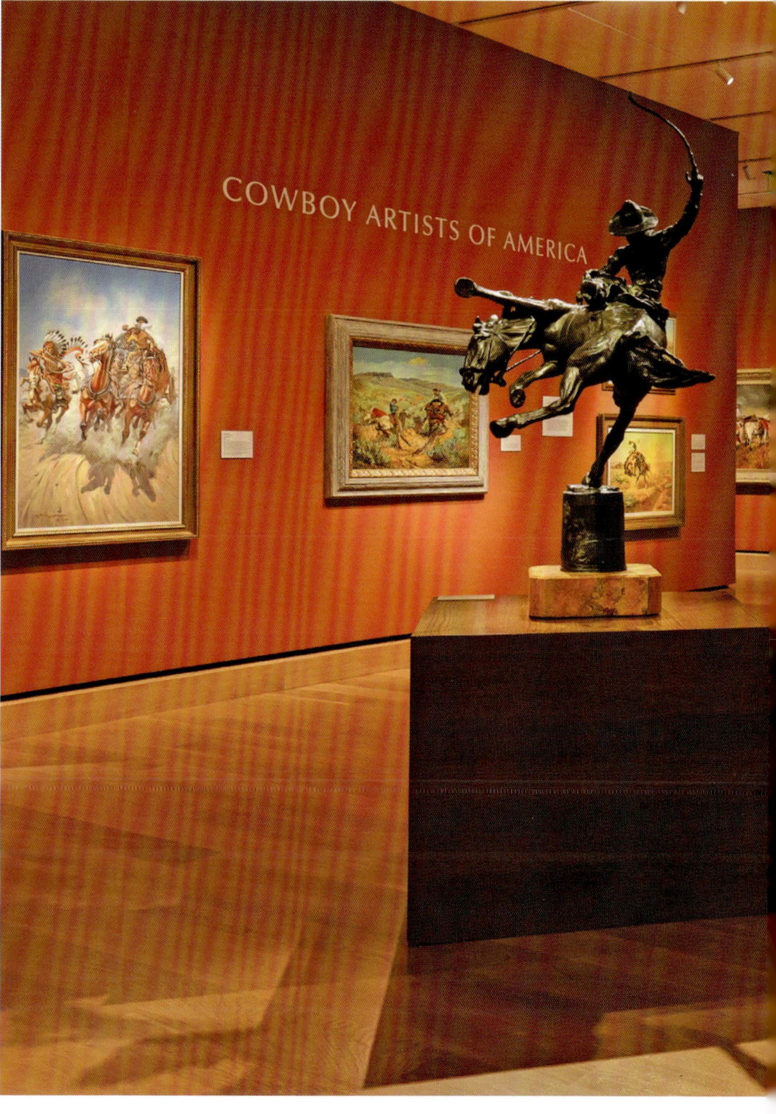

The West and the cowboy are celebrated through bronzes and paintings depicting scenes from this iconic era in the American story.

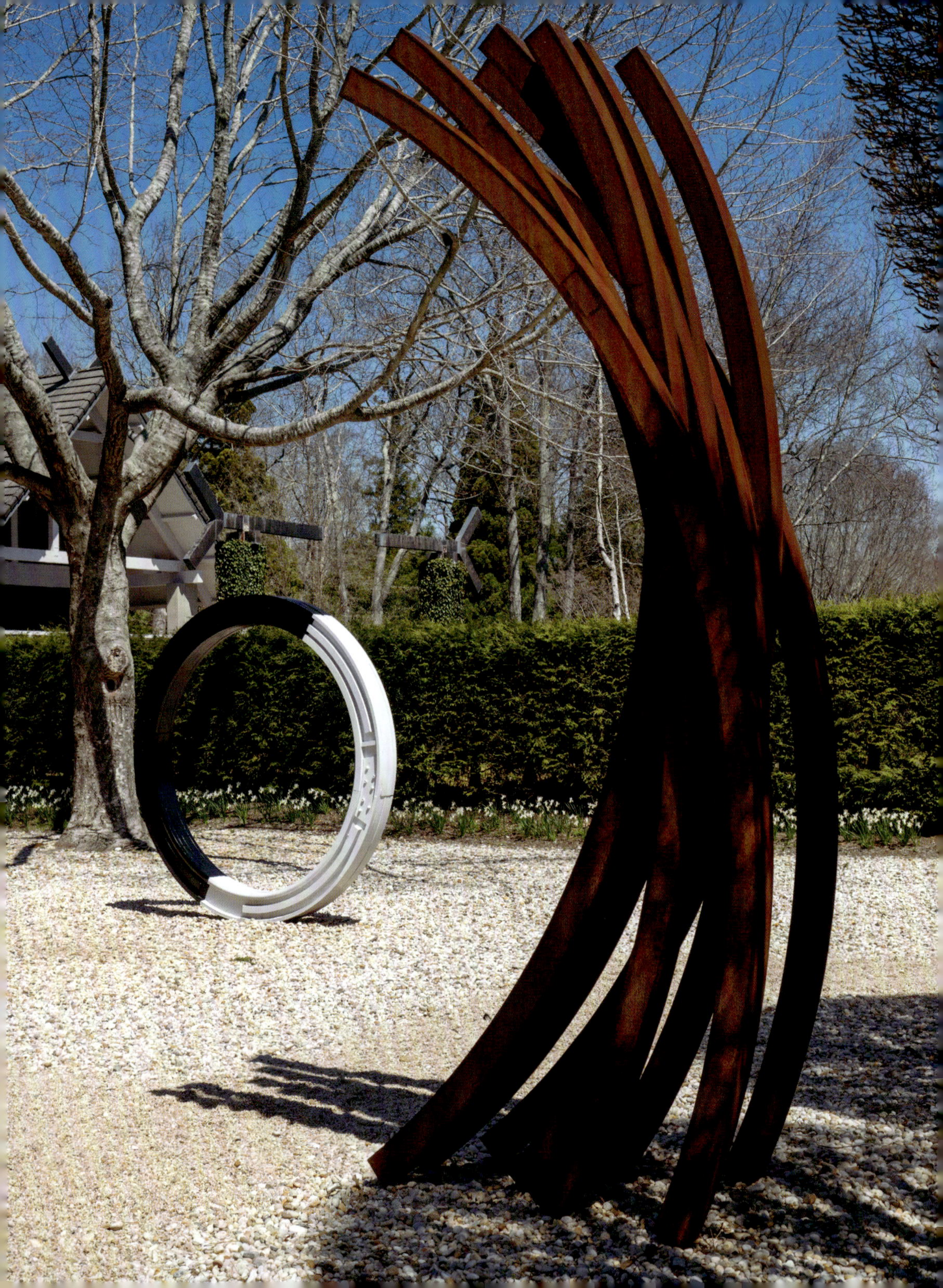

LongHouse Reserve

Hidden in the woods of East Hampton, one needs to know about LongHouse Reserve. Outdoor sculptures set within the curated gardens are a welcome respite from the hubbub of the Hamptons. **LONGHOUSE.ORG**

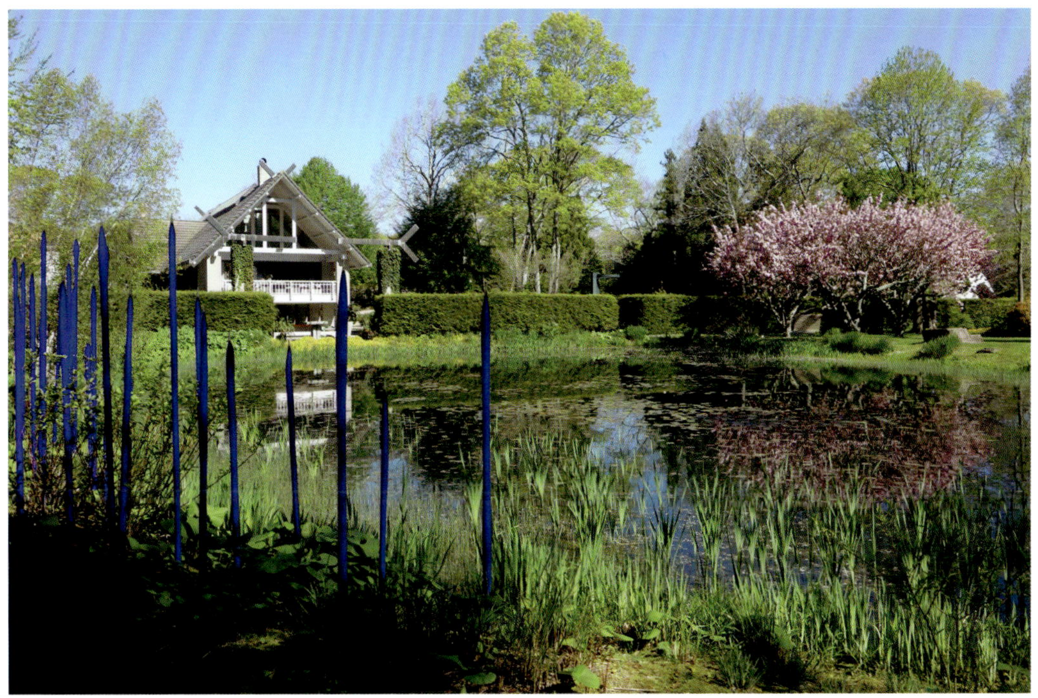

LONGHOUSE RESERVE was created in 1991 by Lack Lenor Larsen, the renowned textile designer and great supporter of artists, to showcase his collection of more than sixty contemporary sculptures. Nestled in the woods on Eastern Long Island, the sculptures are set amid sixteen acres of gardens, established lawns, grasses, and sand dunes to emphasize the connection between nature and visitors.

Until his death in 2020, Larsen lived on site in the main house, where he maintained an eclectic and diverse collection spanning a millennium. Finding inspiration in the 7th century Shinto shrine at Ise in Japan, Larsen built the house on the property in 1986, with Charles Forberg as architect and Joe Tufariello as builder.

At LongHouse, there are permanent works of sculpture on display alongside seasonal loans from artists, collectors, and dealers, all set within the magnificent natural vistas. Be sure to see *Cobalt Reeds,* a blue-colored glass sculp-

Dale Chihuly's *Cobalt Reeds* seen here alongside Peter's Pond. Facing page, Bernar Venet's *83° Arc x 8* in the foreground, and Tony Rosenthal's *Mandala* in background.

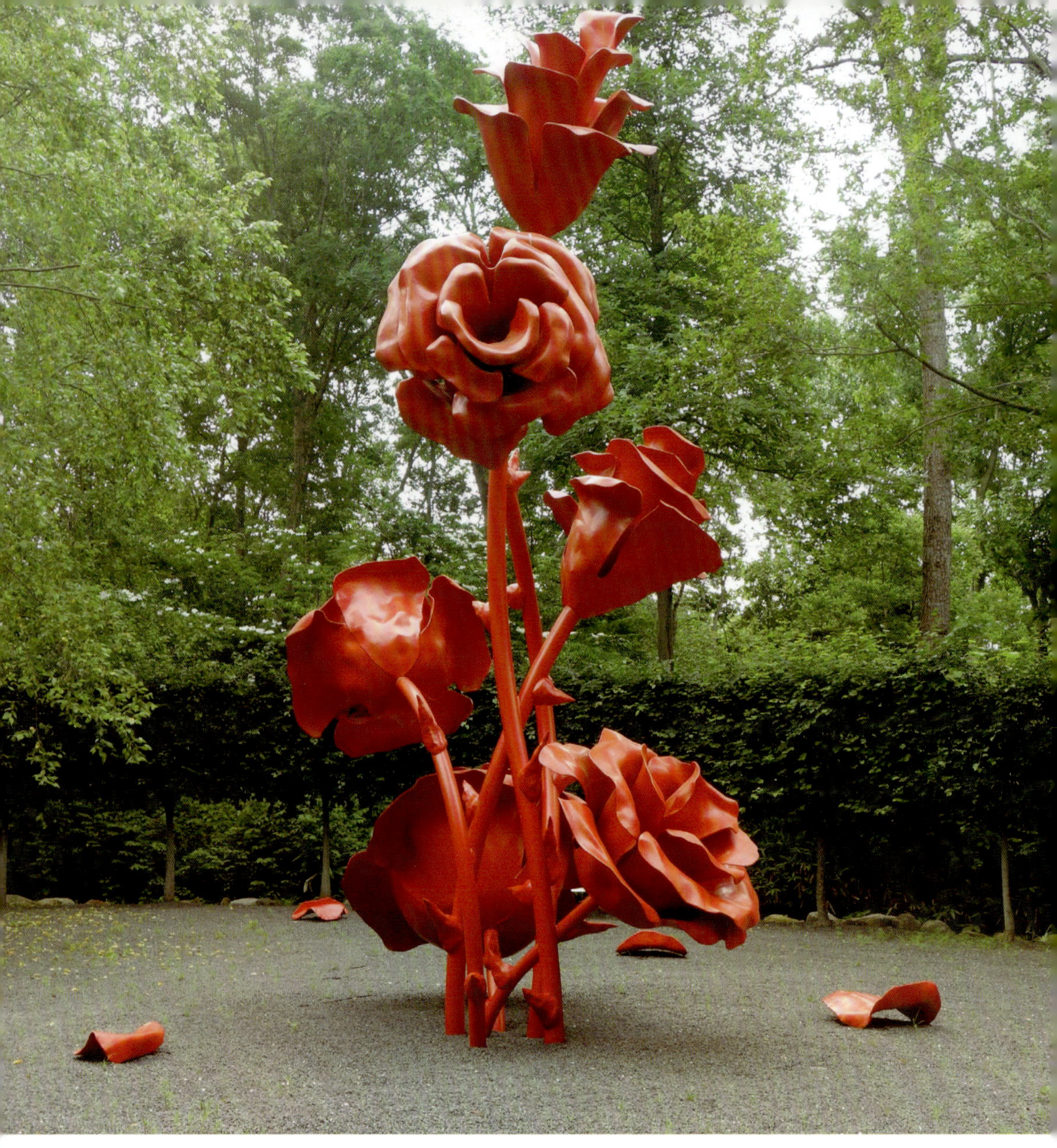

ture by Dale Chihuly from 2000 piercing the sand. Other favorites of mine include an enormous geodesic dome by Buckminster Fuller, *Irregular Progression*, a concrete block piece by Sol LeWitt, and the massive bronze, *Reclining Figure*, by Willem de Kooning.

This is a secretive spot, but only in the best sense of its location in the woods. I think there is so much art to experience here that it would be helpful to engage a docent, but if you choose to walk on your own, you won't be disappointed.

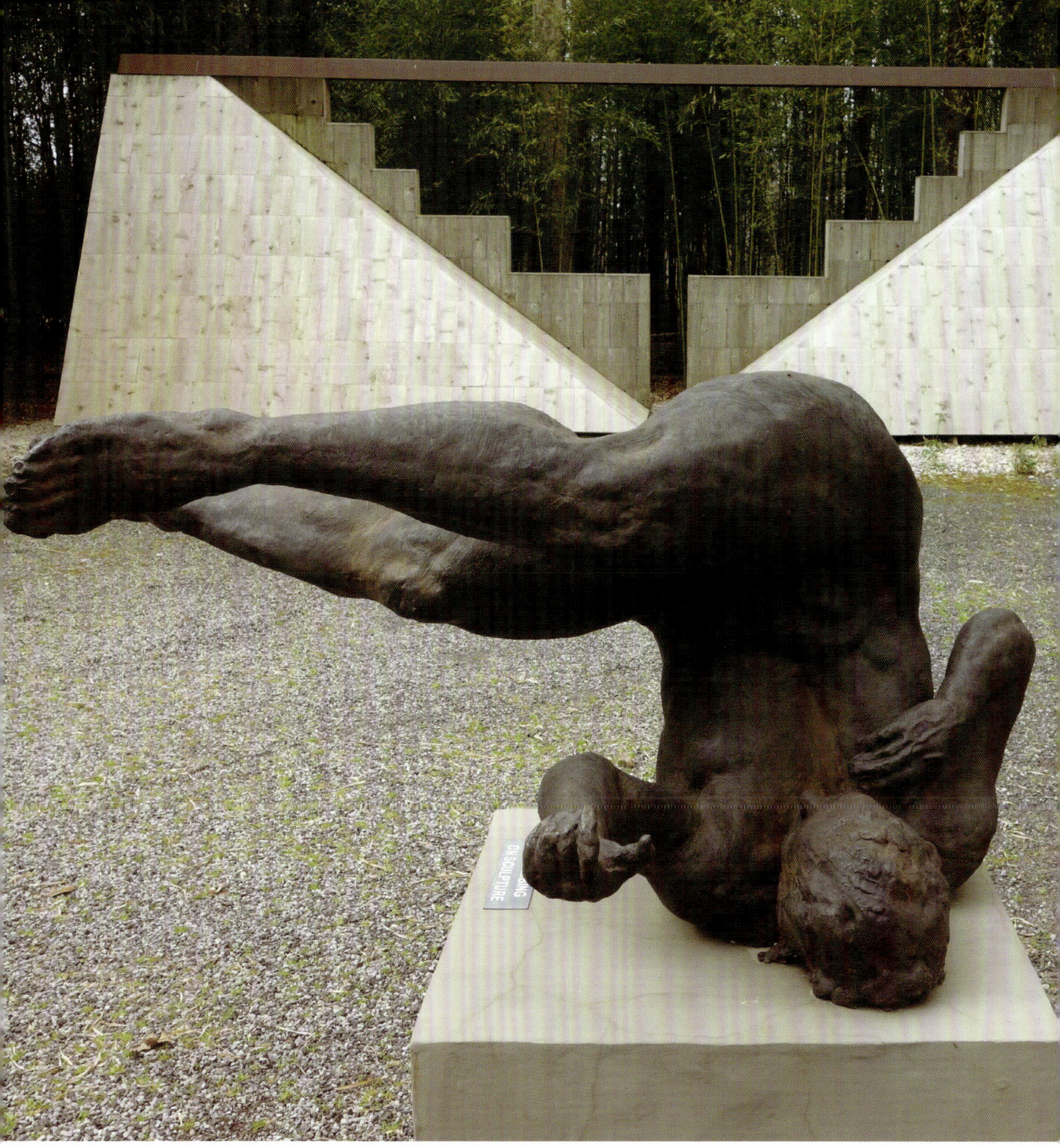

Facing page, a towering rose sculpture by Will Ryman is hidden in one of the secret gardens.

Eric Fischl's unsettling sculpture, *The Tumbling Woman*, 2002, calls attention to the human tragedy of 9/11.

Magazzino Italian Art Foundation

Founders Nancy Olnick and Giorgio Spanu are the visionaries who brought this unparalleled museum of Arte Povera to the Hudson Valley. **MAGAZZINO.ART**

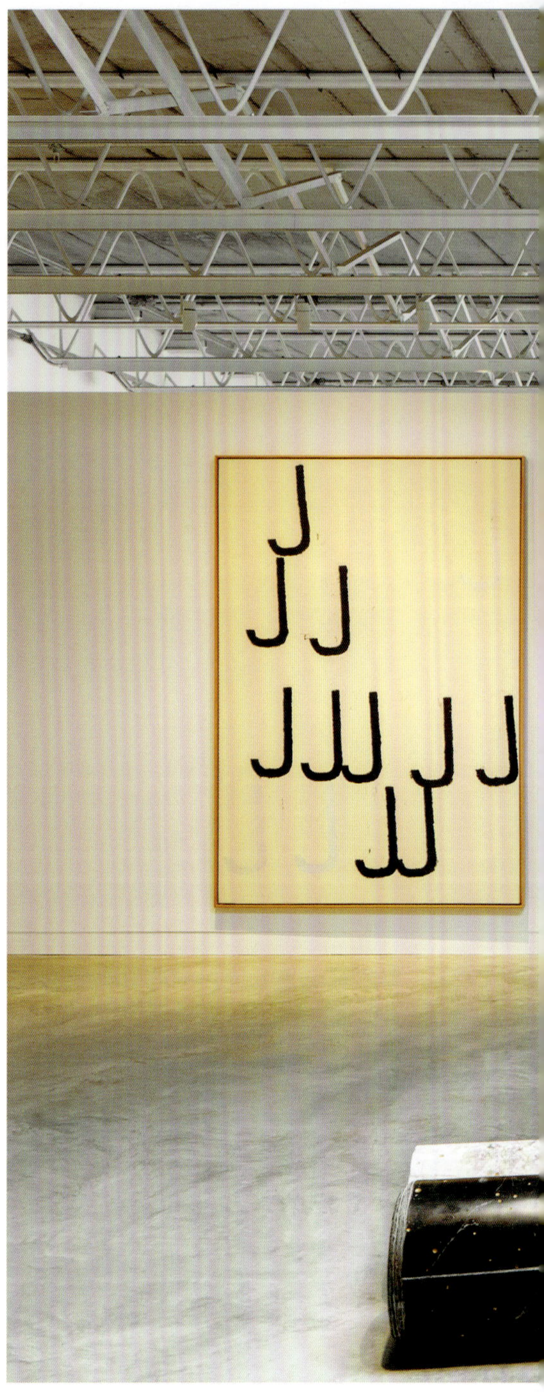

The soaring interior galleries accommodate large contemporary works such as these by Jannis Kounellis.

ALMOST UNKNOWN EXCEPT to those who know, Magazzino (the Italian word for "warehouse") is a one-of-a-kind museum devoted to post–World War II Italian art, Arte Povera. This incredible foundation in the Hudson Valley sits just off the road in Cold Spring, only an hour and a half outside Manhattan. Cofounded by Nancy Olnick and Giorgio Spanu in 2017, the designs for the exhibition spaces and the conversion of the building are by Spanish architect Miguel Quismondo. The new structure and the redesigned uncluttered open spaces reflect the intellectual rigor associated with this period of art.

In addition to the works from the permanent collection on display at all times, there are always temporary installations from the point of view of a meticulous exploration of the enduring global impact of Arte Povera. Rather than distracting from the twenty thousand square feet of art and sculpture with wall text, at Magazzino, there is a written brochure you can download

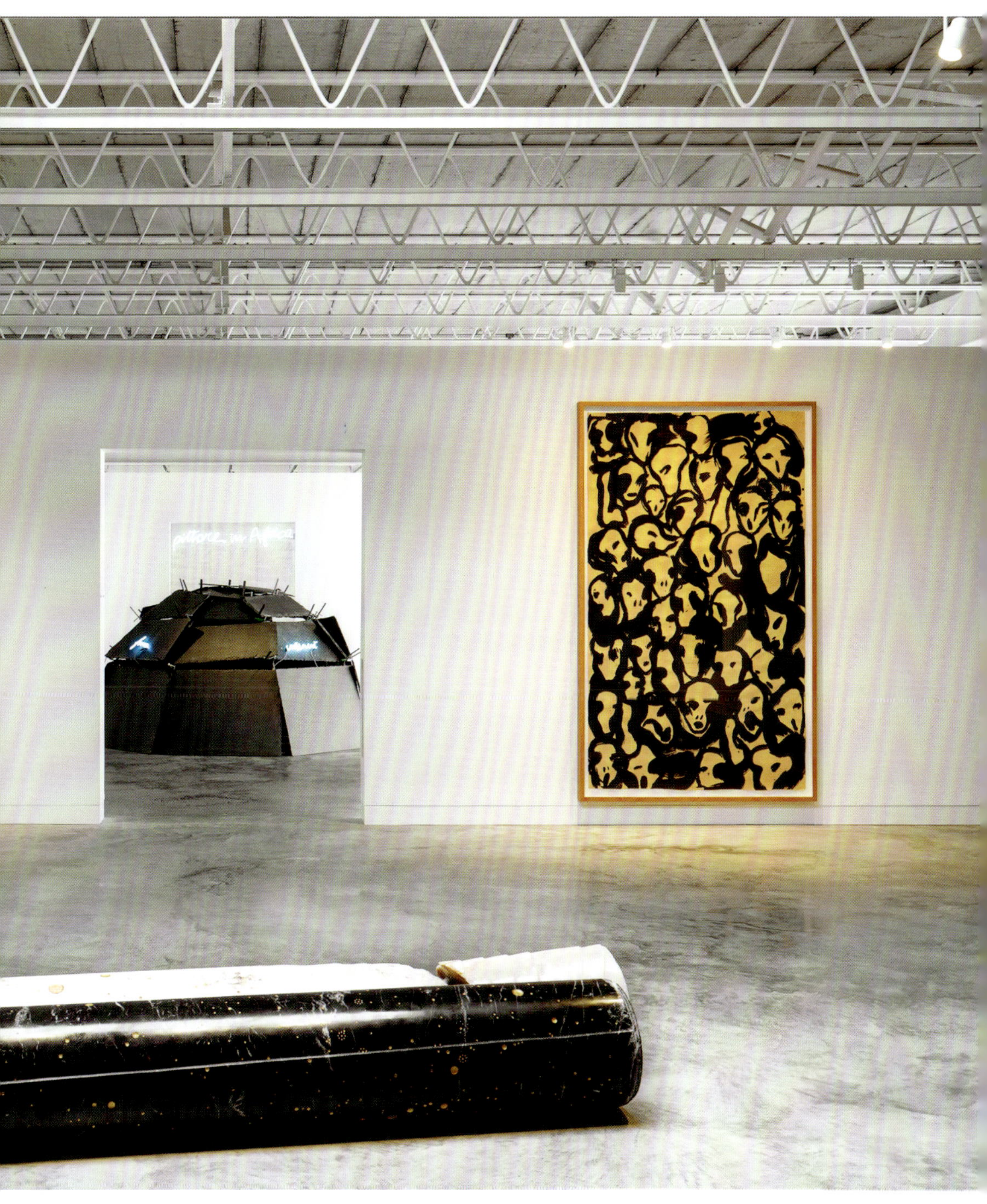

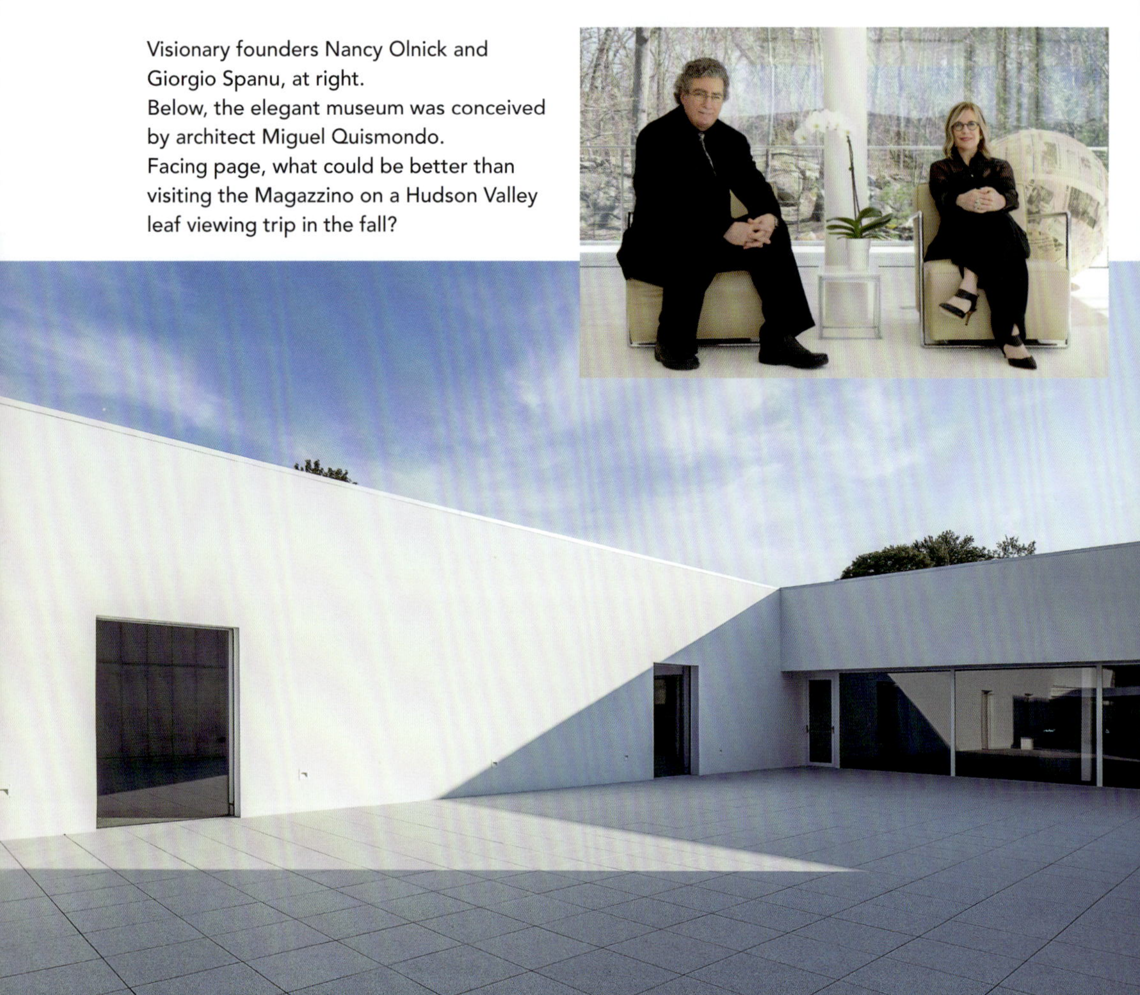

Visionary founders Nancy Olnick and Giorgio Spanu, at right.
Below, the elegant museum was conceived by architect Miguel Quismondo.
Facing page, what could be better than visiting the Magazzino on a Hudson Valley leaf viewing trip in the fall?

onto your phone and follow as you walk through. This activates the experience and presents the art as more than just static objects on the walls and on the floor. To further your knowledge and understanding, Olnick and Spanu maintain an extensive and beautifully designed research library of archival material, open to all visitors, with more than five thousand volumes on Arte Povera.

When I first visited, I could not imagine where else I would see a collection like this of very bold paintings and sculpture with such a specific point of view. When I returned most recently, it was a beautiful autumn day, and we loved seeing the leaves change as we headed north. Upon arrival, we received devices that buzzed if we came too close to another visitor, a reminder that, in these times, it is more important than ever to appreciate art and the efforts that even a smaller institution like Magazzino will take to bring back their beloved guests.

Magazzino is a true cultural hub and community resource, and truly one of those places that if you don't know, you'll never go!

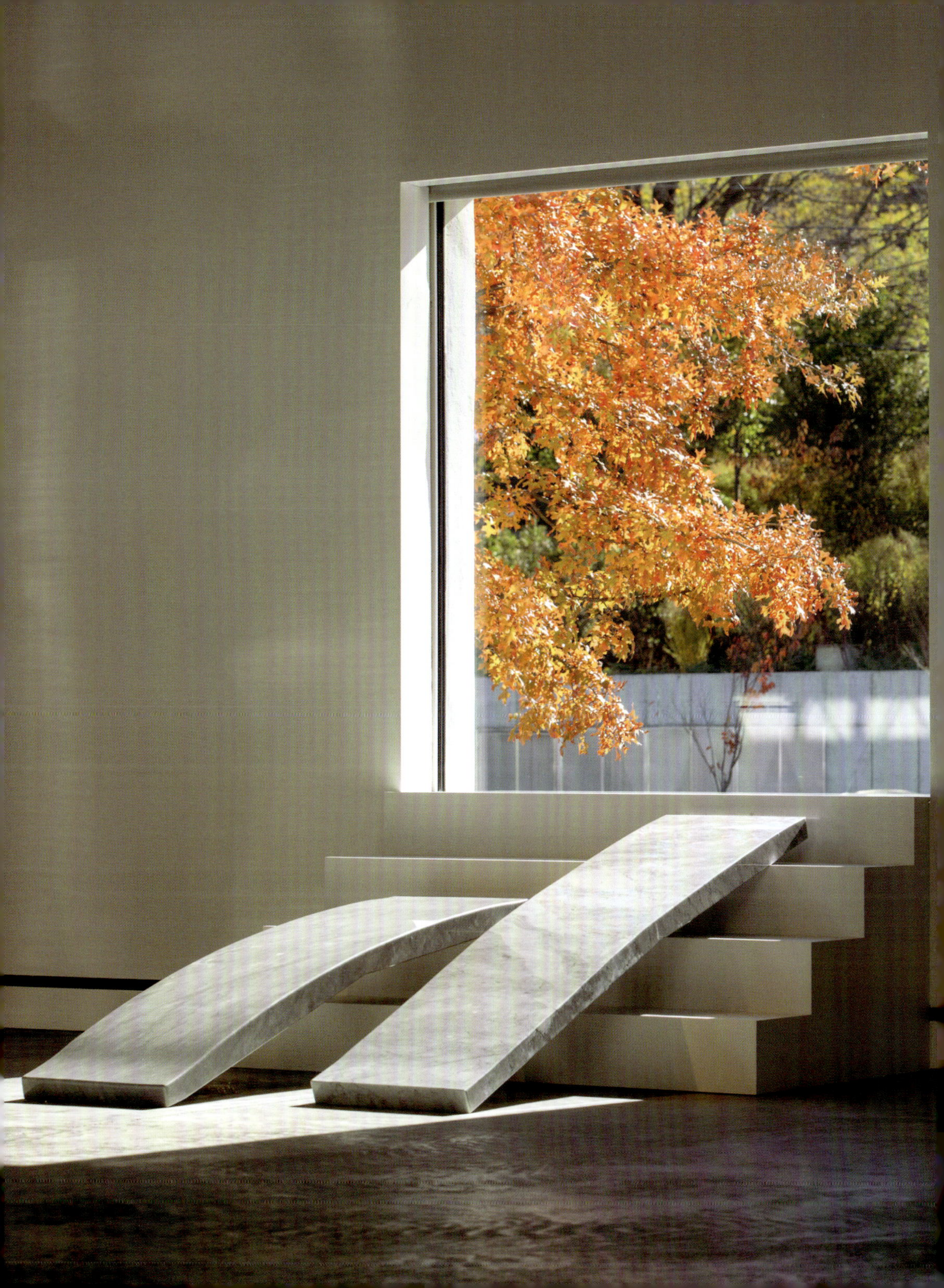

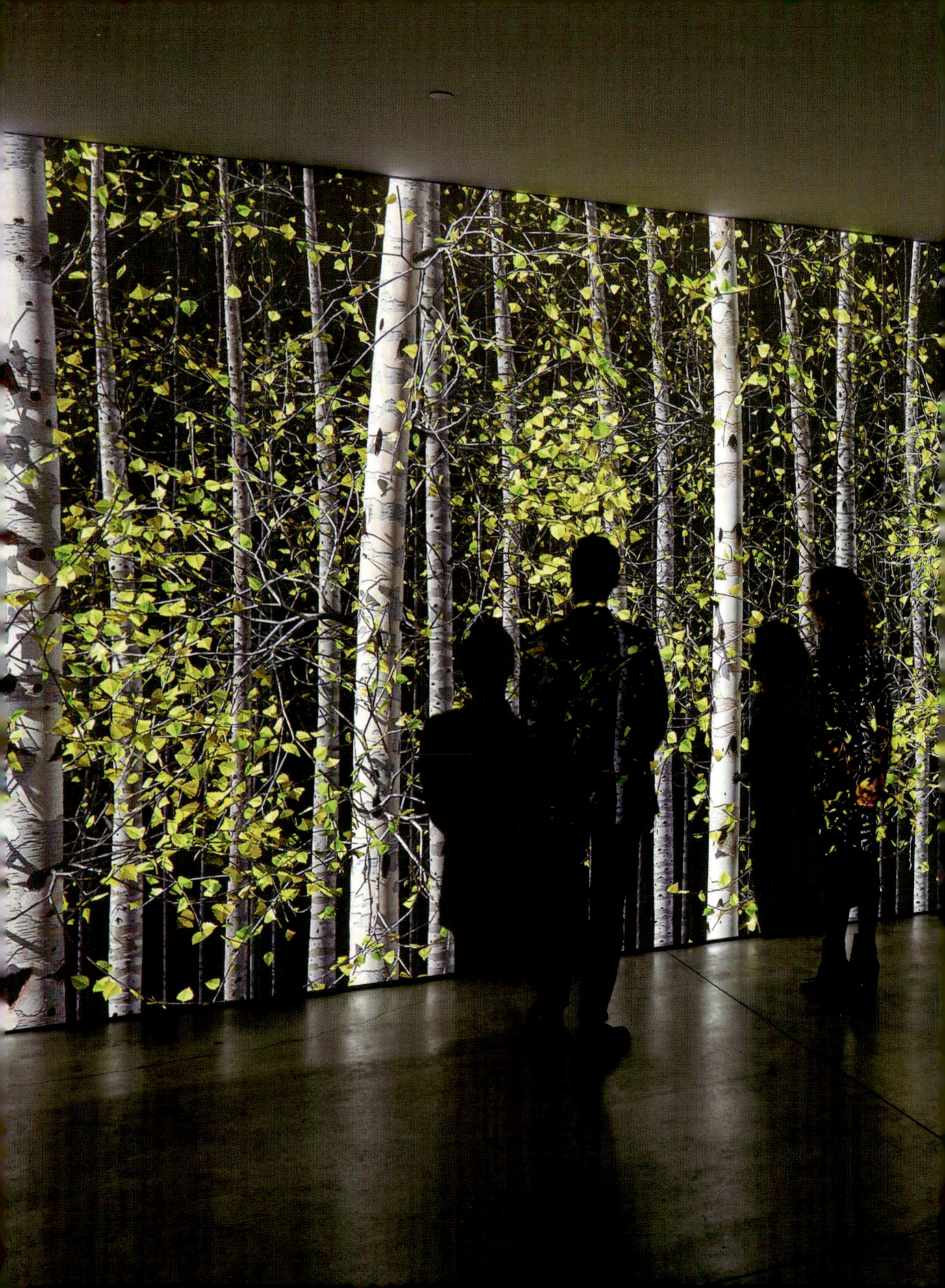

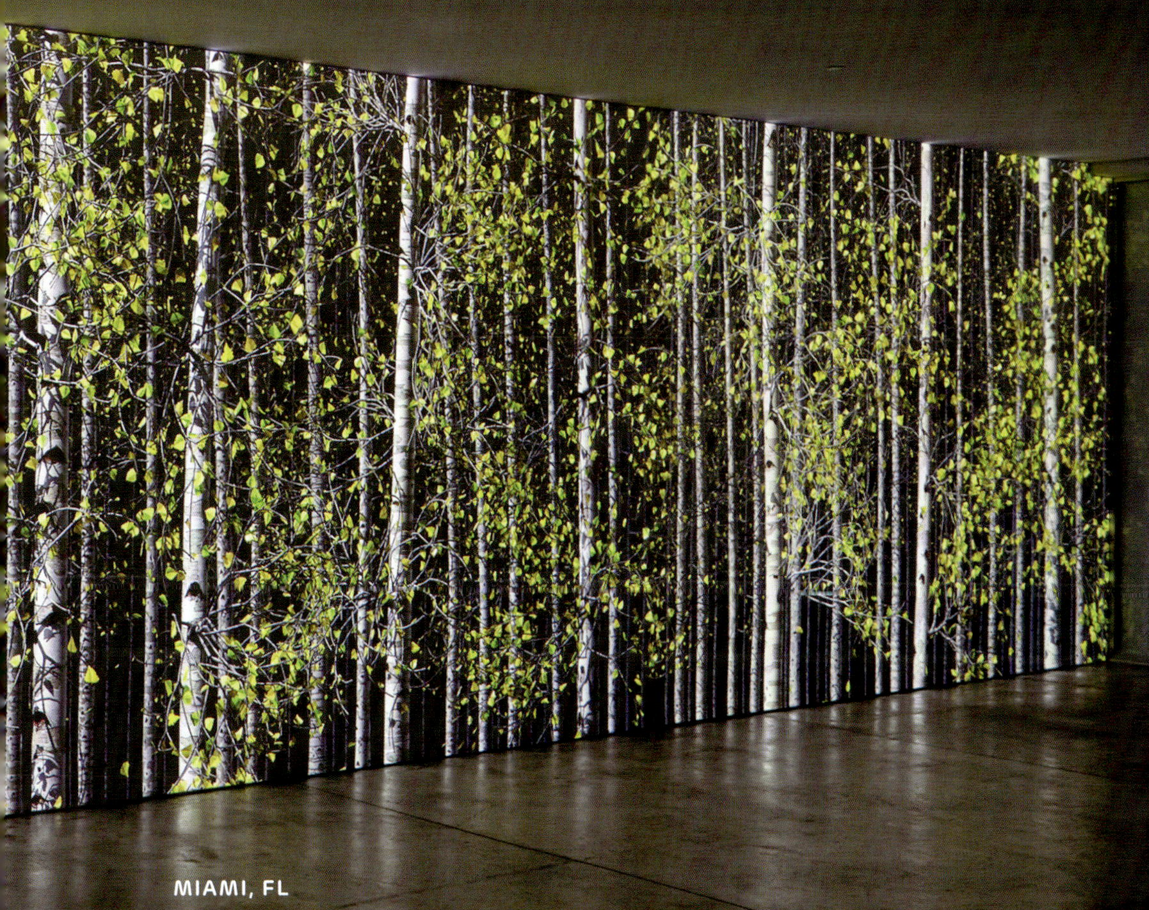

MIAMI, FL

Margulies Collection at the Warehouse

This museum-quality collection of serious art is a testament to Martin Margulies's vision and taste. Large-scale installations fill the oversized spaces in this warehouse in Miami. **MARGULIESWAREHOUSE.COM**

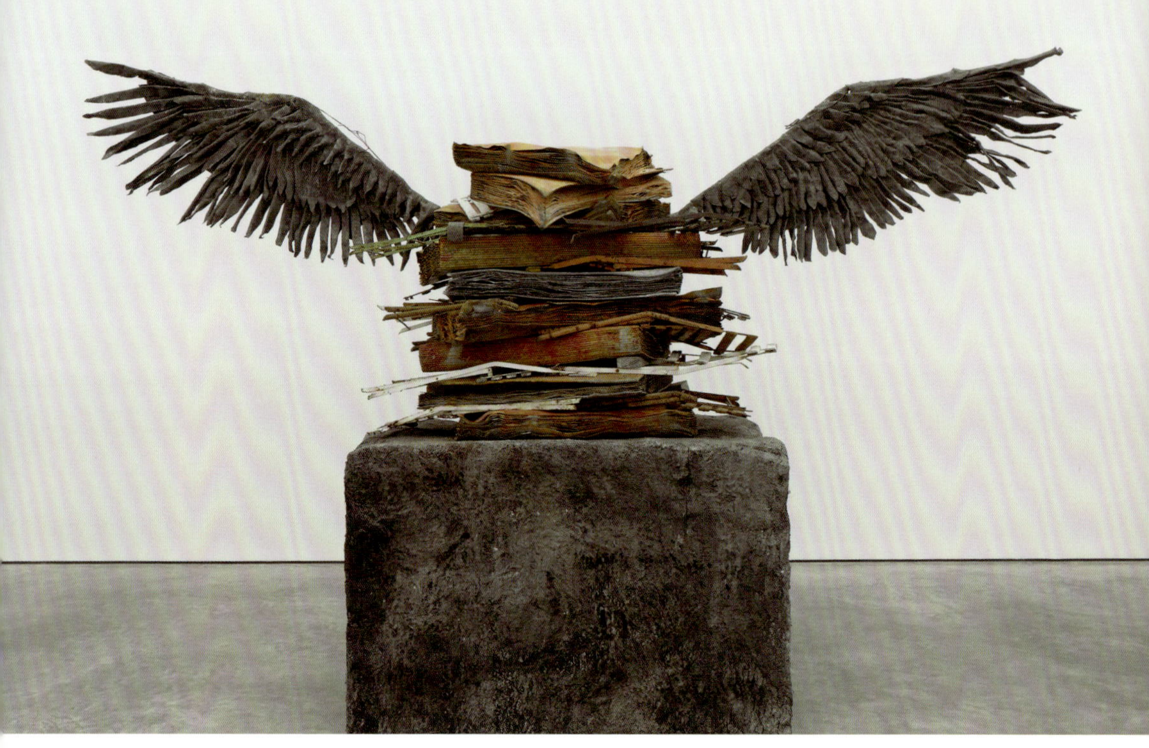

VISITORS TO THE Margulies Collection at the Warehouse are in for a serious art experience. This 55,000-square-foot building in the Wynwood arts district of Miami is home to a wide range of contemporary art, including massive sculptures and huge installations. Commanding attention to the right of the entry is a Magdalena Abakanowicz installation of 250 figures of adults and children. The figures, made of burlap and resin, immediately conjure images of the Holocaust or of nameless immigrants searching for a new homeland. This type of installation set so close to the entry speaks to the seriousness of the collection in the galleries to follow.

Many of the works at the Margulies are masterpieces, especially a large group of works by Anselm Kiefer, which fills galleries. Seeing a significant installation by any artist of this caliber would constitute a museum-quality show any place in the world, but here they are in Miami—collected en masse by

Sprache der Vögel, 1989, by Anselm Kiefer is made of lead, steel, wood and resin. This powerful art assemblage is placed in its own space in the gallery. Facing page, Pier Paolo Calzolari's *Untitled (L'aria vibra)*, exempifies the Italian Arte Povera movement.

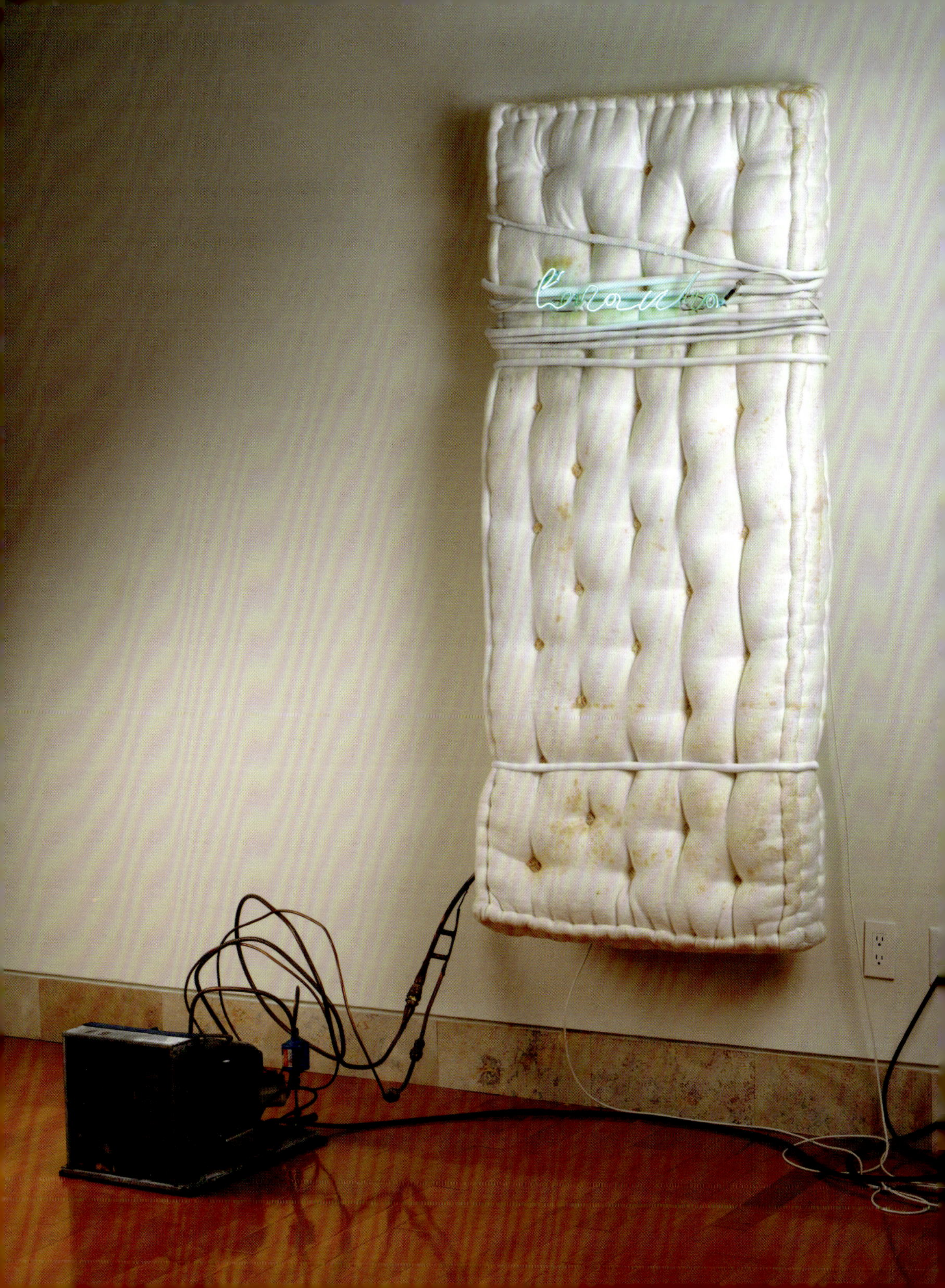

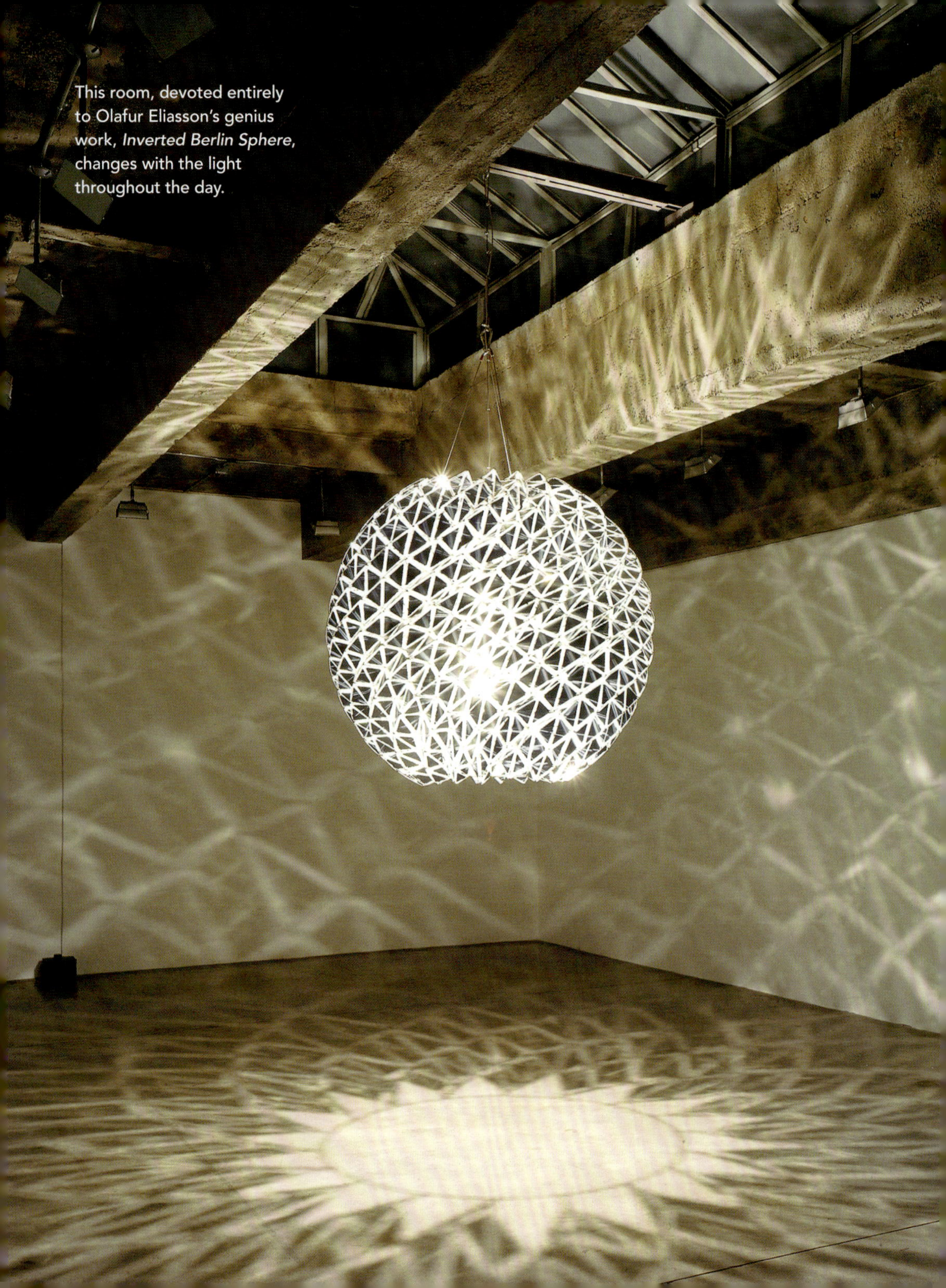
This room, devoted entirely
to Olafur Eliasson's genius
work, Inverted Berlin Sphere,
changes with the light
throughout the day.

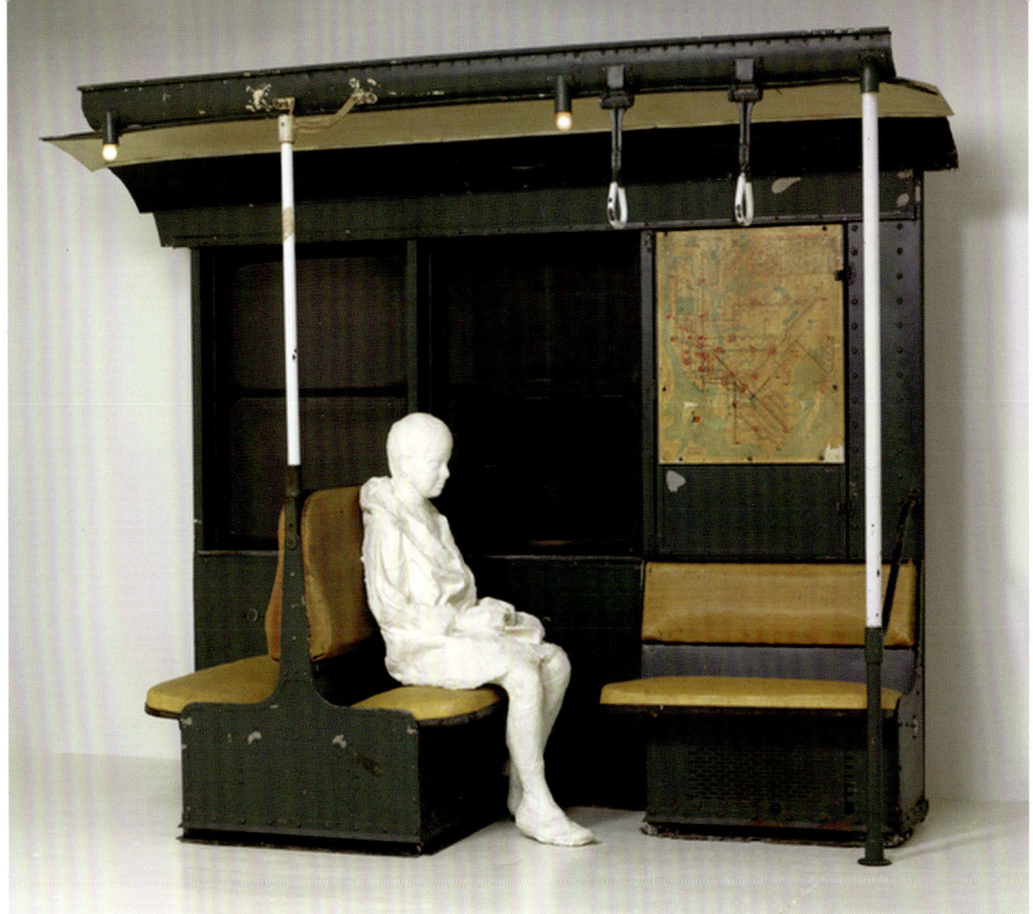

the passionate Martin Z. Margulies, who has tucked them into his art venue for the public to so generously enjoy.

On a lighter note, there is a massive installation by Brazilian artist Ernesto Neto. Made from Lycra, polyamide, black pepper, and cloves, the gargantuan cloth installation makes each viewer smile. His organic form takes over the enormous space and is an unforgettable art experience. Neto states, "What we have in common is more important than what makes us different." I could not agree more.

What I really loved about my visit to the Warehouse was the newly opened storage area. One could peruse the back area and see how the storage racks are constructed as well as the salon-style way the hundreds of photographs that are part of the museum's collection have been mounted. There is even a seating area for the visitor to sit and appreciate this unique environment.

At the Margulies, outstanding educational programs, public lectures, and tours for schools and museum groups, are part of their mission. The collections are regularly shared through gifts and loans to national and international museums and other educational institutions. A prime example of Margulies's generosity was donating the work of Kehinde Wiley, *Saint John the Baptist*, 2014, to the National Museum of African American History and Culture.

Allow plenty of time when visiting this venue for an unparalleled art experience.

George Segal's beloved installation, *Subway*, 1968, conjures a sense of isolation in an empty subway car.

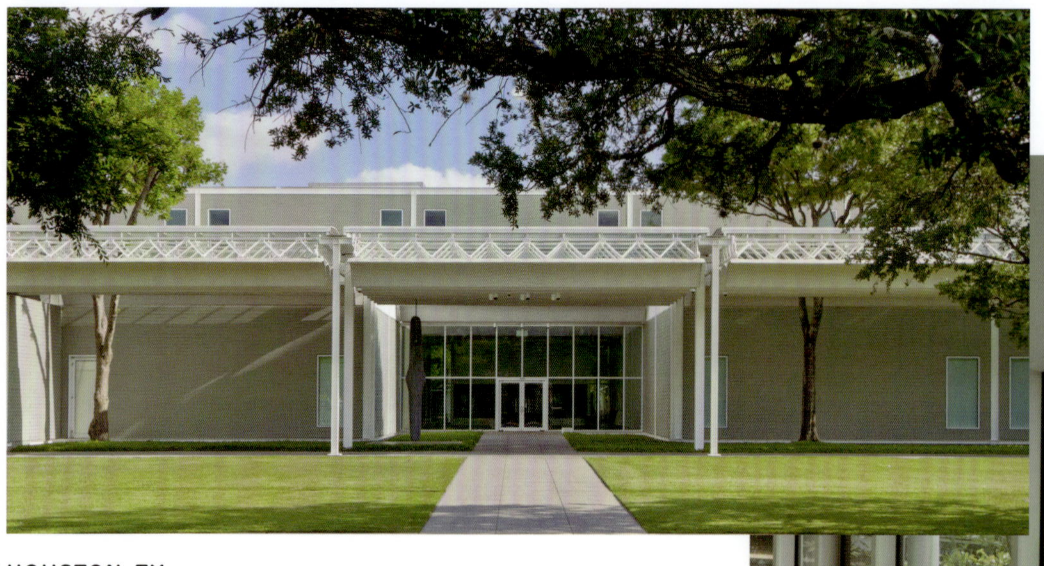

The Menil Collection

Like a campus of museums, each
one filled with the best-of-the-best
modern art. Visitors from all over
the world come to pay homage and
to experience the Rothko Chapel.
MENIL.ORG

THE WORLD FAMOUS Menil Collection in Houston, Texas, is an art history introduction to the greatest artists and works of the twentieth century. The museum houses John and Dominique de Menil's collection of some of the most important examples of cubism, surrealism, and pop art, ranging from paintings, sculpture, prints, and drawings to rare books and photographs.

The de Menils left France during WWII and arrived in America. They settled in Texas to be near Dominique's family business, Schlumberger Limited, which established its new headquarters in Houston. Over the years, the couple's collection grew to more than seventeen thousand pieces of art. In the heyday of their purchases, they were known to buy out entire shows by Dan Flavin and Donald Judd.

The entrance to the main building of the museum, which was designed by Renzo Piano, is carefully planned with a very horizontal impression, rather than a huge and soaring feeling, which can be

Architect Renzo Piano's vision for the museum's main building is horizontal and light-filled; a perfect introduction to the other buildings that make up the art campus, including the Rothko Chapel and the Drawing Institute.

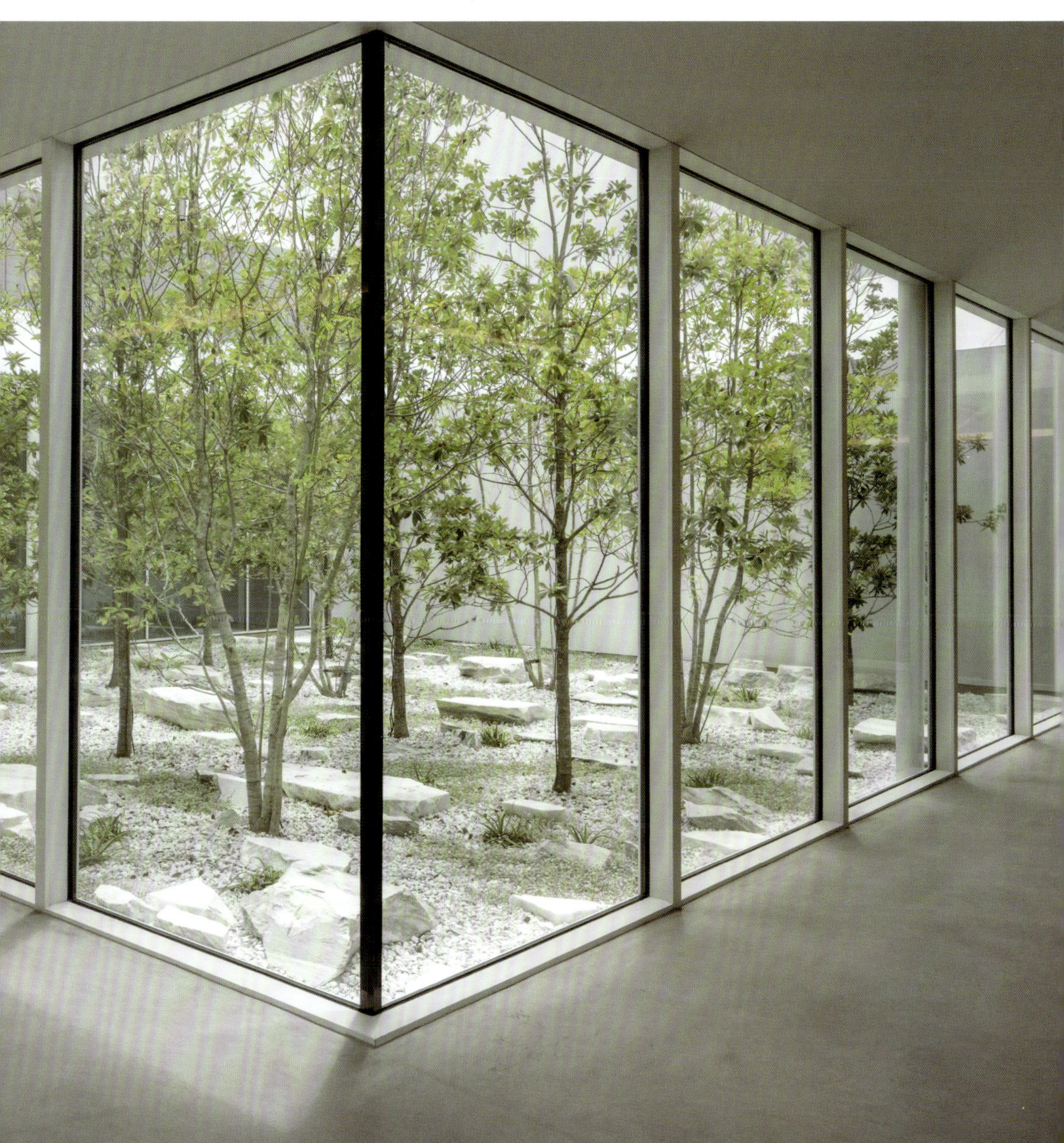

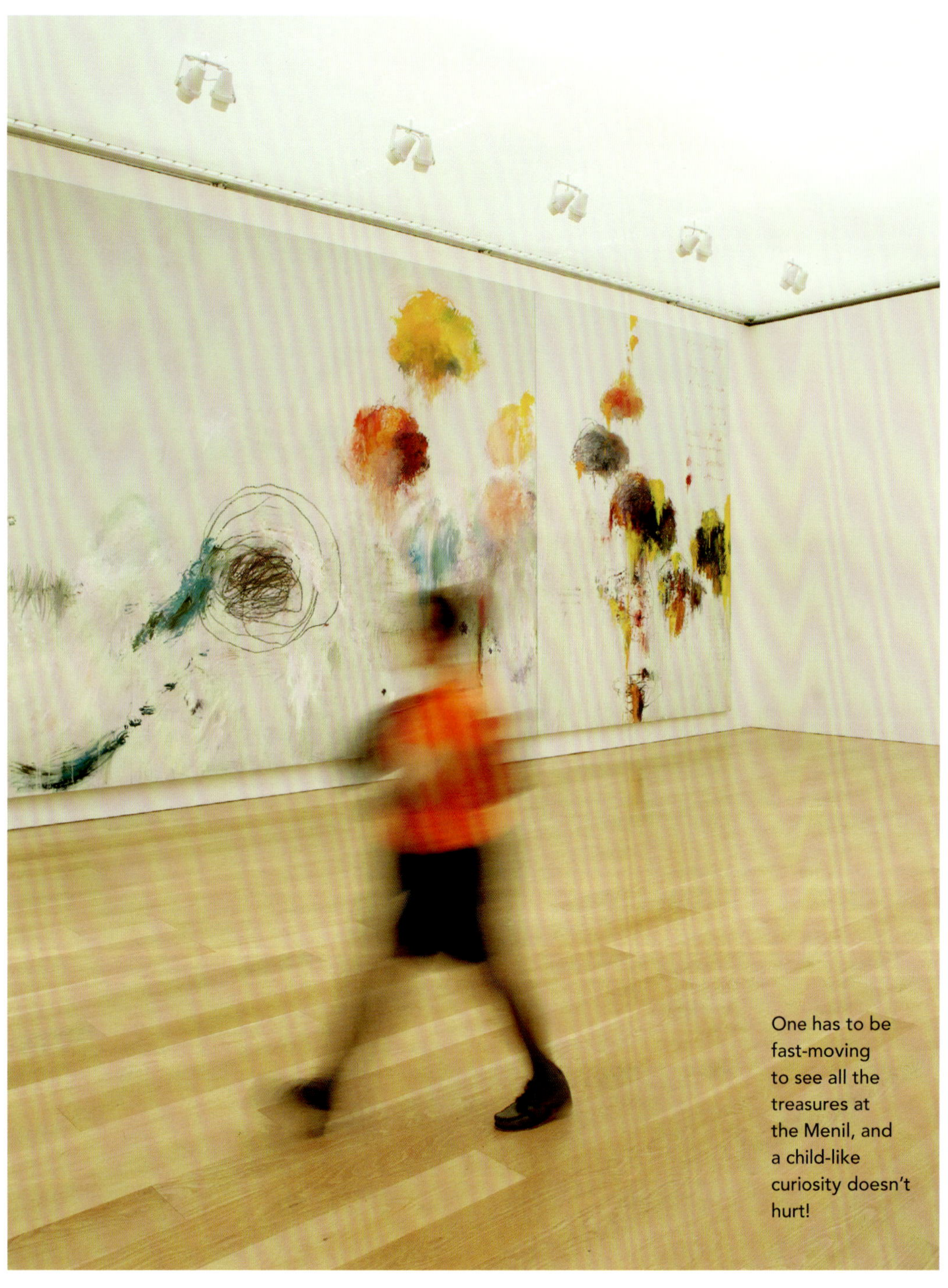

One has to be
fast-moving
to see all the
treasures at
the Menil, and
a child-like
curiosity doesn't
hurt!

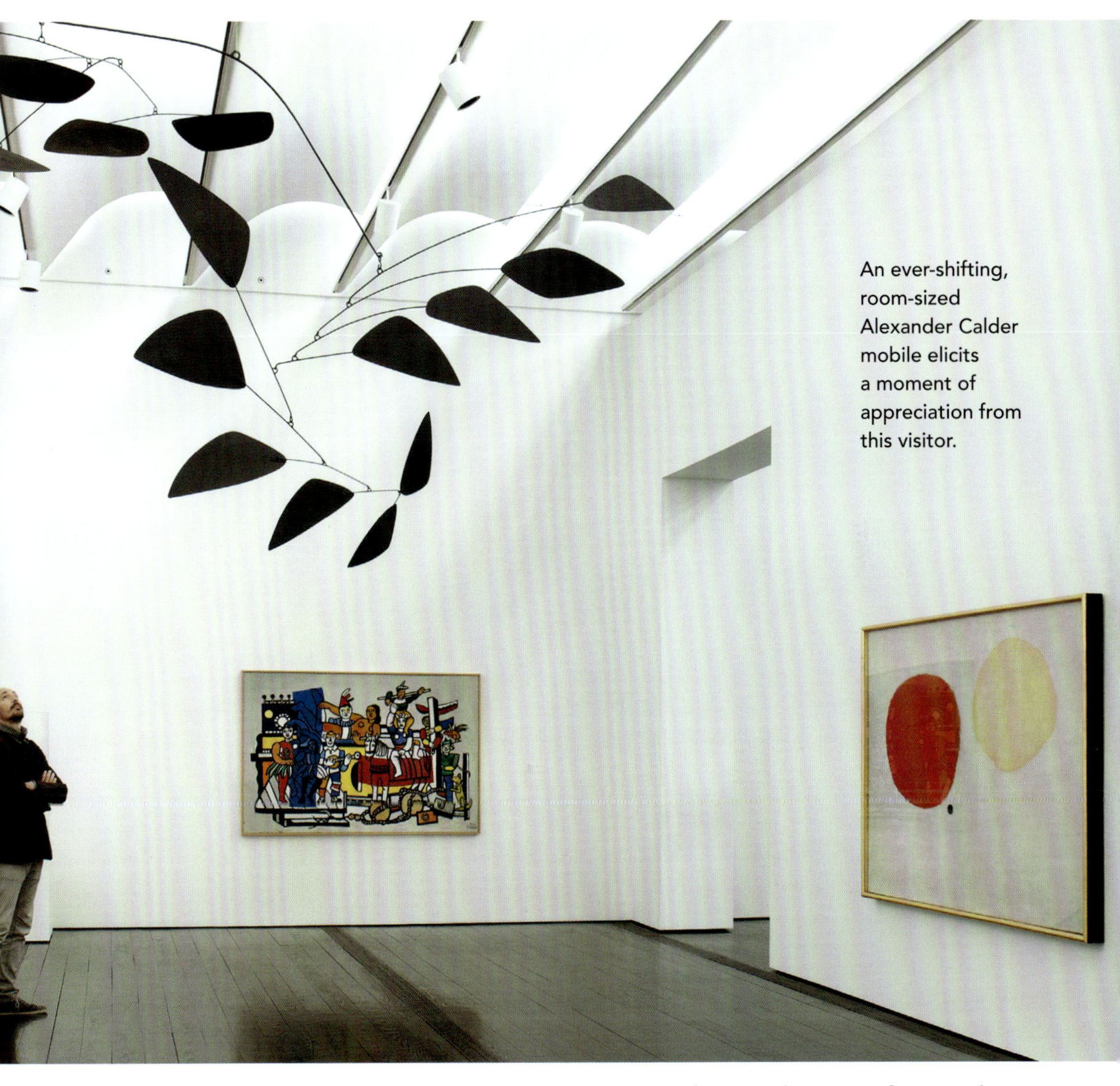

overwhelming. This human-scaled consideration elicits a humble response upon entering. In addition to the main buildings, the Menil Collection includes the Drawing Institute and the Rothko Chapel and many other buildings. There is so much art to see and absorb on this art campus and so many buildings to navigate, I recommend doing research on their excellent website to choreograph your visit.

Their daughter Philippa de Menil has her parents' DNA for art and support of artists. She and her husband, Heiner Friedrich, started the Dia Foundation, and Philippa solely funded the foundation in 1974.

One could easily spend a whole day visiting the various buildings of the brilliant Menil Collection. If you do plan a full excursion, be sure to have a delicious lunch at the minimalist designed restaurant Bistro Menil, but book reservations before you visit because it is a very popular venue.

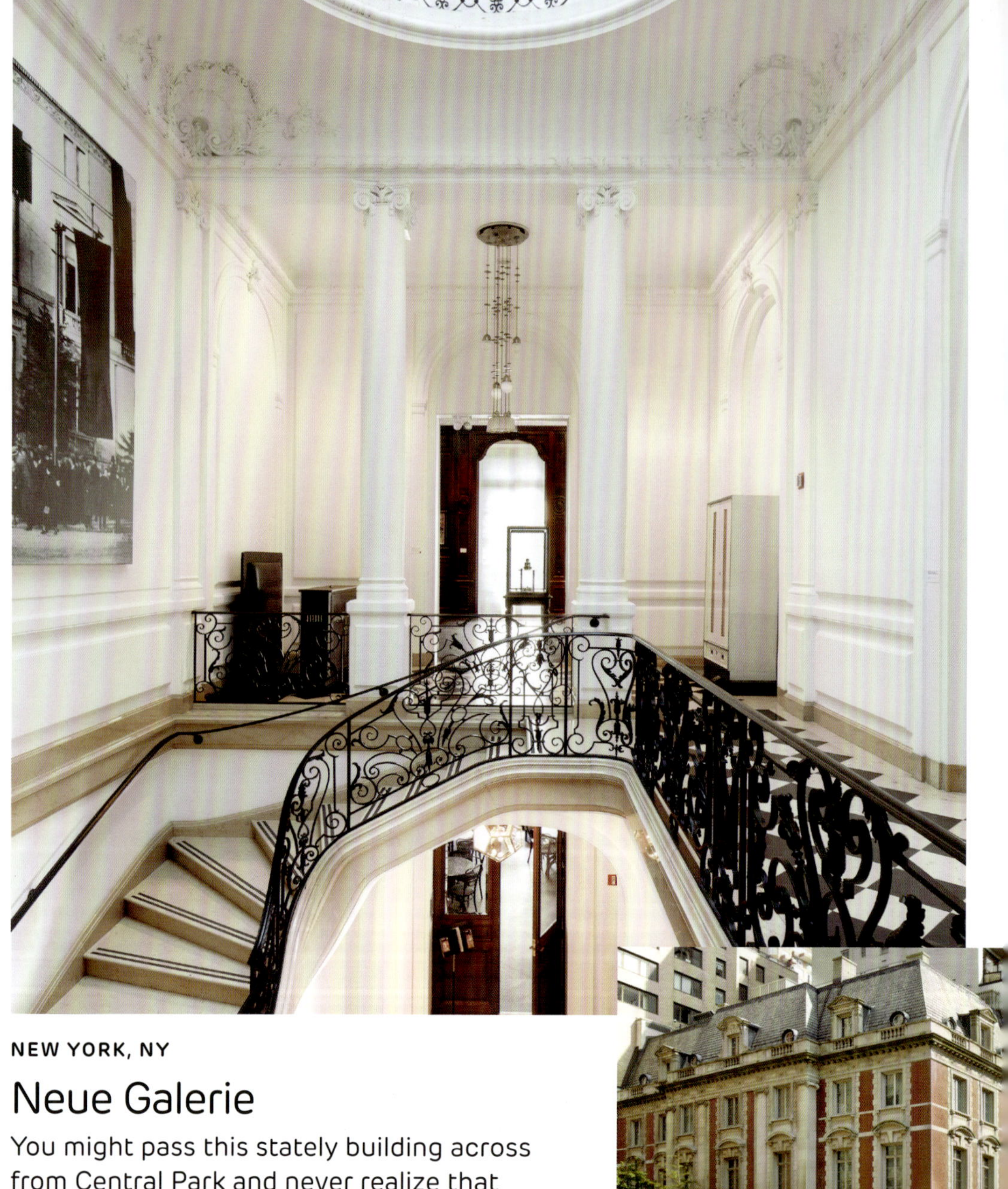

Neue Galerie

You might pass this stately building across from Central Park and never realize that inside—and open to the public—is the most wonderful collection of German and Austrian art in America. **NEUEGALERIE.ORG**

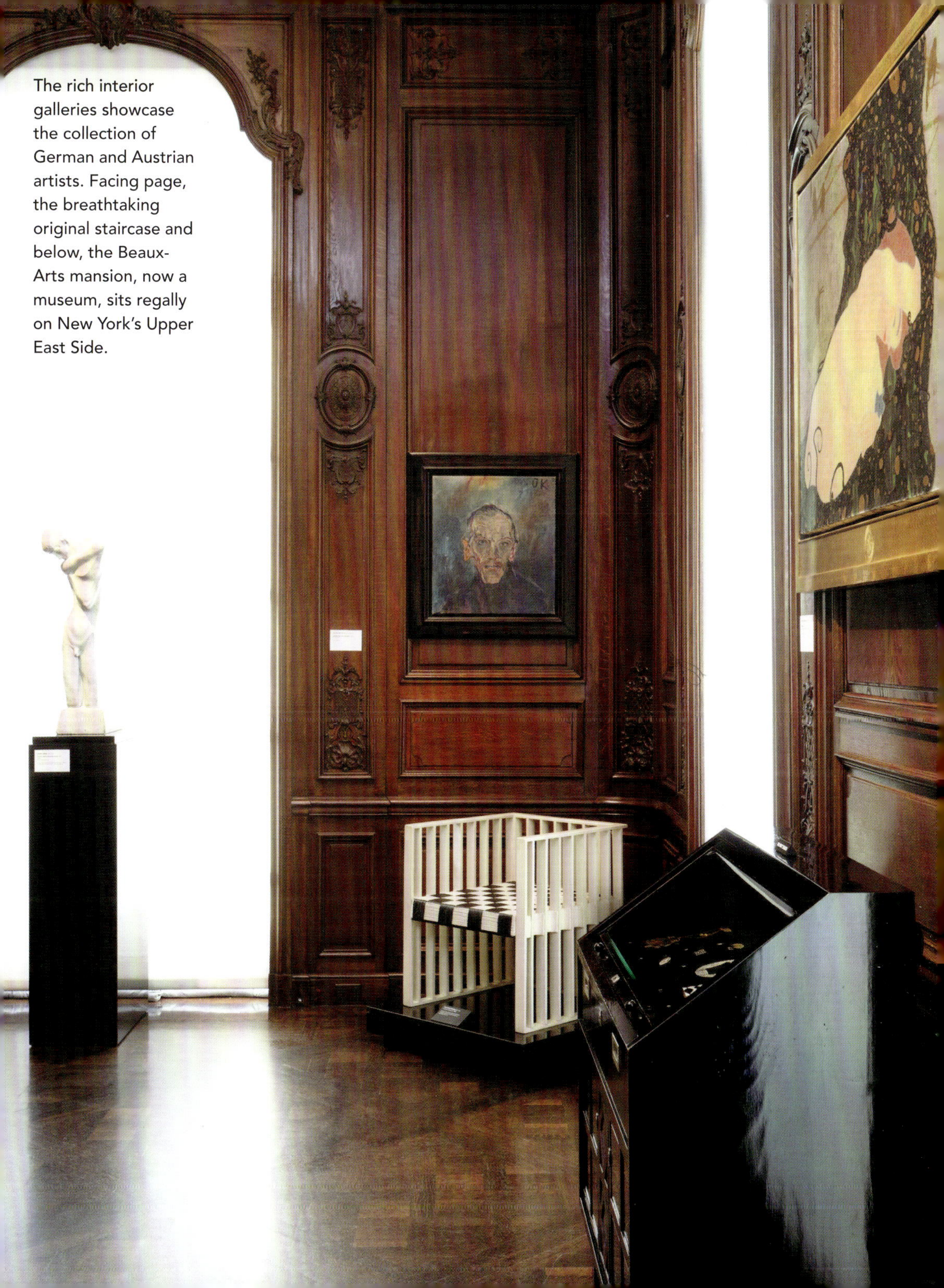

The rich interior galleries showcase the collection of German and Austrian artists. Facing page, the breathtaking original staircase and below, the Beaux-Arts mansion, now a museum, sits regally on New York's Upper East Side.

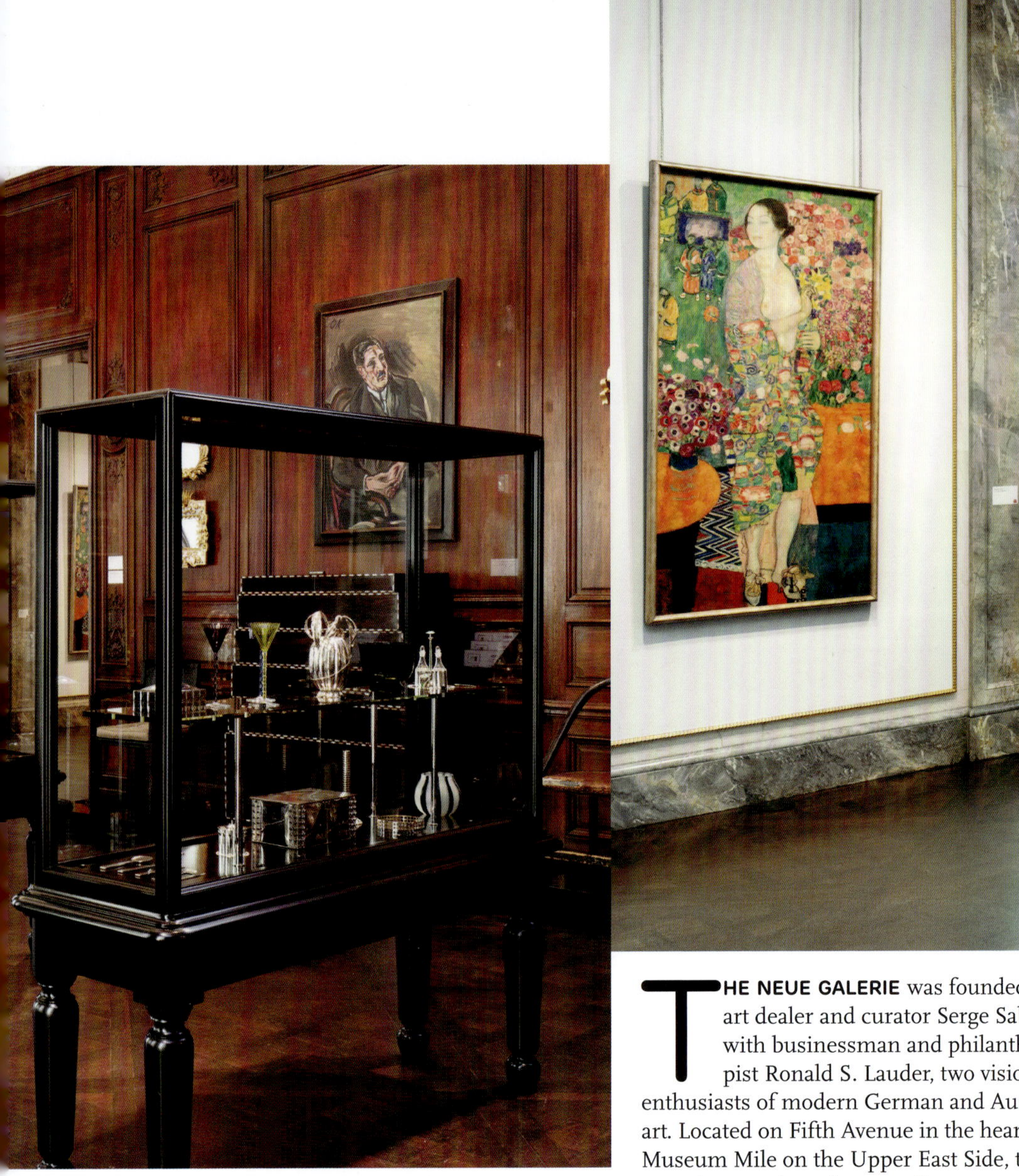

Decorative objects from the early 20th century invite a closer inspection. At right, paintings by Gustave Klimt including the *Portrait of Adel Bloch Bauer I*, on the far wall.

THE NEUE GALERIE was founded by art dealer and curator Serge Sabarsky with businessman and philanthropist Ronald S. Lauder, two visionary enthusiasts of modern German and Austrian art. Located on Fifth Avenue in the heart of Museum Mile on the Upper East Side, the Neue is an early and extraordinary example of collectors opening a space to showcase artwork for the public.

The museum is housed in an historic 1914 Carrere and Hastings Beaux Arts mansion purchased by the museum's founders in 1994. A complete renovation by renowned architect Annabelle Selldorf was commis-

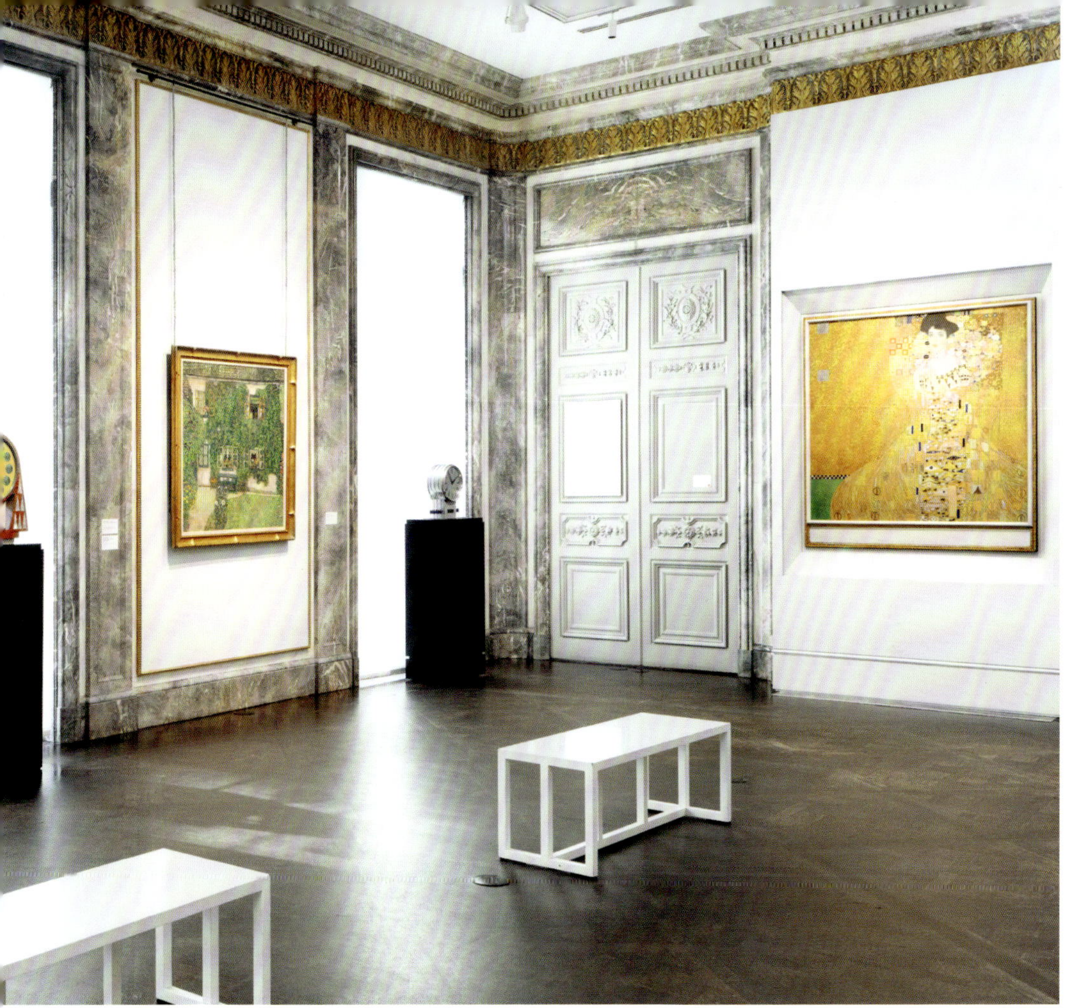

sioned to create an elegant townhouse home for masterpieces by Der Blaue Reiter, the Bauhaus, and the Deutscher Werkbund. Over the years, it has become a premier exhibition space as well as a center of research for German and Austrian art from the early part of the twentieth century.

The litmus test for the permanent collection and for temporary installations is that they be relevant to the art and artists of that period. When you enter, the world shifts and you are transported to the early twentieth century and the world of German art and design. I always like to begin my visit and set the mood with Viennese coffee and pastries in the museum's charming café before walking up the breathtaking staircase to see the collection.

One of the biggest draws for me is the extraordinary portrait of Adele Bloch-Bauer by Gustave Klimt. The fantastic story of the painting became a book and a popular movie, *The Woman in Gold*. The circuitous history of the painting, including various lawsuits against the Austrian government, is told in entertainingly great detail in the movie. The story ended when Ronald Lauder purchased the work at auction for $135 million dollars in June 2006. Sharing this portrait and all the Neue Galerie's art so generously with the public is a great gift to the city of New York.

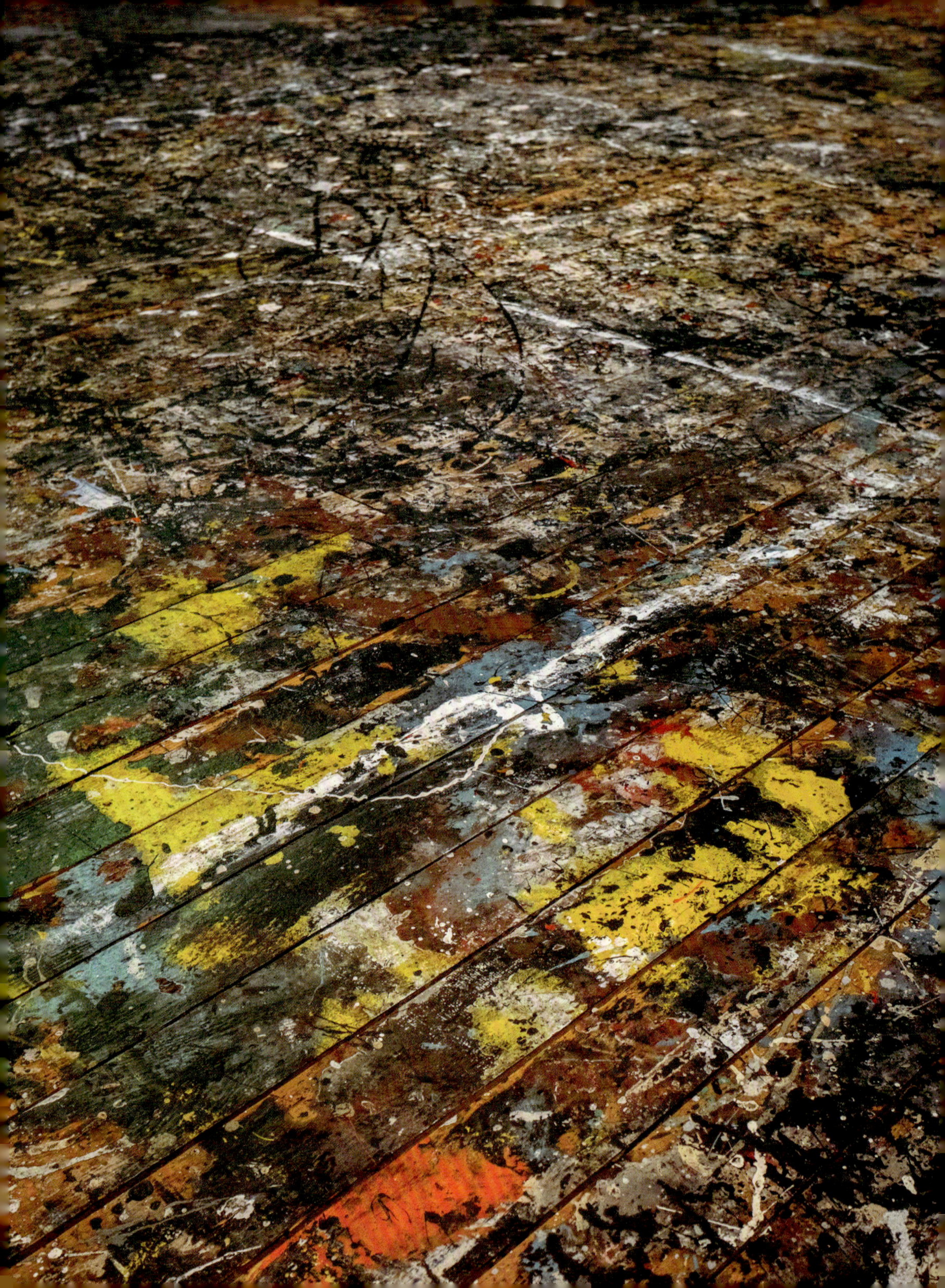

Pollock-Krasner House And Study Center

The best part about a visit to Pollock-Krasner House is the studio where Pollock created his famous paintings, but their warm and charming home offers perspective on the couple's life together. **PKHOUSE.ORG**

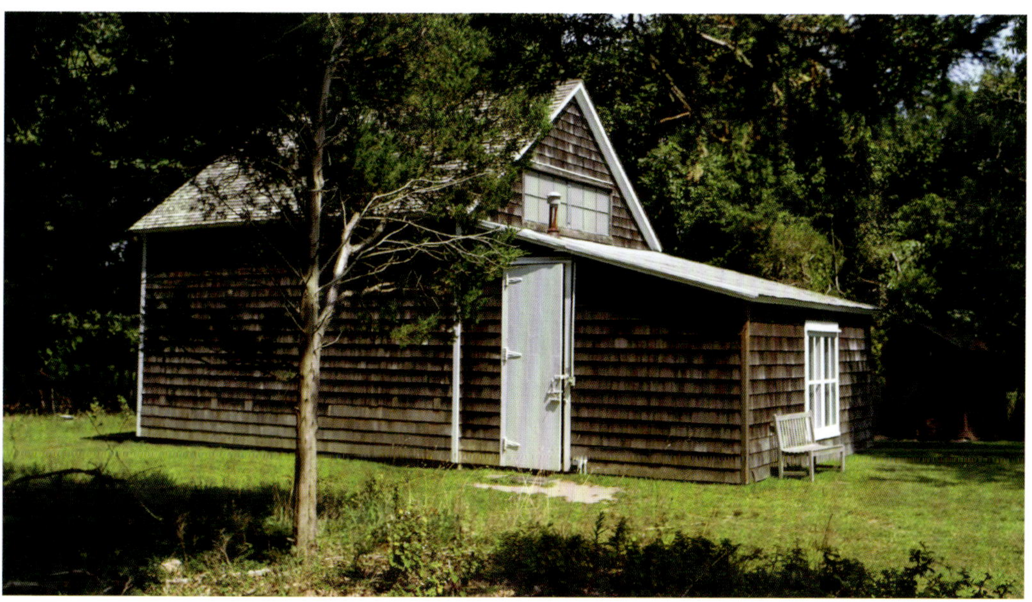

Jackson Pollock's studio in a converted barn. Facing page, remnants of paint on the rough studio floor tell the story of his paintings.

THE POLLOCK-KRASNER HOUSE and Study Center is an incredible shrine to Jackson Pollock and Lee Krasner. Located north of East Hampton in the Springs area of Eastern Long Island, their home and workspaces are preserved and maintained for visitors to study the life and processes of the artists.

It's very easy to make a reservation, which is required for your visit. Our well-informed guide sat with us outside in the shade of a large tree and told us all about the artists' lives as well as the history of the house. The time he spent explaining their stories contributed to a very personal feeling that is sustained throughout the tour. Our guide then brought us into the famous barn studio to see the splattered floor with the residue of Pollock's famous paintings. It was exciting to see on the studio floor the

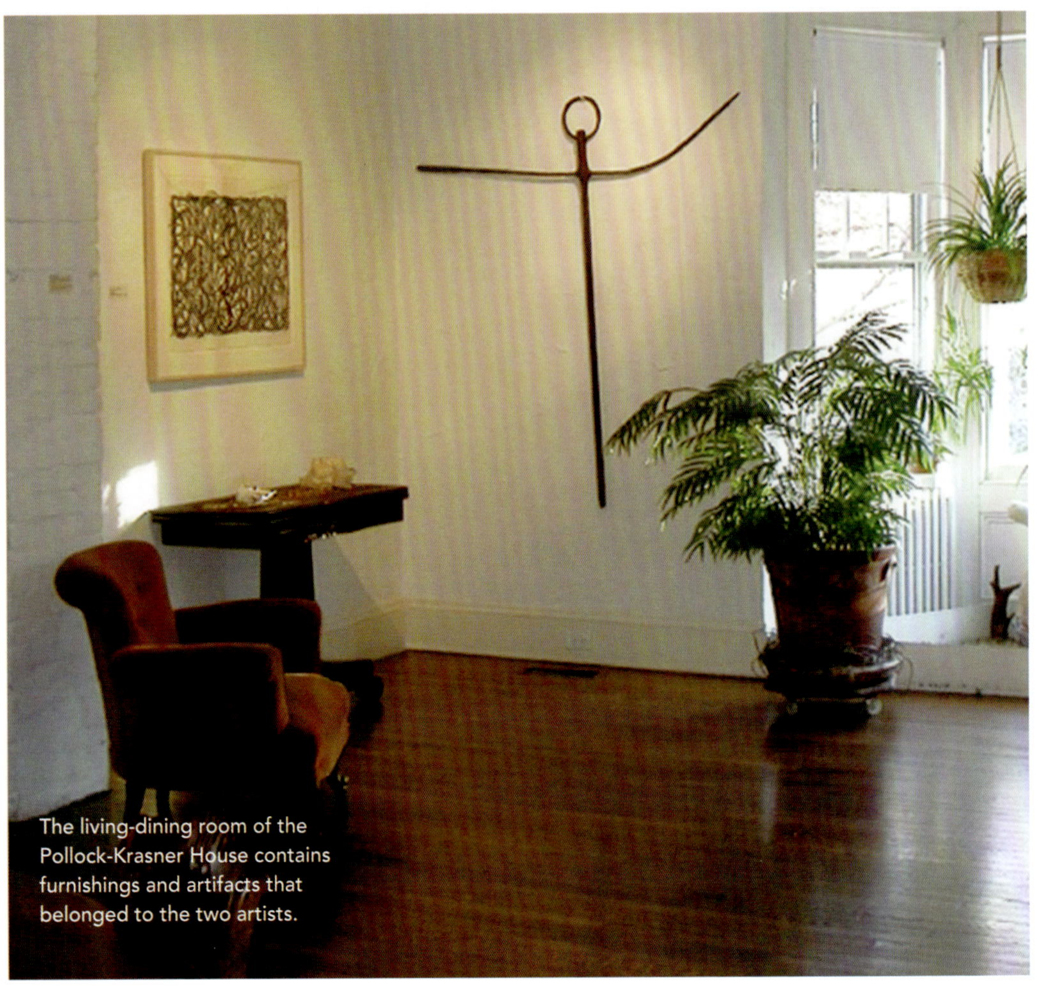

The living-dining room of the Pollock-Krasner House contains furnishings and artifacts that belonged to the two artists.

evidence of the actual shift in art history and the making of art brought about by Pollock's genius.

The house they lived in, especially the upstairs, is cozy and well preserved. I enjoyed seeing Krasner's upstairs studio and a computer art presentation of the works she painted in that location. There is no way to overstate the remarkable quality of being inside an artist's house and studio, especially one like this that is basically untouched and preserved over these years. I highly recommend a visit to Pollock-Krasner House, and be sure to allow at least an hour and a half for a full tour and individual exploration. I suggest

taking an extra half hour after your tour to drive about a mile further north on Accobonac Road to stop at the Green River Cemetery where Pollock was buried after his fatal car crash.

Facing page, in the master bedroom, the wicker Boston Rocker and cheval glass mirror were purchased by Krasner after Jackson's death. In the mirror is a reflection of her 1969 lithograph, *Primary Series: Rose Stone*, hanging over the bed. The portrait was painted by Igor Pantuhof, her lover in the 1930s. The evening dress was custom made for her by a Madison Avenue dressmaker in 1967.

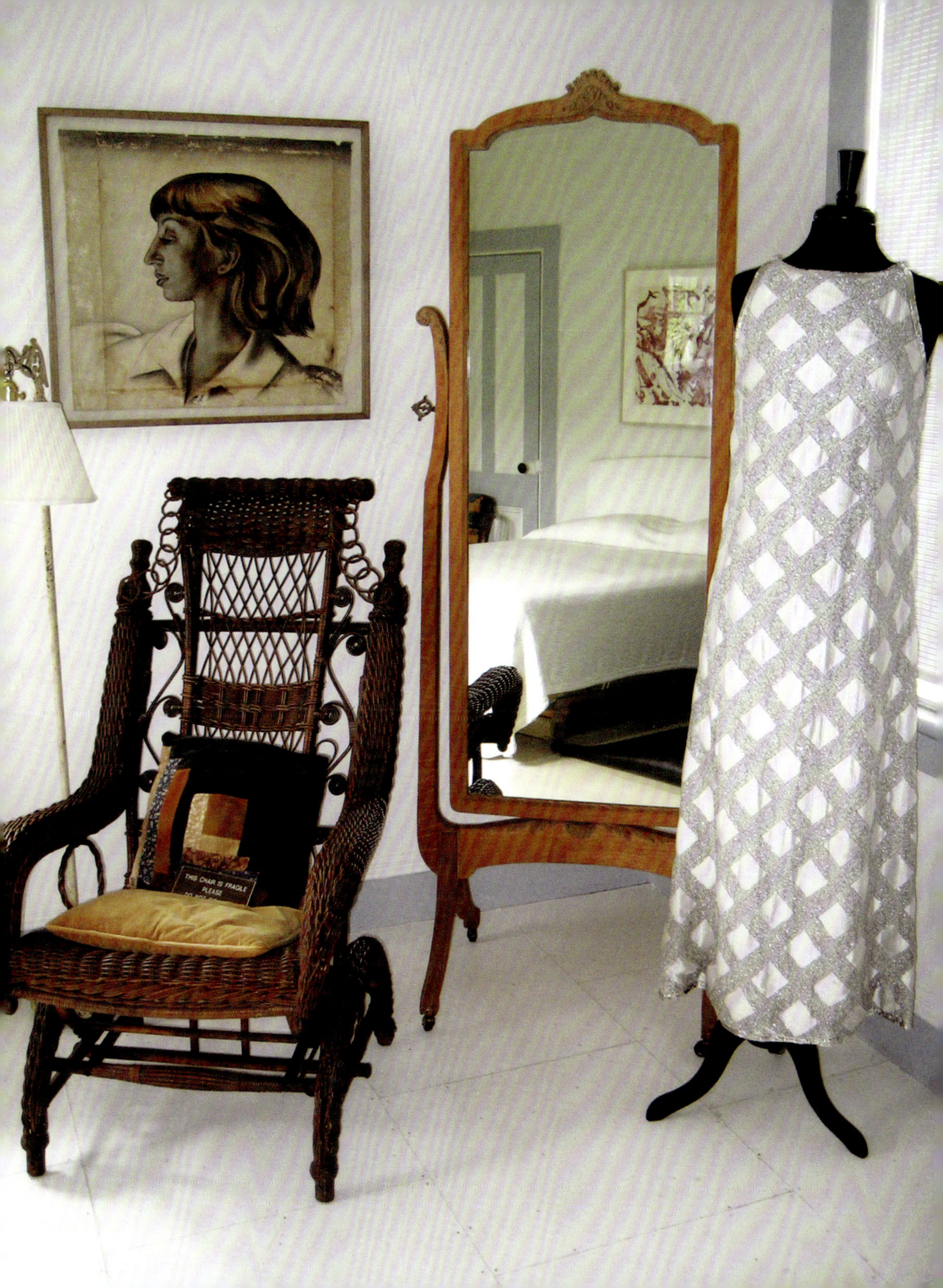

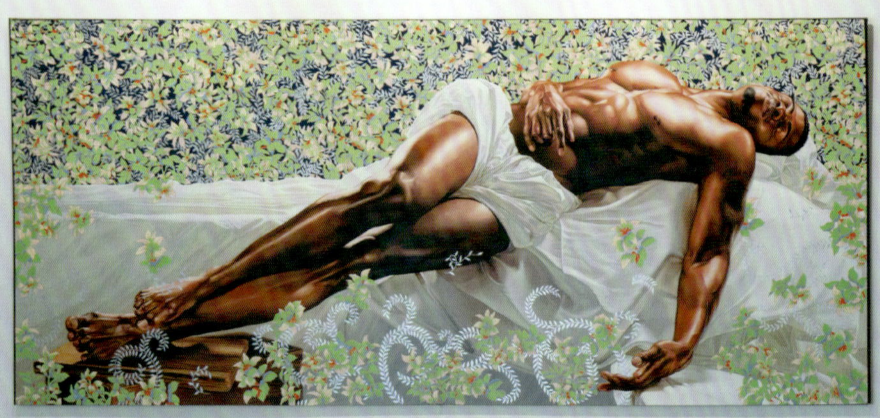

Only a museum this size and scale can accommodate extra-large contemporary works of art by Kehinde Wiley and Gilbert and George. In the far gallery, a Keith Haring.

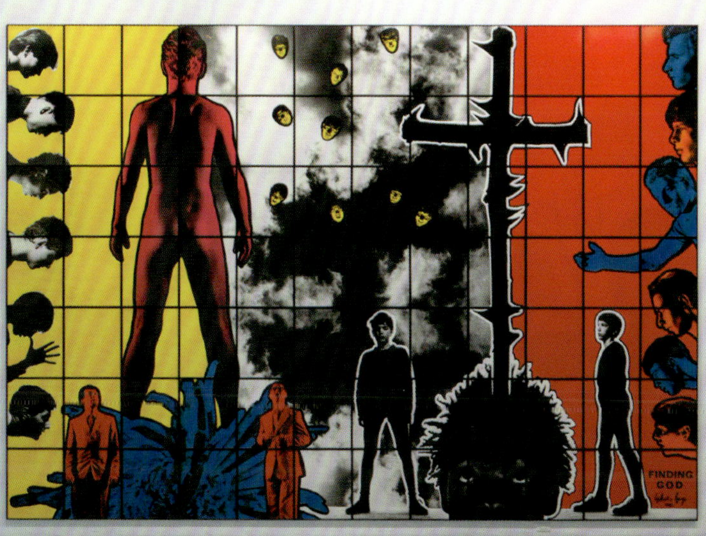

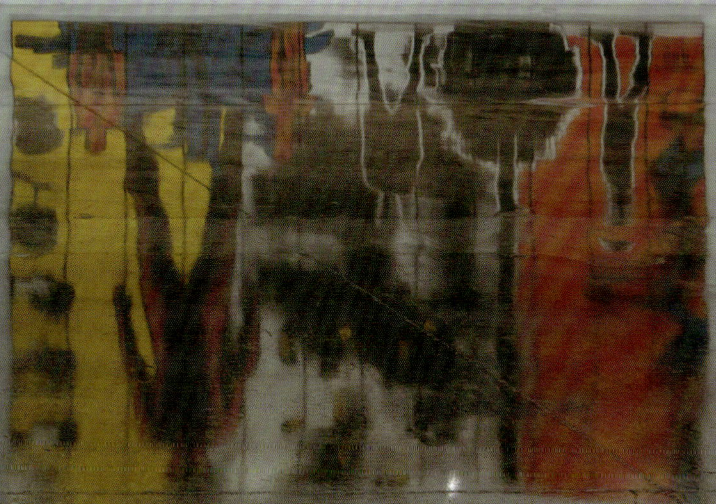

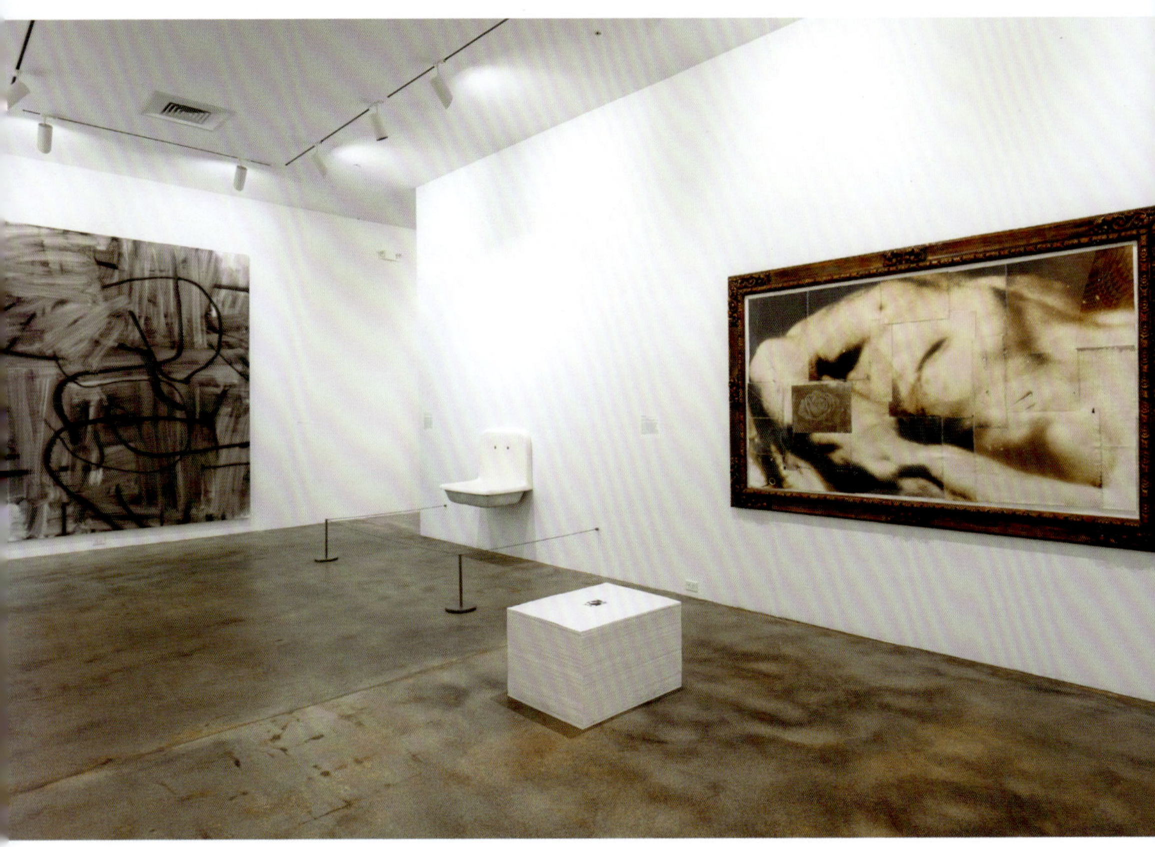

MIAMI IS ONE OF MY favorite destinations to see art. Every December during the week of Art Basel, I am always excited to visit the many private collections opened to the public in Miami and its surrounding areas. In 1993, Mera and Don Rubell opened the Rubell Family Collection/Contemporary Art Foundation. The Rubells were pioneers in the private art sector due to their passion, not just for acquiring contemporary art by a wide range of artists early in their careers, but especially for welcoming the public to see their private collection. Mera was also instrumental in bringing Art Basel to Miami.

Every Thursday after Miami Art Basel's VIP opening, I would visit the Rubell Family Collection. Their daughter, artist Jennifer Rubell, always greeted us with a fabulous installation based on breakfast food. While every visit was tremendous fun, I will never forget one year when she gave us containers of plain yogurt, which we held out to collect honey that was dripping from the ceiling. After one of these extravagant "hello" experiences, we would tour the newest installation of their Artist in Residence series, view newly curated shows, and of course see familiar art favorites from the Rubell collection.

In 2019, the Rubells moved their entire collection of more than 7,000 works by more than 1,000 artists to a

The galleries are full of thought-provoking work by contemporary artists.
Facing page, Yayoi Kusama's metal spheres create detours in and out of the galleries.

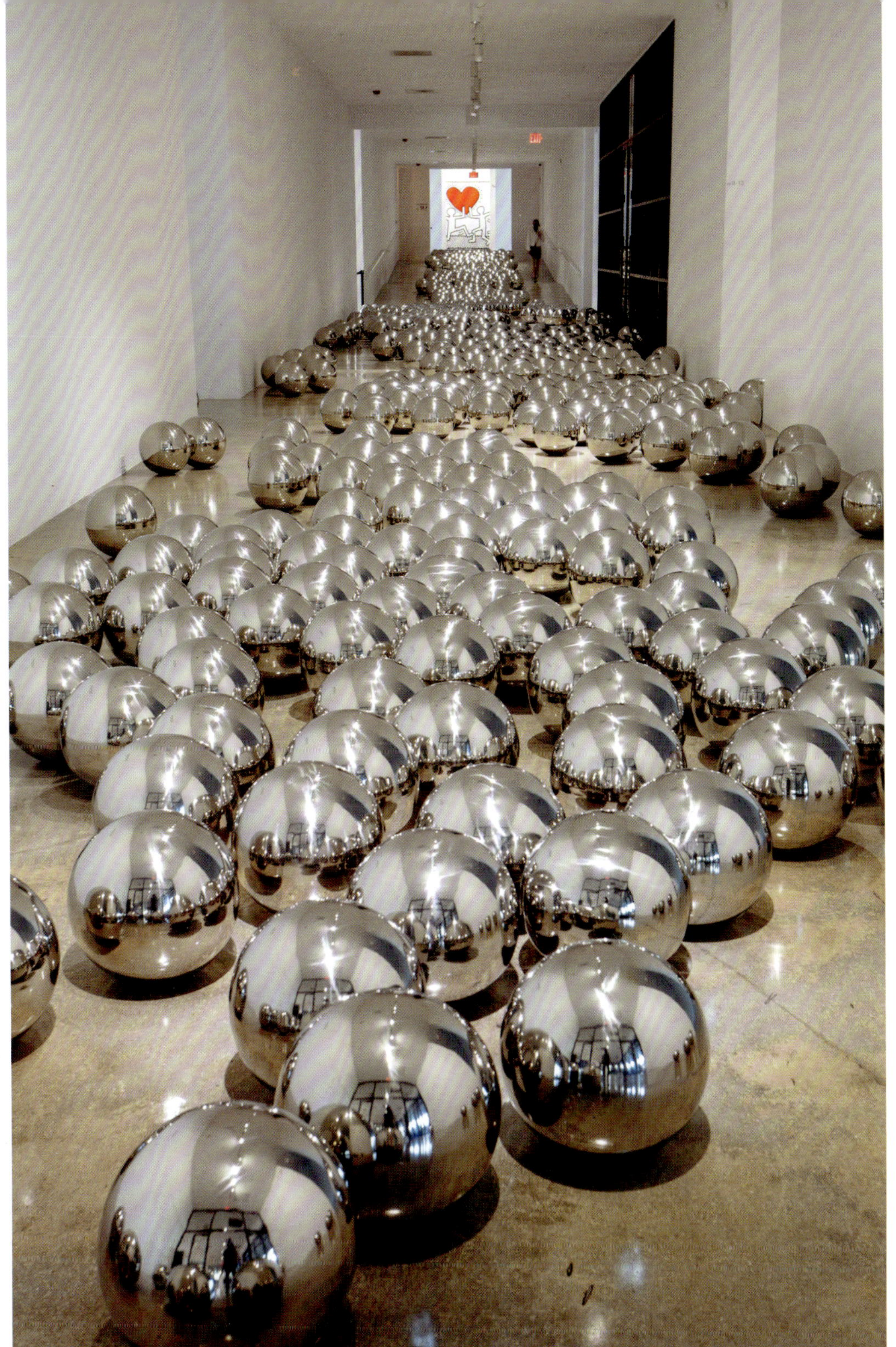

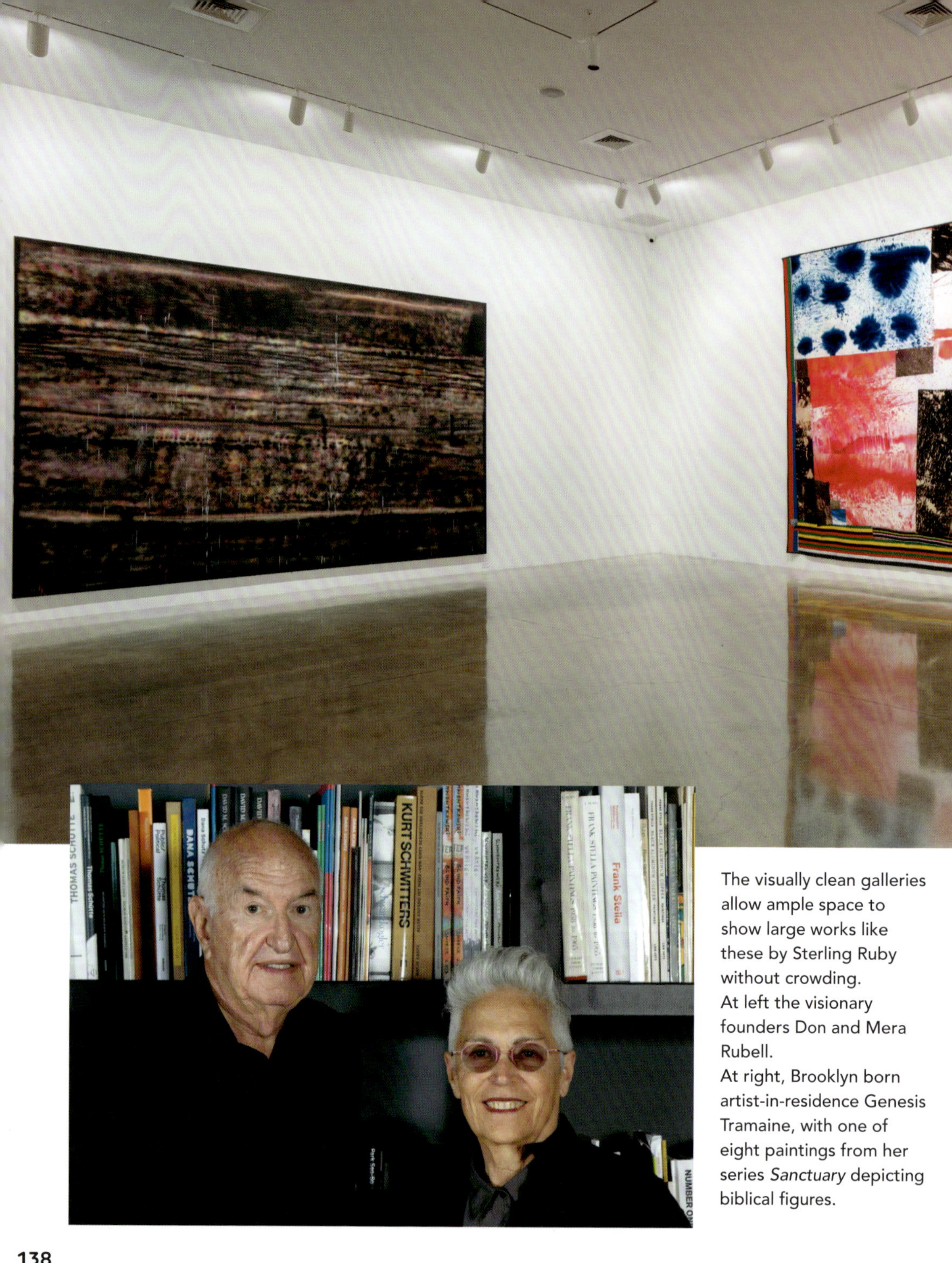

The visually clean galleries allow ample space to show large works like these by Sterling Ruby without crowding.
At left the visionary founders Don and Mera Rubell.
At right, Brooklyn born artist-in-residence Genesis Tramaine, with one of eight paintings from her series *Sanctuary* depicting biblical figures.

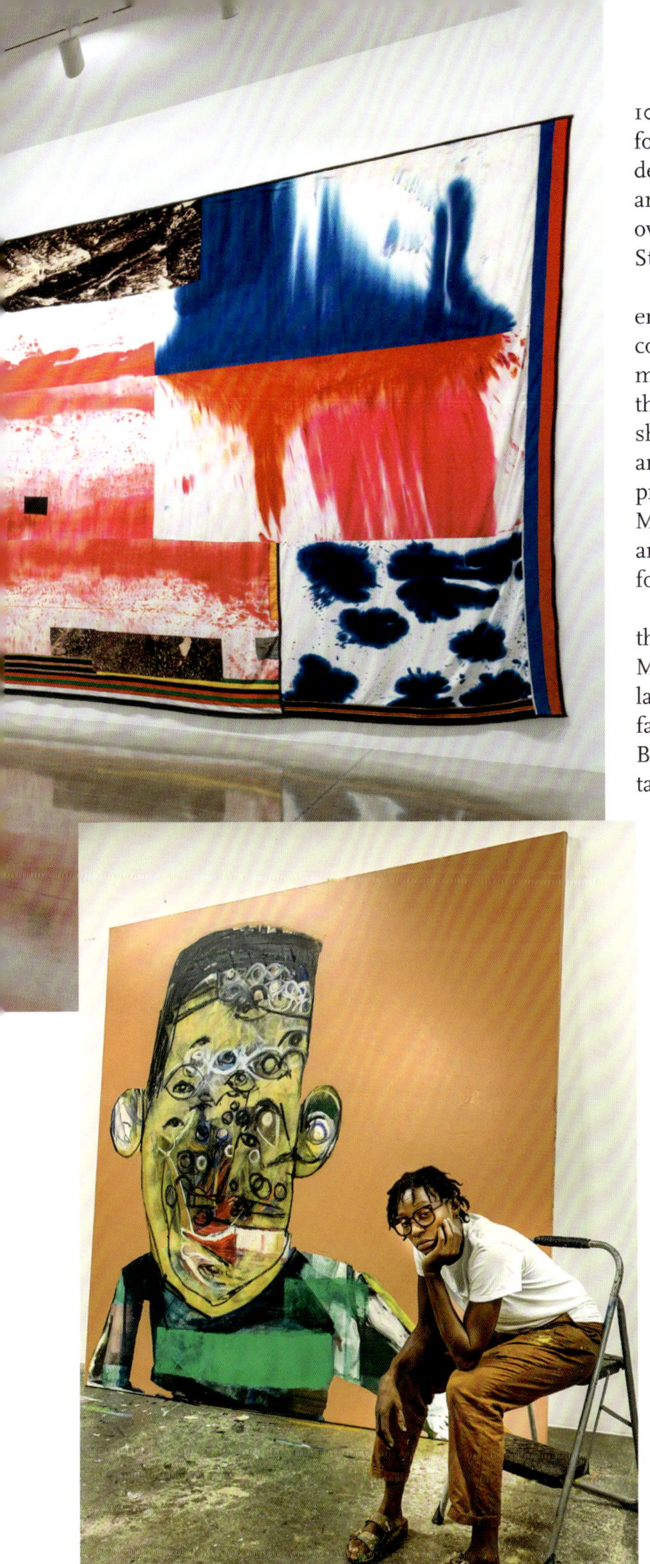

100,000-square-foot warehouse transformed by Selldorf Architects. It's hard to describe how vast some of the galleries are and how they effortlessly accommodate the overscale masterpieces by artists such as Sterling Ruby and Kehinde Wiley.

Renamed the Rubell Museum to emphasize its public mission, this private collection acts—in all the best ways—very much like any art institution. They lend their works worldwide, create and curate shows that are sent to other art institutions, and they generously sponsor community programs and internships. The Rubell Museum is considered the gold standard and the model for private museums and foundations in America.

Be sure to plan a few hours to enjoy the collection in full when you visit Miami. Make a stop in the garden to appreciate the landscape from the chairs, pillows, and sofas. I also love going to Leku, the Museum's Basque cuisine restaurant, to refuel after taking in all the magnificent art.

Interestingly, their son Jason has clearly inherited his parents collecting DNA, and his life, like his parents', is filled with art and experiences about art. I had the privilege of listening to him speak about his parents' Artists in Residence programs, which allowed him to understand an artist's creative process in great depth. After each residency, artists would be given a show at their museum. Inspired by his parents, Jason told us that his first major purchase when he was young was a work by George Condo, which a very kind gallerist allowed him to pay for in small monthly installments. Years later while on his honeymoon in Japan, he and his new wife made a stop at Takashi Murakami's studio and bought a beautiful painting, which was a very meaningful moment for him, and a reminder of the power of art to not just inspire us, but also to help define our lives.

Storm King Art Center

This excursion doesn't disappoint. One will always remember the vistas and sculptures, and, especially, the interplay of art and nature. **STORMKING.ORG**

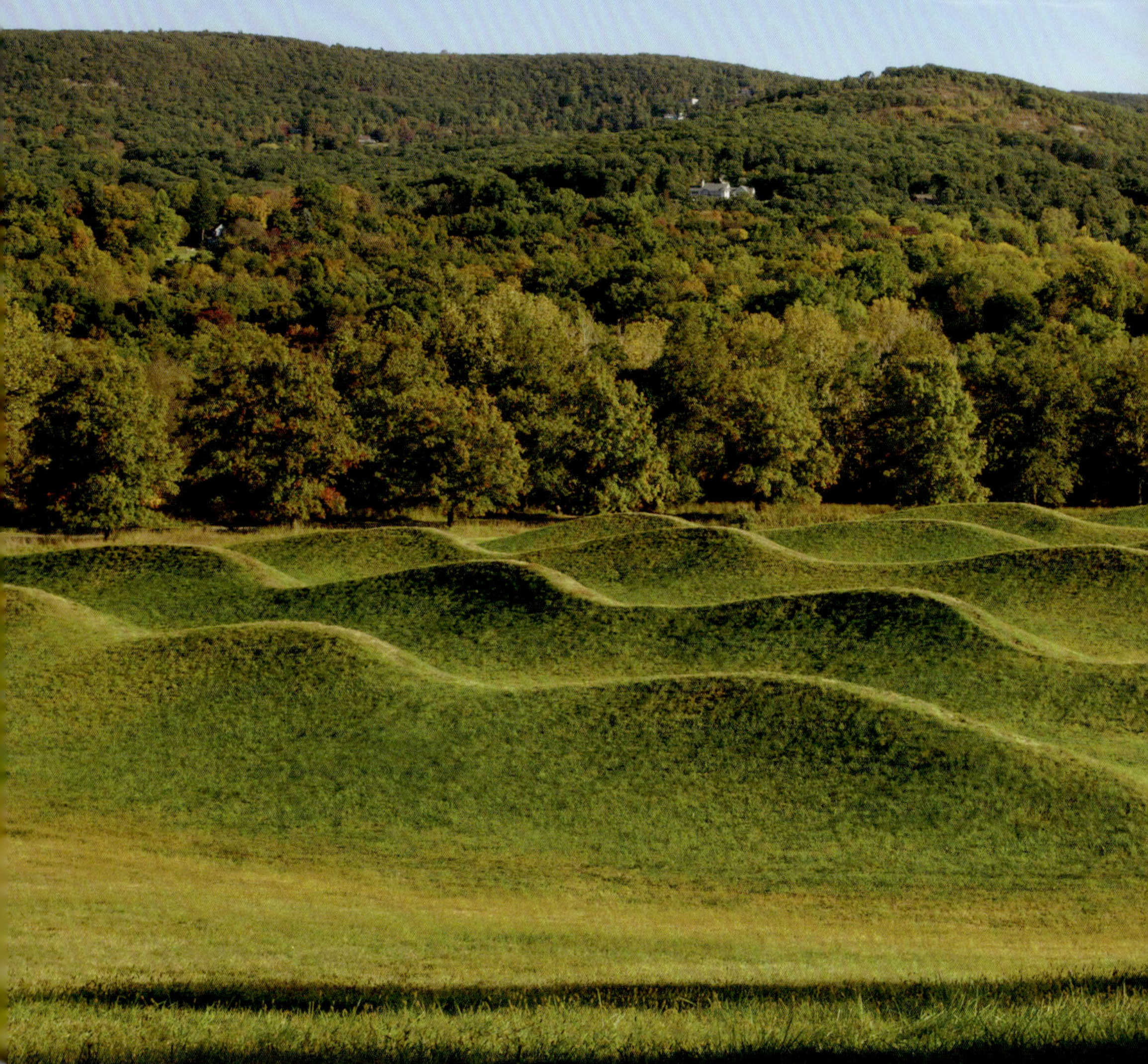

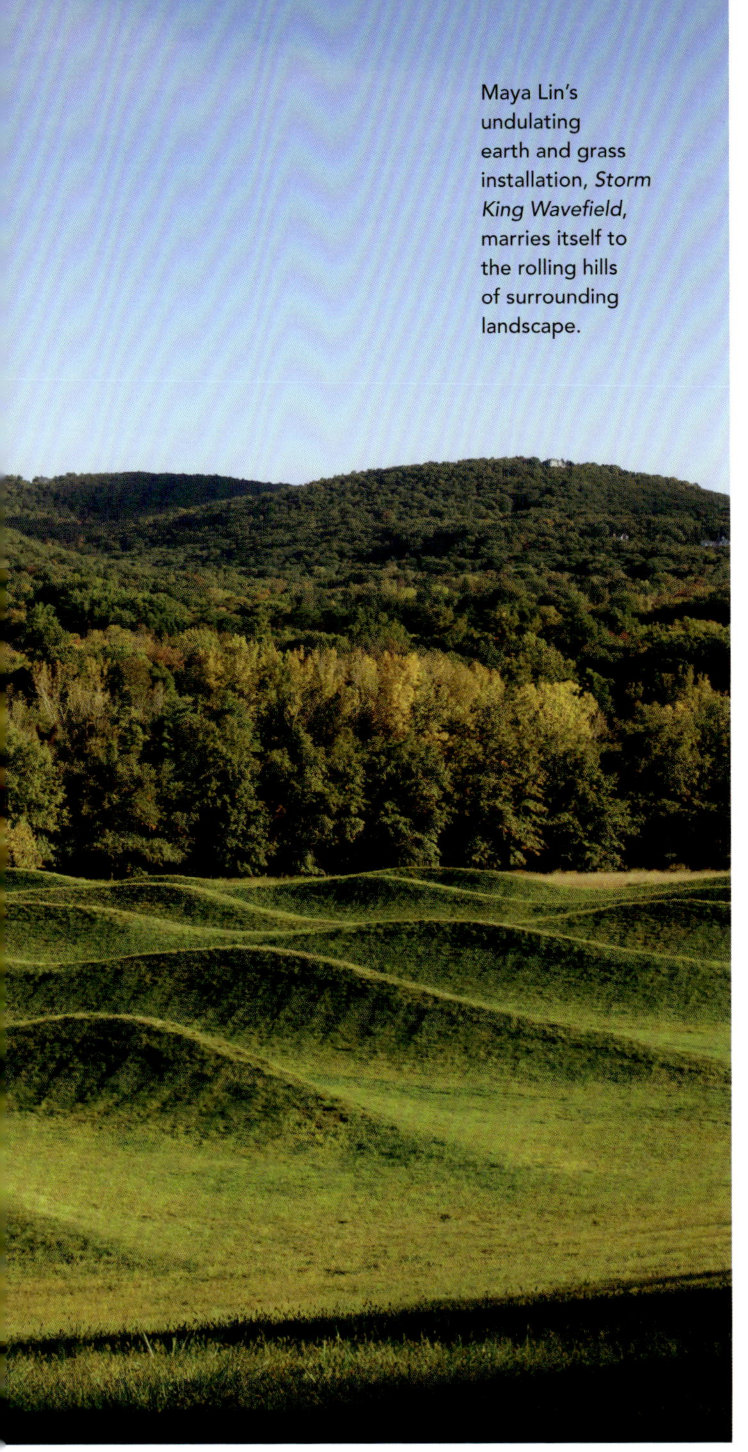

A VISIT TO STORM KING in New Windsor, New York, is not just a unique art experience; it's also tremendous fun and a great way to get your 10,000 steps for the day. Five hundred acres filled with large-scale sculpture and site-specific commissions beckon and are yours to explore—just follow the paths on foot or on bicycle to enjoy. There is no better way to fully understand an artist's commitment to site and scale than to see their work in situ like at Storm King. The connection between art, nature, and people is obvious here, in the very best sense, and the visitor need only approach each piece with an open mind to admire the work.

The first impression of Storm King is of its enormous vistas stretching out toward the sculptures set amid the rolling hills and meadows. Sky-scraping steel sculptures by Mark di Suvero punctuate the expansive landscape from the parking area. You can't help but guess what they are or what they could be. Do they move? Are they representational? It really doesn't matter. Just walk closer and let their sheer size amaze you.

There are so many great sculptures in stone and metal, it's hard to even call out the favorites. We loved the intimate garden of David Smith sculptures just as much as the gigantic work by Menashe Kadishman, called *Suspended*, where visitors lined up for their photos as if they were in Pisa, Italy. Alexander Liberman's vibrantly kinetic and confrontational *Iliad* could not be more different from Maya Lin's *Storm King Wavefield*, which you almost don't realize you are near until you are on top of it, yet each feels perfectly placed.

From Barbara Hepworth to Noguchi, from Zhang Huan to Andy Goldsworthy, there is a seemingly endless array of dynamic sculpture to explore. Storm King is an international destination designed to contribute to the cultural life and prosperity of the Hudson Valley region by forging relationships with artists and encouraging the development of their ideas. Whether you approach from an intellectual point of view or from the simple desire to let your kids run around for the day and have a picnic on the benches, Storm King is not to be missed.

Built in the tradition of dry stone walls, Andy Goldsworthy's *Storm King Wall* winds snake-like through the trees to emerge on the near side of this lake, 2,278 feet from it's beginning.

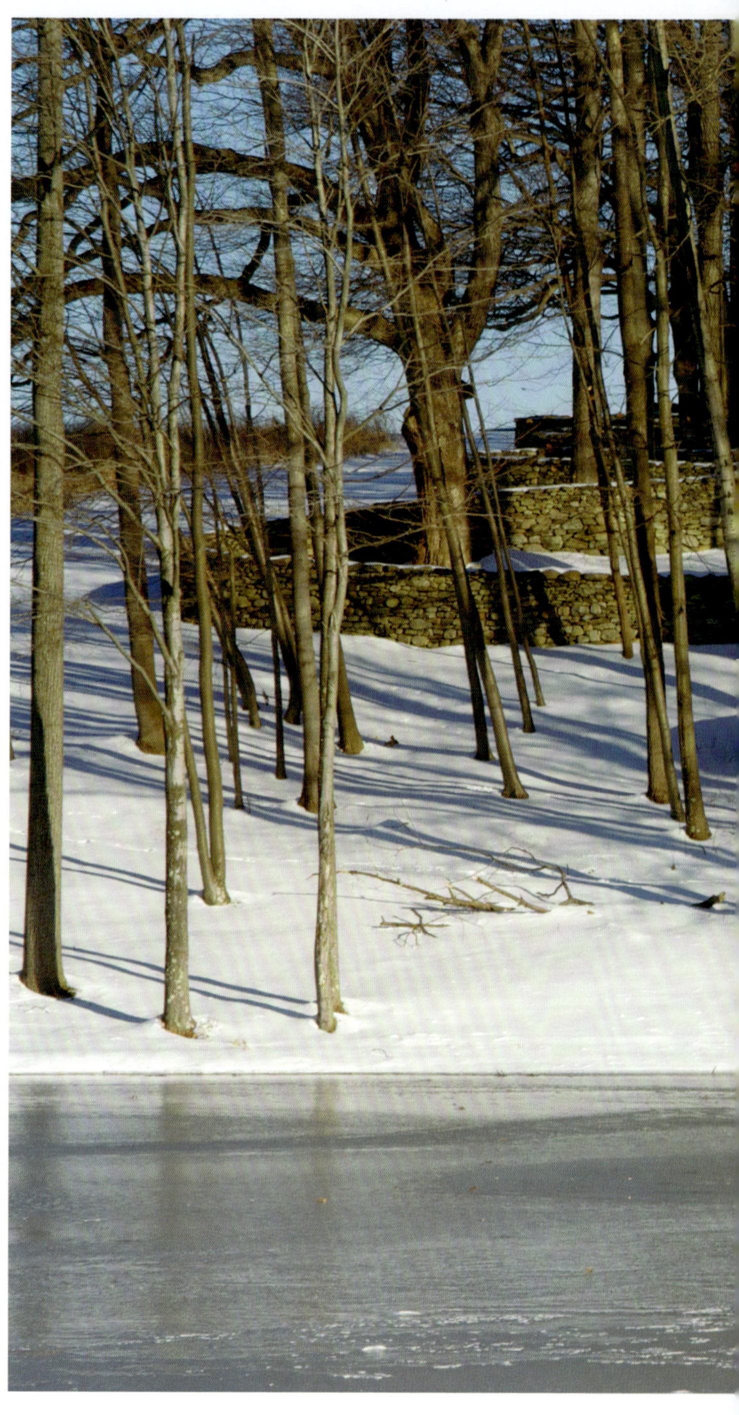

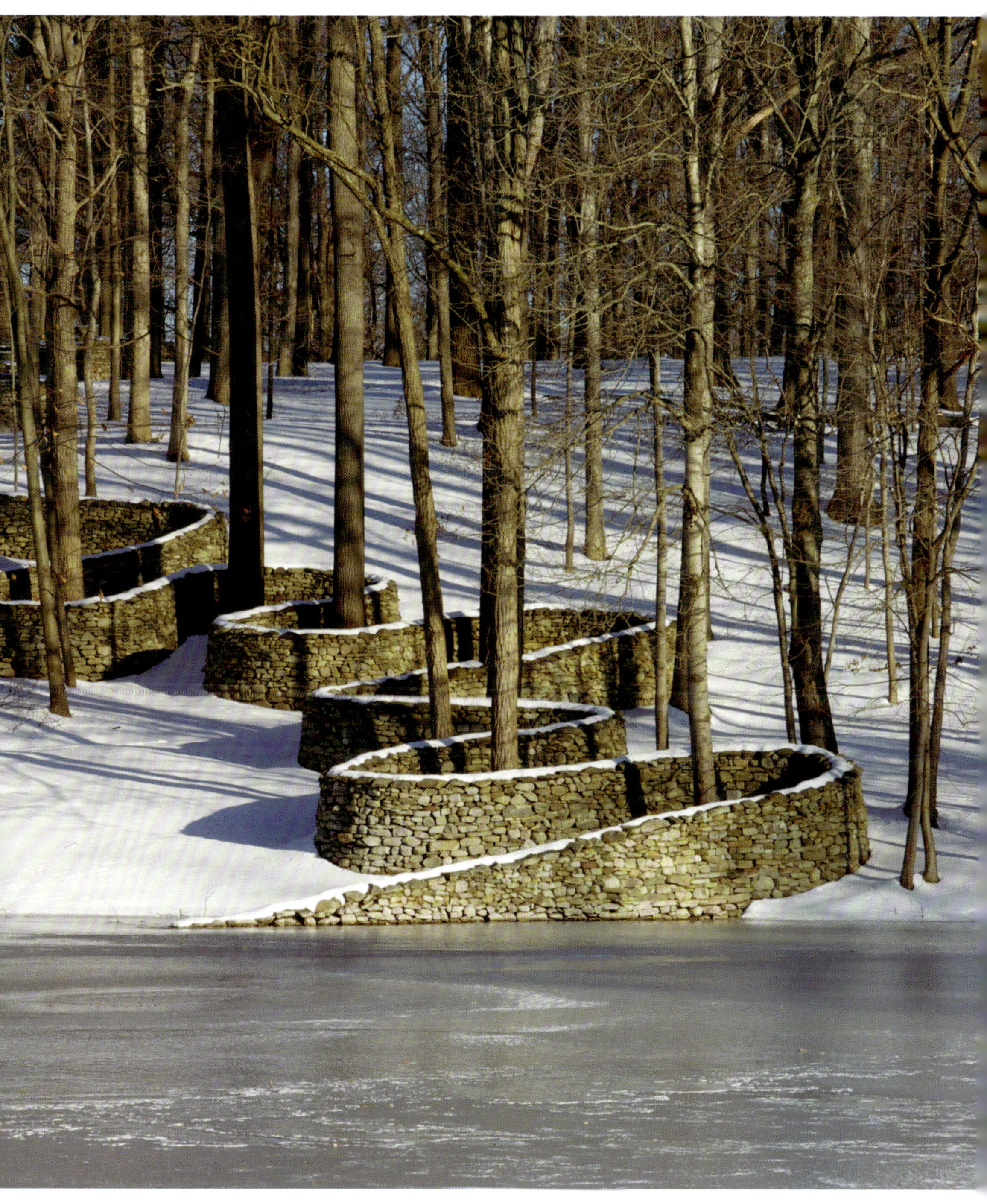

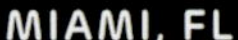

Superblue

Superblue is generating a new art medium by bringing together scientists, graphic designers, and mathematicians to create experiential and meditative art. **SUPERBLUE.COM**

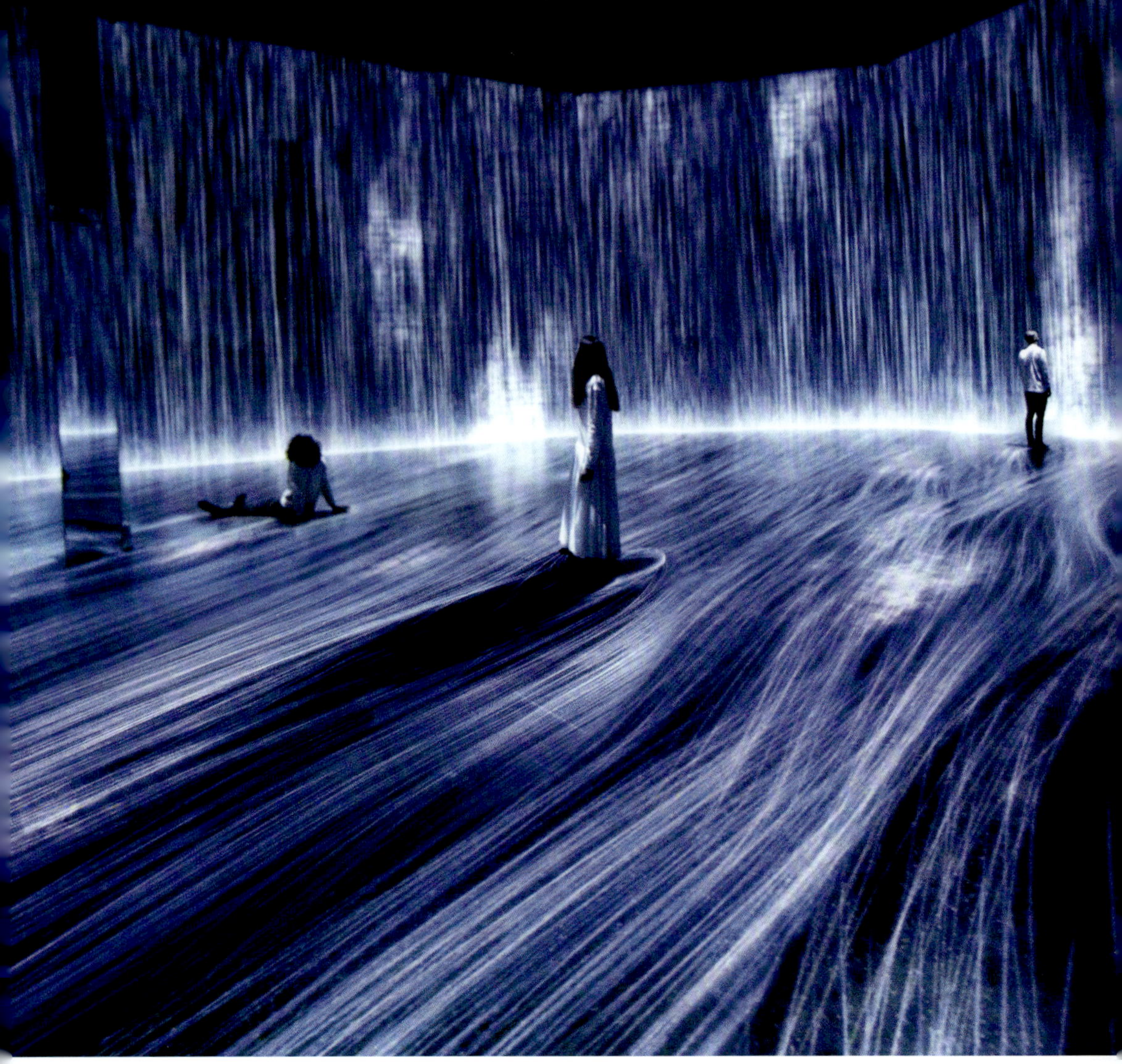

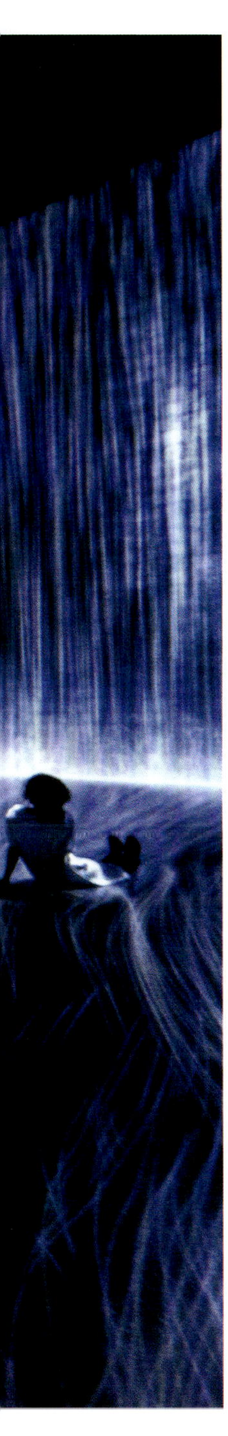

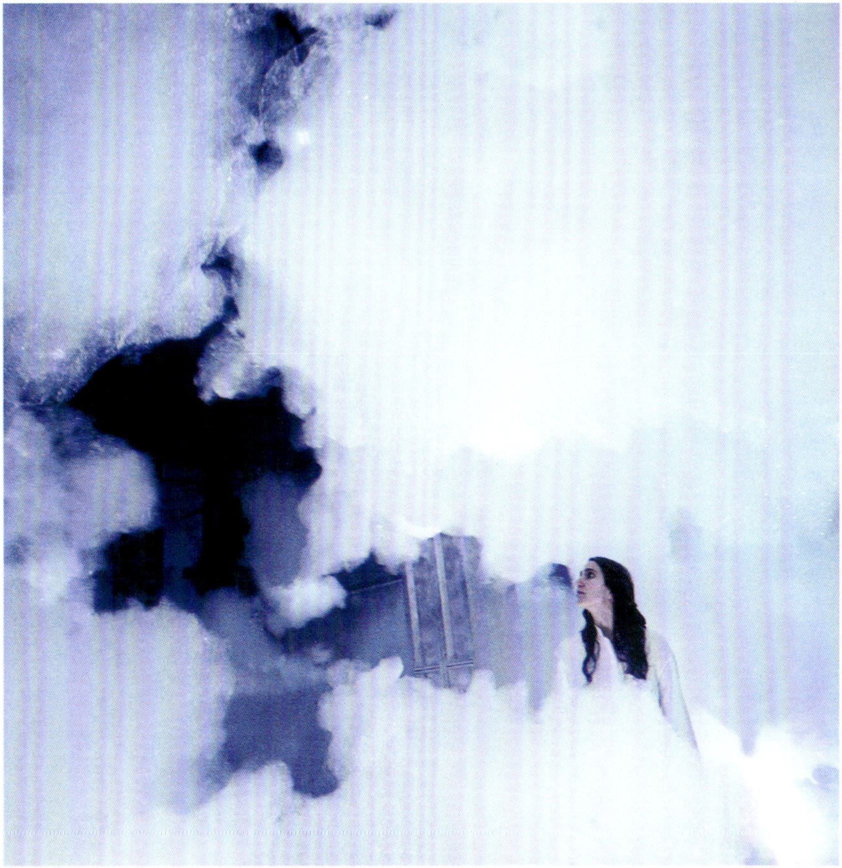

THE FIRST TIME I SAW an interactive art experience was in Menlo Park, California, in 2018. It was under the auspices of Pace gallery and the art installation was created by teamLab, a Japanese art cooperative formed in 2001 that includes fine artists, computer programmers, graphic artists, and electronic technicians. Today, Superblue is an umbrella company for digital artists, including teamLab, all of whom create computer driven art, which I think is a very exciting way to experience the rapidly growing field of immersive art.

Superblue in Miami opened in 2021 in a perfect location across from the Rubell Museum. The voluminous space is 31,000 feet long with 30-foot ceilings. Our family was allowed to visit early before it was completed. We were captivated by the beautiful videos and the various installations.

The highlight for us was the interactive piece by teamLab titled *Massless Clouds Between Sculpture and Life*. We dressed

The interactive exhibits are a thrilling sensory overload of visual stimulation and pure beauty.

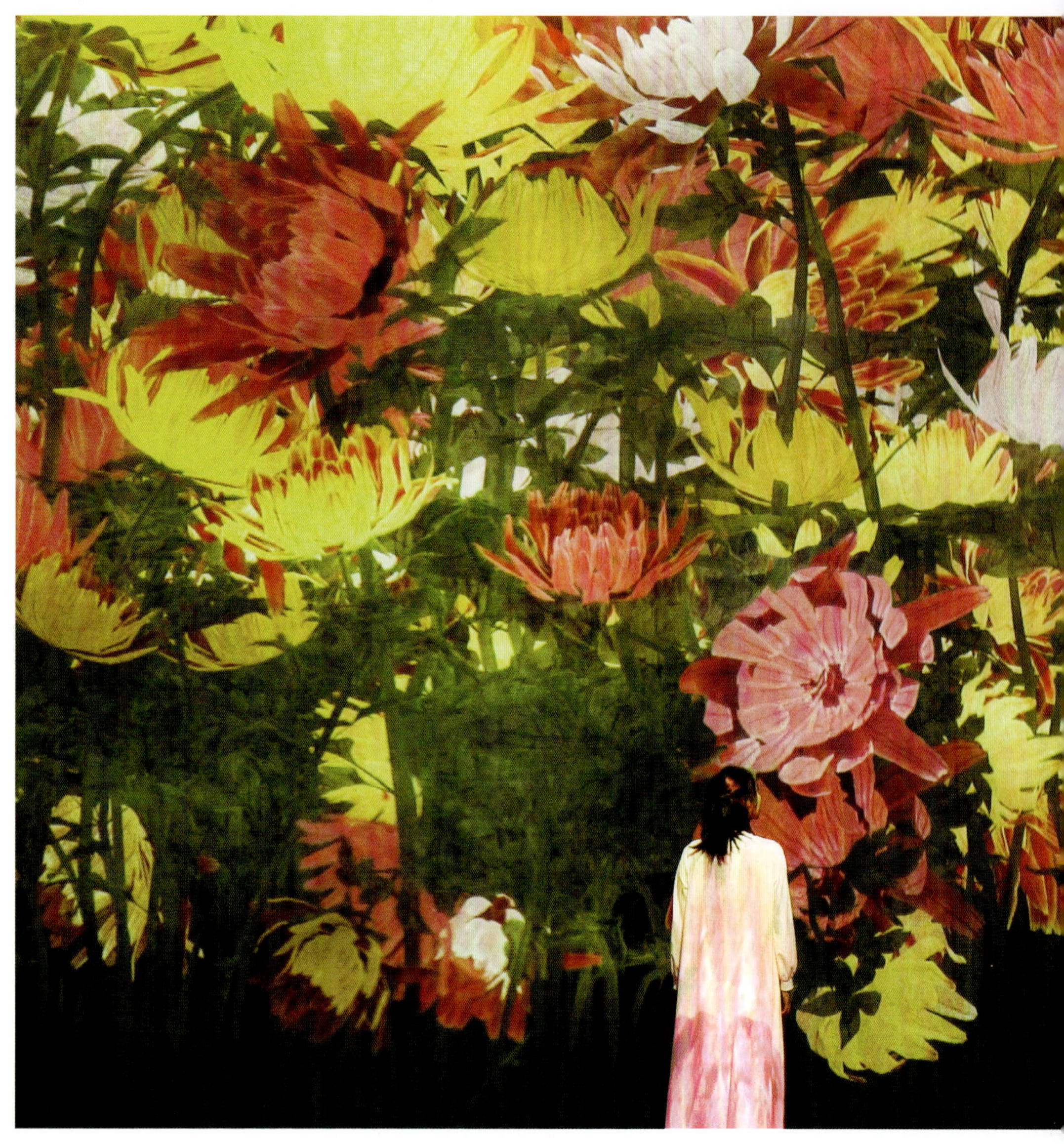

in full-body protective gear and stepped into the chamber. We had a uniquely mesmerizing experience pretending we were in the sky enveloped by clouds, which were made from bubbles. The adults loved it as much as the children.

In another installation, computers generated flowers on large screens. As we walked through the galleries, the flowers moved with our bodies as if they were responding to the heat emitted by our actions, dispersing and regrouping into other formations. This felt like a commentary on ecology and global warming.

A money-making venture, Super-

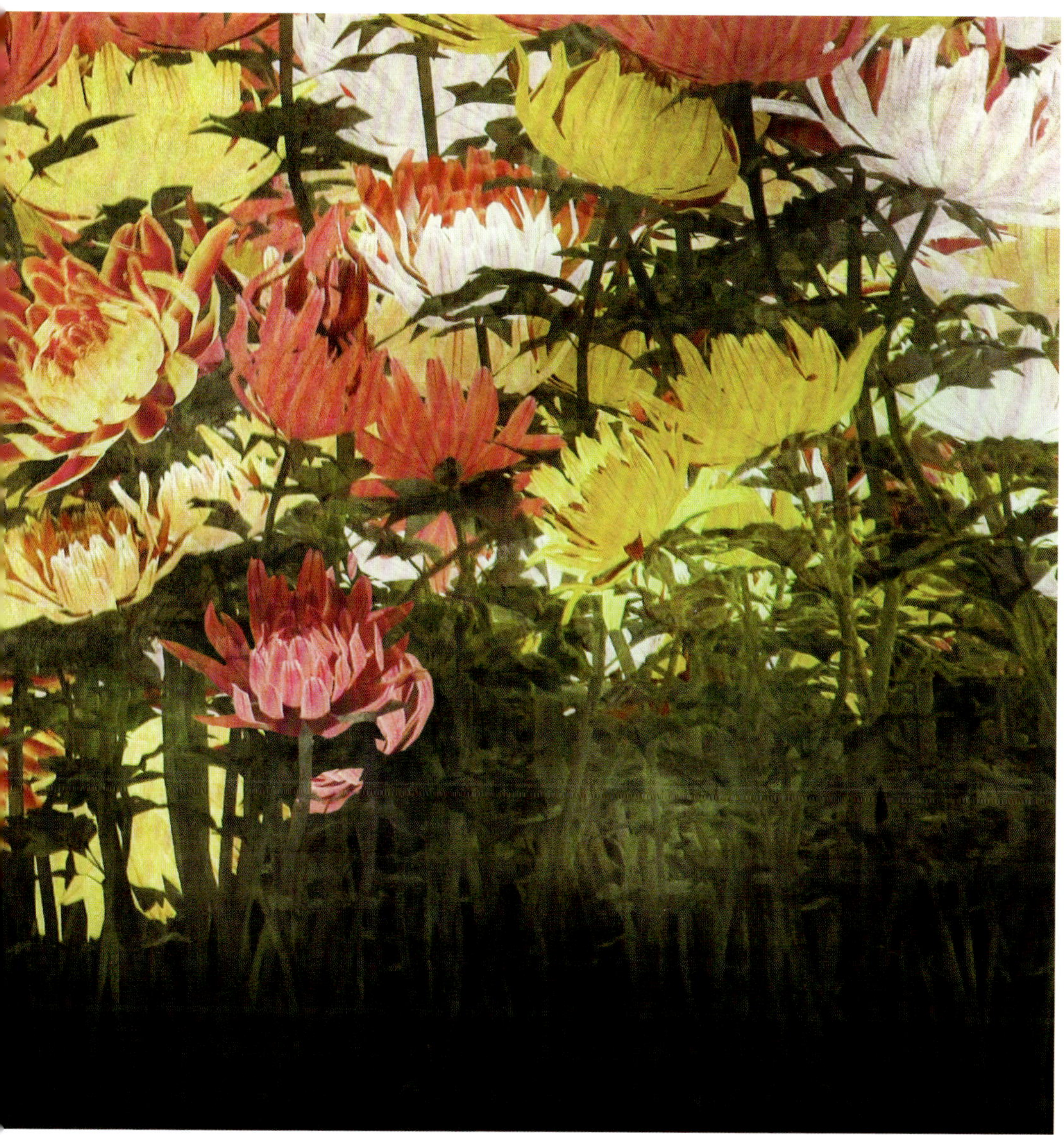

blue is currently in Miami, at the Shed in New York City, and in London. I am sure that there will soon be Superblues in many cities across the globe.

Book early because it is a very popular venue. You do not want to be shut out of this meditative and otherworldly way to interact with art.

A visitor meditates on the abundant and transitory realm of the natural world.

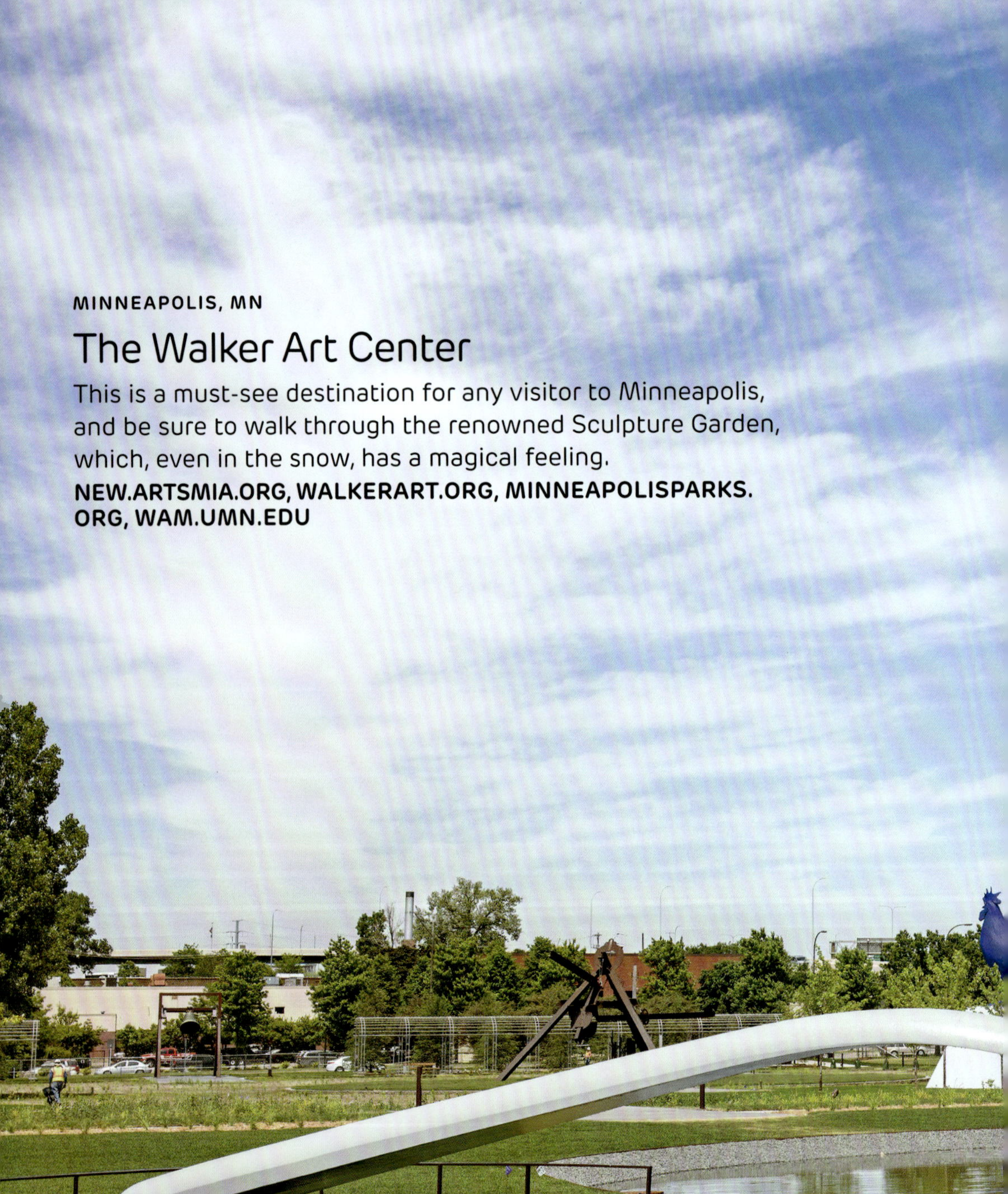

MINNEAPOLIS, MN
The Walker Art Center
This is a must-see destination for any visitor to Minneapolis, and be sure to walk through the renowned Sculpture Garden, which, even in the snow, has a magical feeling.
NEW.ARTSMIA.ORG, WALKERART.ORG, MINNEAPOLISPARKS.ORG, WAM.UMN.EDU

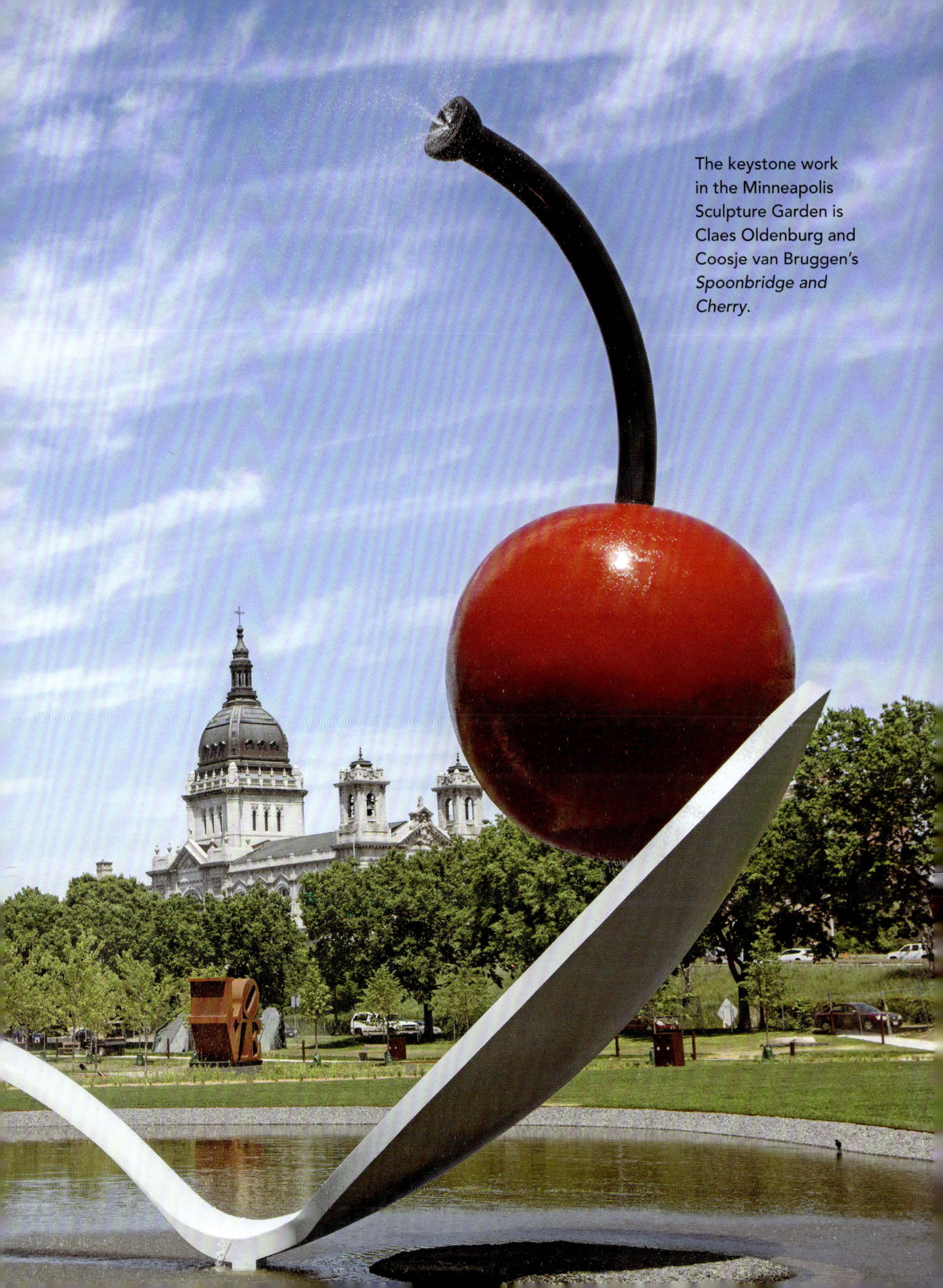

The keystone work in the Minneapolis Sculpture Garden is Claes Oldenburg and Coosje van Bruggen's *Spoonbridge and Cherry.*

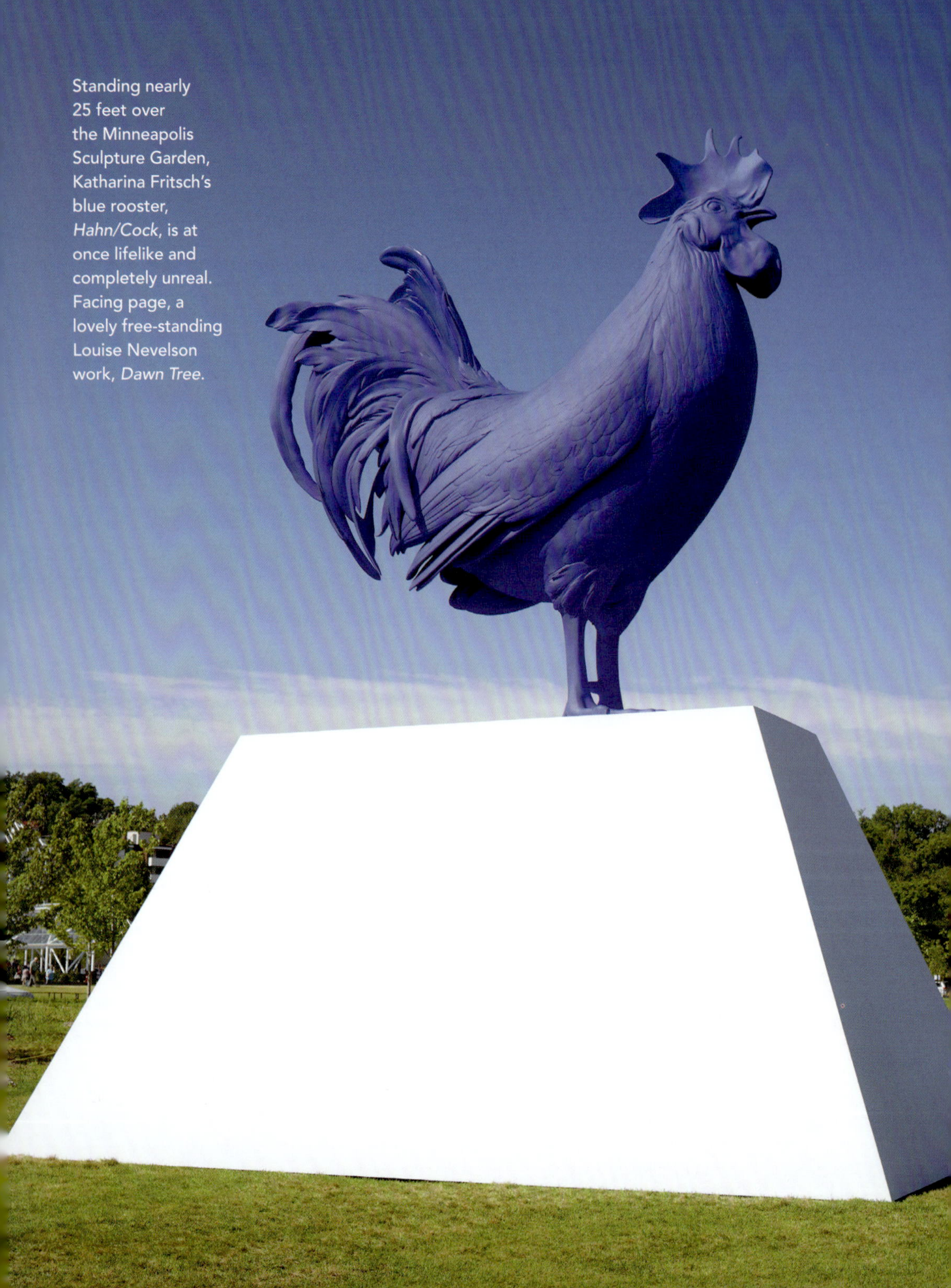
Standing nearly
25 feet over
the Minneapolis
Sculpture Garden,
Katharina Fritsch's
blue rooster,
Hahn/Cock, is at
once lifelike and
completely unreal.
Facing page, a
lovely free-standing
Louise Nevelson
work, *Dawn Tree*.

RECENTLY, we flew from New York to Minneapolis to spend a day looking at art. Our friends were shocked but quite impressed. The early flight from La Guardia arrived at 10 a.m., leaving us with a full day to enjoy some terrific art experiences.

Our first stop was the Minneapolis Institute of Art. This encyclopedic museum can give the Metropolitan Museum real competition. The grand building boasts soaring ceilings, marble clad halls, and on the second floor, an awe-inspiring collection of Asian art. We saw an outstanding print show celebrating twenty years of Highpoint Editions. The works were marvelous, and the museum set up a print studio with a printing press to demonstrate the process of making monotypes.

The Walker Art Center, our main event for the day, opened at 11 a.m. and would have been our second stop, but first we had to visit the Minneapolis Sculpture Garden located just across the road. It was a gorgeous fall day for us to enjoy this eleven-acre park that was once a marshland and is now home to more than forty sculptures from the Walker Art Center's collection. In partnership with the city's Minneapolis Park & Recreation Board, they created a top destination with no entry fee for the community and visitors.

The park was filled with families and groups enjoying the natural setting. The carefully considered native plants are interwoven with sculpture by famed artists such as Tony Cragg, Mark di Suvero, Barry Flanagan, Jenny Holzer, and Claes Oldenburg.

After, we walked across the road to the Walker Art Center where Julie Mehretu's mid-career retrospective was on view. I had seen the exhibition at the Whitney Museum in New York previously, and the show looked equally compelling at the Walker. I especially enjoyed a video where Mehretu explains her process.

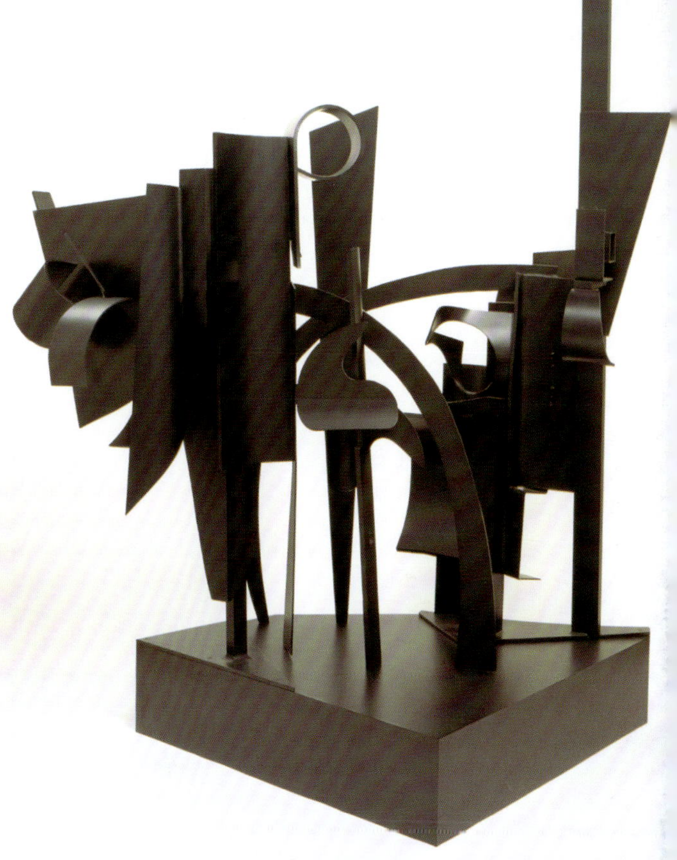

Their impressive permanent collection has works by Willem de Kooning, Kerry James Marshall, Georgia O'Keeffe, and a spectacular and very large Joan Mitchell oil painting, *Posted*, from 1977.

We wanted to check out the Frank Gehry–designed Frederick R. Weisman Art Museum at the university of Minnesota before we left, but it was unfortunately closed due to renovations. We drove by to marvel at the gleaming silver structure and compared it to Gehry's other architectural works.

Overall, we had a fabulous art day, and it was geographically enlightening to realize that Minnesota is not that far away from the East Coast and is very accessible. A good reminder that there are art experiences all over the country and that one should not be intimidated by a seemingly far-off location. It is always worth the trip!

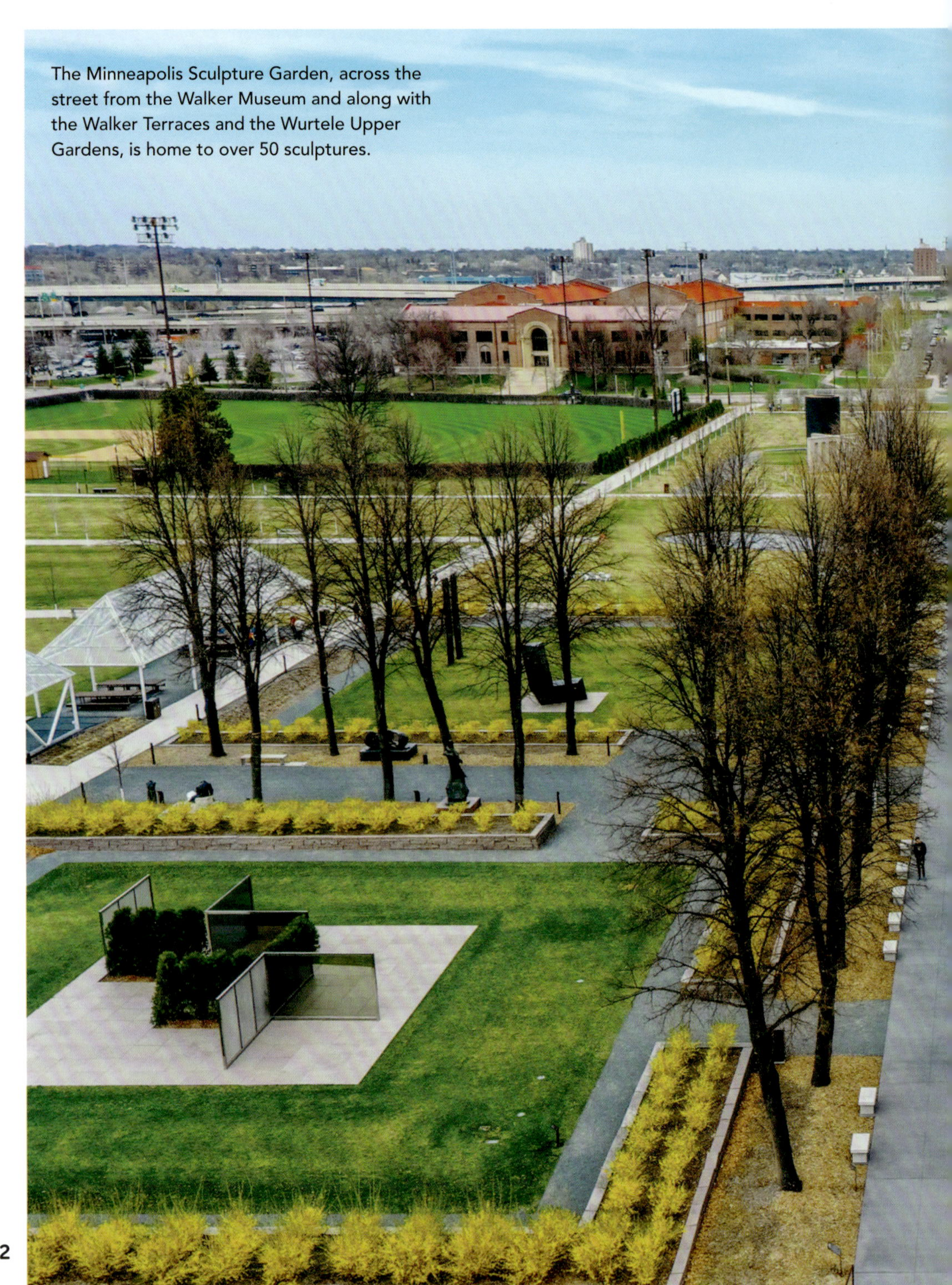

The Minneapolis Sculpture Garden, across the
street from the Walker Museum and along with
the Walker Terraces and the Wurtele Upper
Gardens, is home to over 50 sculptures.

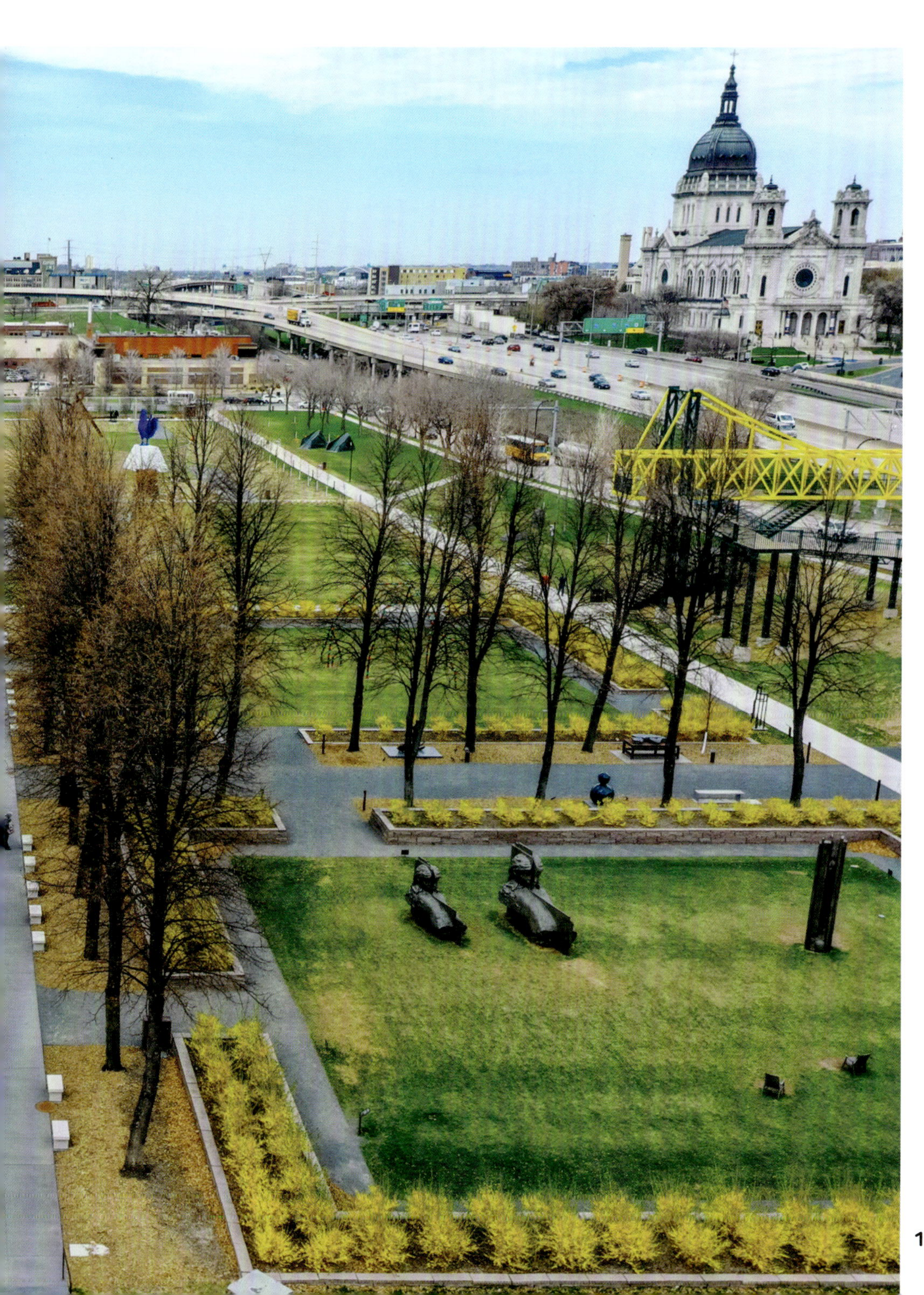

Acknowledgments

I want to thank Marta Hallett, my publisher, who got excited when I presented the concept of cultural art travel in America to her, and who believed that it could be a book.

Thank you to Stephen Fay for the inspired art direction and design of this book.

Thank you to Margaux King whose tenacity and organization in the middle of the Covid crisis helped us acquire the photographs for the book.

Thank you to Tracey Pruzan who took my words and helped them flow in a more cogent and lyrical manner. Her professional expertise of how a book project is constructed was invaluable. She organized the chapters for publishing and continuously had her eye on the finished project. Working on the book with Tracey was every minute a joyful experience.

Photo Editor Marie-Helene Rousseau is a brilliant and gifted diplomat. Magically, she was able to obtain the consents from museums, artists, estates and foundations to allow us to use the images that are the structure of this book. Rousseau accomplished this in the most elegant and creative manner, and she never gave up.

Thank you to my husband Gregory Fischbach who cheered me on when things were challenging. Greg flew with me to Minneapolis, where I had never been, to see the Sculpture Garden and the Walker Art Center.

Thank you to my lawyer, Karen Gantz who brought me to G Editions.

Thank you to the amazing collectors, creators, and owners of the many private museums, foundations, and art spaces that I visited and that enriched my life.

Seeing the Rubell museum in Miami and being exposed to the newest and most creative artists is something that I look forward to every year.

Thank you to a dearest friend, Margie Neu who traveled with me by train to see the incredible American Visual Arts Museum in Baltimore and to revisit the Barnes Foundation in Philadelphia in one overnight trip.

Thank you to Nancy Olnick and Giorgio Spanu who are the energetic creators of Magazzino, a private museum that focuses on post WWII Italian art in Cold Springs, New York. Spending the day with them and observing their enthusiasm and passion was one of the highlights of this process.

Art travel has been a fun and stimulating part of my life. I am so happy that I can share my experiences with you.

Love, Linda

Credits

Page 9
Courtesy of the Frist Art Museum.

American Visionary Art Museum

Page 10
Aurora Borealis Mosaic Wall, by youth apprentices of Maryland Dept. of Juvenile Services with facilitator, artist Mari Gardner, photo Dan Meyers.

Page 11
Main Building Interior, photo Shawn Levin.

Page 12
MASP Exhibit Doc, photo Nick Prevas.

Page 13
JRVC, David Hess, *Birds Nest Balcony,* photo Alain Jaramillo. Flicks From The Hill, photo Nick Prevas.

Anderson Collection at Stanford University

Pages 14-15
Exterior of the Anderson Collection, photo Linda A. Cicero.

Pages 16-17
Interior gallery photos, courtesy of the Anderson Collection at Stanford University. Family portrait of the Andersons, photo Linda A. Cicero.

Art Barge and Victor D'Amico Institute of Art

Pages 18-19
Courtesy of The Victor D'Amico Institute of Art.

Barnes Foundation

Page 20-21
Ensemble view, Room 22, north wall (detail), Philadelphia, 2012. Image © The Barnes Foundation
Ensemble view, Room 19, west wall (detail), Philadelphia, 2012. Image © The Barnes Foundation
Vincent van Gogh. *The Postman* (Joseph-Étienne Roulin), 1889.

The Brant Foundation

Pages 22-23
Installation view of "Remembering Henry's Show: Selected Works 1978-2008," photo Tom Powel Imaging.
Urs Fischer, *To Be Titled (Big Clay No.3),* 2008-2011. © Urs Fischer, photo Christopher Burke.

Pages 24-25
Photo Sean Keenan, photo Tom Powel Imaging.

Courtesy of the The Brant Foundation, Greenwich, CT USA.

The Broad

Pages 26-27
Lobby, exterior, photo Mike Kelley.

Pages 28-29
Robert Therrien, *Under the Table,* 1994, The Broad Art Foundation, photo Joshua White.
Jeff Koons, *Rabbit,* 1986, The Eli and Edythe L. Broad Collection and *Balloon Dog (Blue),* 1994-2000, The Broad Art Foundation, photo Ryan Miller.
The Vault, photo Mike Kelley.

The Bunker Artspace

Page 30
The Bunker Artspace, East Gallery Inaugural Exhibition, 2017. Pictured: Artworks by Bharti Kher, Nick Cave, and Alex Da Corte. Image courtesy of The Bunker Artspace.

Page 31
The Bunker Artspace, Lobby Inaugural Exhibition, 2017. Pictured: Artworks by Richard Hughes, Tom Friedman, Studio Job, Tony Oursler, Monika Sosnowska, Jose Alvarez (D.O.P.A.), and Alex Da Corte. Images ©Firooz Zahedi.

Page 32
The Bunker Artspace, 2019 Opening Performance "Delia Brown: Chamber Music." Images ©Firooz Zahedi.

Page 33
The Bunker Artspace, East Gallery, 2019.
"Inner Space/Outer Space," curated by Simon Watson.
Pictured: Artworks by Tavares Strachan, Naotaka Hiro, and Dona Nelson.

Charles M. Schulz Museum and Research Center

Pages 34-37
All images courtesy of Charles M. Schulz Museum and Research Center, Santa Rosa CA.

Chihuly Collection

Pages 38-39

Chihuly Collection and Morean Glass Studio. Dale Chihuly, *Florida Rose Crystal Tower*, 2010, Chihuly Collection presented by the Morean Arts Center, St. Petersburg, Florida, photo ©2017 Chihuly Studio.

Pages 40-41

Dale Chihuly, *Azul de Medianoche Chandelier*, 2002 and *Drawing Wall*, 2010, Chihuly Collection presented by the Morean Arts Center, St. Petersburg, Florida, installed 2010, photo ©2017 Chihuly Studio. Morean Shopping, photo Beth Reynolds.

Clyfford Still Museum

Pages 42-45

All photos courtesy Clyfford Still Museum.

Crystal Bridges Museum of American Art

Pages 46-47

View of restaurant from Walker Landing with Keith Haring, *Two-Headed Figure*, courtesy of Crystal Bridges Museum of American Art.

Pages 48-49

Early American Art Galleries, Contemporary Art Gallery, courtesy of Crystal Bridges Museum of American Art.

The Dalí Museum

Pages 50-53

All images ©2021, Salvador Dalí Museum, Inc., St. Petersburg, FL.

De la Cruz Collection

Pages 54-55

Installation view of A Possible Horizon 2020-2021 exhibition featuring work by Aaron Curry, Felix Gonzalez-Torres © Estate of Felix Gonzalez-Torres, courtesy of the Felix Gonzalez-Torres Foundation, Sterling Ruby, Manfred Pernice, Isa Genzken, and Nate Lowman, courtesy of the de la Cruz Collection.

Pages 56-57

Installation view of "A Possible Horizon 2020-2021" exhibition featuring work by Glenn Ligon (© Glenn Ligon, courtesy of the artist, Hauser & Wirth, New York, Regen Projects, Los Angeles, Thomas Dane Gallery, London, and Galerie Chantal Crousel, Paris) and Felix Gonzalez-Torres (© Estate of Felix Gonzalez-Torres, courtesy of the Felix Gonzalez-Torres Foundation.) Courtesy of the de la Cruz Collection.

Installation view of "A Possible Horizon 2020-2021" exhibition featuring work by Martin Kippenberger, Rufino Tamayo, Dana Schutz, Albert Oehlen, Gabriel Orozco, Salvador Dali, Felix Gonzalez-Torres (© Estate of Felix Gonzalez-Torres, courtesy of the Felix Gonzalez-Torres Foundation), and Rudolf Stingel. Courtesy of the de la Cruz Collection.

Di Rosa Center For Contemporary Art

Pages 58-59

Photo Colson Griffith.

Page 60

Photo Israel Valencia, Infinity Visuals.

Page 61

Photo Grace Hendricks.

Dia Beacon

Pages 62-63

Sam Gilliam, *Double Merge*, 1968. Installation view, Dia:Beacon, Beacon, New York, 2019. © Sam Gilliam/Artists Rights Society (ARS), New York, photo Bill Jacobson Studio, New York, courtesy Dia Art Foundation.

Page 64-65

John Chamberlain, *Daddy in the Dark*, 1988. Dia Art Foundation, gift of Louise and Leonard Riggio. © 2023 Fairweather & Fairweather LTD/Artists Rights Society (ARS), New York, photo Bill Jacobson Studio, New York, courtesy Dia Art Foundation, New York. Bruce Nauman, *Left or Standing, Standing or Left Standing*, 1971. Dia Art Foundation, partial gift, Lannan Foundation, 2013. © Bruce Nauman/Artists Rights Society (ARS), New York, photo Bill Jacobson Studio, New York, courtesy Dia Art Foundation, New York.

Dia Bridgehampton and the Dan Flavin Art Institute

Pages 66-67

Exterior, photo Bill Jacobson.
Dan Flavin, Installation view at Dan Flavin Art Institute, photo by Florian Holzherr, © 2023 Stephen Flavin/Artists Rights Society (ARS), New York.

The Donum Estate

Pages 68-70

© The Donum Estate.

Pages 70-71

Zhan Wang, *Artificial Rock No. 126*, 2007-13, photo Robert Berg.

The FLAG Art Foundation

Pages 72-73
Elmgreen & Dragset, *Changing Subjects*, 2016, photo S. Probert.

Pages 74-75
E. Kelly, *B&W Works*, 2018, photo S. Probert. © Ellsworth Kelly Foundation, courtesy Matthew Marks Gallery.
Installation view of Awol Erizku: *New Flower/Images of the Reclining Venus* at The FLAG Art Foundation, 2015, photo ArtEcho LLC.

Frederick R. Weisman Art Foundation

Pages 76-79
All photos courtesy of the Frederick R. Weisman Art Foundation.

Frist Art Museum

Pages 80-83
Courtesy of the Frist Art Museum.

Getty Center and Getty Villa

Page 84
Getty Center, photo Stacey Rain Strickler, © J. Paul Getty Trust.

Page 85
Central Garden at the Getty Center Central Garden © Robert Irwin, photo © 2008 J. Paul Getty Trust.

Pages 86-87
Outer Peristyle at the Getty Villa, photo Tahnee L. Cracchiola © 2018 J. Paul Getty Trust.
Tablinum at the Getty Villa, photo Elon Schoenholz © 2018 J. Paul Getty Trust

Hess Art Collection at the Hess Persson Estates

Page 88-89
Photo Olaf Nagel, Ostfildern Germany. Courtesy of the Hess Art Collection.

Pages 90
Photo Robert Russo, Mill Valley CA. Courtesy of the Hess Art Collection.

Page 91
Photo Robert Ceballos, Napa CA. Courtesy of the Hess Art Collection.

Page 92
Photo Ray Marcinkowski, Santa Rosa CA. Courtesy of the Hess Art Collection.

Page 93
Homage, Leopoldo Maler, photo Ray Marcinkowski, Santa Rosa CA. Courtesy of the Hess Art Collection.

Isabella Stewart Gardner Museum

Page 94-95
Courtyard, Isabella Stewart Gardner Museum, Boston, photo Sean Dungan.
Raphael Room, Isabella Stewart Gardner Museum, Boston, photo Sean Dungan.

Page 96-97
Little Salon, Isabella Stewart Gardner Museum, Boston, photo Sean Dungan.

Page 98
Titian Room, Isabella Stewart Gardner Museum, Boston, photo Sean Dungan.

Page 99
Spanish Cloister, Isabella Stewart Gardner Museum, Boston, photo Sean Dungan.

The Isamu Noguchi Foundation And Garden Museum

Pages 100-103
All photos Nicholas Knight. ©The Isamu Noguchi Foundation and Garden Museum, New York/ARS.

The James Museum Of Western & Wildlife Art

Page 104-107
All photos courtesy of the James Museum.

Page 105
Logan Maxwell Hagege, *Light on the Round Clouds*, 2013, oil on canvas, 40" x 60," courtesy of the James Museum.

LongHouse Reserve

Page 108
Photo Gary Mamay.

Page 109
Photo Joanne Sohn.

Page 110
Photo Will Ryman.

Page 111
Photo Joanne Sohn.

Magazzino Italian Art Foundation

Pages 112-113
Installation view of the exhibition Arte Povera at Magazzino Italian Art, Cold Spring, New York, photo Alexa Hoyer. Courtesy Magazzino Italian Art, Cold Spring, NY.

Page 114
Giorgio Spanu and Nancy Olnick, photo Marco Anelli.
Magazzino Italian Art, photo Montse Zamorano.
Courtesy Magazzino Italian Art, Cold Spring, NY.

Page 115
Luciano Fabro's *Due nudi che scendono le scale*,
1987–1989, Bardiglio marble. Part of the exhibition
Arte Povera at Magazzino Italian Art, Cold Spring,
New York, photo Alexa Hoyer. Courtesy Magazzino
Italian Art, Cold Spring, NY.

Margulies Collection at the Warehouse
Pages 116-117
Jennifer Steinkamp, *Blind Eye 3*, 2019, video
installation, dimensions variable. Collection Martin Z.
Margulies.

Page 118
Anselm Kiefer, *Sprache der Vögel*, 1989, lead, steel,
wood, oil, plaster, resin and acrylic. Collection Martin
Z. Margulies.

Page 119
Pier Paolo Calzolari, *Untitled (L'aria vibra)*,
Melton, refrigerating unit and copper pipes, neon,
transformer, lead. Collection Martin Z. Margulies,
photo Peter Harholdt.

Page 120
Olafur Eliasson, *Inverted Berlin Sphere*, 2005, stainless
steel, mirror, wire, cable, bulb, dimmer. Collection
Martin Z Margulies.

Page 121
George Segal, *Subway*, 1968, plaster, metal, glass.
Collection Martin Z. Margulies. © 2023 The George
and Helen Segal Foundation/Licensed by VAGA
at Artists Rights Society (ARS), NY, photo Peter
Harholdt.

The Menil Collection
Pages 122-123
Menil Collection front entrance, photo Kevin Keim.
The Menil Collection, interior view, photo Don
Glentzer.

Page 124-125
Interior view of The Menil Collection, Houston, photo
Richard Barnes.
The Menil Collection, interior view of the Cy Twombly
Gallery, photo Don Glentzer.
All images courtesy of the Menil Collection, Houston.

Neue Galerie
Page 126
Grand Staircase of Neue Galerie New York, courtesy of
the Neue Galerie New York.

Neue Galerie New York, Building Exterior, photo Hulya
Kolabas, courtesy of the Neue Galerie New York.

Page 127
The Neue Galerie, Second Floor Galleries, March
2019. Courtesy of the Neue Galerie New York.

Pages 128-129
The Neue Galerie, Second Floor Galleries, "Modern
Worlds: Austrian and German Art, 1890-1940."
Courtesy of the Neue Galerie New York.

Pollock-Krasner House
And Study Center
Page 130-131
Photo Weber Visuals. © 2019 Weber Studios.

Page 132-133
Pollock-Krasner House and Study Center, East
Hampton, NY. Used by permission.

Rubell Museum
Pages 134-135
Gallery 23 at the Rubell Museum. Works by (from left)
Kehinde Wiley, Keith Haring and Gilbert & George,
photo Chi Lam, courtesy of the Rubell Museum.

Page 136
Untitled (Join), 1990, by Felix Gonzalez-Torres
in conjunction with Michael Jenkins. Installed in
Inaugural Exhibition. Rubell Museum, Miami, FL.
4 Dec. 2019 – 18 Nov. 2020. Photo Chi Lam, courtesy
of the Rubell Museum.

Page 137
Yayoi Kusama: Narcissus Garden, photo Chi Lam,
courtesy of the Rubell Museum.

Page 138-139
Gallery 25, the Rubell Museum, photo Chi Lam,
courtesy of the Rubell Museum.
Don and Mera Rubell, photo Chi Lam, courtesy of the
Rubell Museum.
Artist Genesis Tramaine, photo @shleyzilla, courtesy
of the Rubell Museum.

Storm King Art Center

Pages 140-141

Maya Lin, *Storm King Wavefield*, 2007-08, Earth and grass, 240,000 sq. ft. (11-acre site). Gift of the Ralph E. Ogden Foundation, Janet Inskeep Benton, The Philip and Muriel Berman Foundation, The Brown Foundation Inc. of Houston, Texas, Amb. and Mrs. W. L. Lyons Brown, Jr., Callahan and Nannini Quarry Products, Charina Endowment Fund, The Donohue Family Foundation, Edmund G. Glass, the Hazen Polsky Fund, Paul and Barbara Jenkel, the Kautz Family Foundation, The Lipman Family Foundation, Martin Z. Margulies, Margaret T. Morris Foundation, Roy R. and Marie S. Neuberger Foundation, Inc., Peckham Family Foundation, Jeannette and David Redden, Gabrielle H. Reem, M.D. and Herbert J. Kayden, M.D., The Richard Salomon Family Foundation, Inc., Sara Lee and Alex H. Schupf, Anne and Constantine Sidamon-Eristoff and Mr. and Mrs. Thomas W. Smith. © Maya Lin Studio, courtesy Pace Gallery, photo Jerry L. Thompson, © Storm King Art Center, Mountainville, New York.

Pages 142-143

Andy Goldsworthy, *Storm King Wall*, 1997-98, Fieldstone, 60 in. x 2278 ft. 6 in. x 32 in. (152.4 cm x 694.5 m x 81.3 cm). Gift of the Ralph E. Ogden Foundation, Mr. and Mrs. Joel Mallin, Mrs. W. L. Lyons Brown, Jr., Mr. and Mrs. James H. Ottaway, Jr., the Margaret T. Morris Foundation, The Horace W. Goldsmith Foundation, the Hazen Fund, the Joseph H. Hazen Foundation, Inc., Mr. and Mrs. Ronald N. Romary, Dr. Wendy Schaffer and Mr. Ivan Gjaja, and an anonymous foundation.© Andy Goldsworthy, courtesy Galerie Lelong & Co., New York, photo Jerry L. Thompson, © Storm King Art Center, Mountainville, New York.

Superblue

Pages 144

teamLab, *Universe of Water Particles, Transcending Boundaries*, 2017, Interactive Digital Installation, sound Hideaki Takahashi © teamLab, courtesy Pace Gallery.

Pages 145

teamLab, *Massless Clouds Between Sculpture and Life*, 2020. Installation view of Every Wall is a Door, Superblue Miami, 2021, sound teamLab. © teamLab, Courtesy of Pace Gallery.

Pages 146-147

teamLab, *Proliferating Immense Life—A Whole Year per Year*, 2020, Interactive Digital Installation, sound Hideaki Takahashi ©teamLab, courtesy Pace Gallery.

The Walker Art Center

Pages 148-149

Oldenburg, Claes and van Bruggen, Coosje, *Spoonbridge and Cherry*, 1985-1988. Collection Walker Art Center, Minneapolis. Gift of Frederick R. Weisman in honor of his parents, William and Mary Weisman, 1988. Aluminum, stainless steel, paint. © Claes Oldenburg and Coosje van Bruggen.

Page 150

Fritsch, Katharina, *Hahn/Cock*, 2013/2017. Collection Walker Art Center, Minneapolis. Purchased with funds provided by the Pohlad Family, the Frederick R. Weisman Collection of Art, the Wilf Family Foundation, the Duncan and NivinMacMillan Foundation, and the T. B. Walker Acquisition Fund, 2017. Fiberglass, polyester resin, paint, stainless-steel armature. Dimensions 173-1/4 x 173-1/4 x 59". © 2023 Artists Rights Society (ARS), New York/VG Bild-Kunst, Bonn.

Page 151

Louise Nevelson, *Dawn Tree*, 1976. Collection Walker Art Center, Minneapolis, Gift of Judy and Kenneth Dayton, 1998. Aluminum, paint. Dimensions: 103-5/8 x 92-1/2 x 62-3/4". © 2023 Estate of Louise Nevelson/ Artists Rights Society (ARS), New York.

Pages 152-153

Entrance to the Minneapolis Sculpture Garden, photo Bobby Rogers, courtesy Walker Art Center.